Multiculturalism

Multiculturalism

The Political Theory of Diversity Today

Andrew Shorten

polity

First published in 2022 by Polity Press

Polity Press
65 Bridge Street
Cambridge CB2 1UR, UK

Polity Press
101 Station Landing
Suite 300
Medford, MA 02155, USA

ISBN-13: 978-1-5095-5175-0
ISBN-13: 978-1-5095-5176-7 (pb)

A catalogue record for this book is available from the British Library.

Library of Congress Control Number: 2021946298

Typeset in 10.5 on 12pt Sabon
by Fakenham Prepress Solutions, Fakenham, Norfolk NR21 8NL
Printed and bound in Great Britain by TJ Books Ltd, Padstow, Cornwall

The publisher has used its best endeavours to ensure that the URLs for external websites referred to in this book are correct and active at the time of going to press. However, the publisher has no responsibility for the websites and can make no guarantee that a site will remain live or that the content is or will remain appropriate.

Every effort has been made to trace all copyright holders, but if any have been overlooked the publisher will be pleased to include any necessary credits in any subsequent reprint or edition.

For further information on Polity, visit our website:
politybooks.com

For Catherine

Contents

Acknowledgements

This book was mostly written in the gentle surroundings of the Groot Begijnhof in Leuven. For this opportunity, I must thank the University of Limerick for providing sabbatical leave, and the Institute of Philosophy at KU Leuven for hosting me. I was especially grateful for the opportunity to learn from the political philosophers in the RIPPLE research group there, whose numerous seminars were both stimulating and a model of collegiality. Helder De Schutter deserves special thanks for making us feel welcome and helping with the practicalities.

Material in the book was first road-tested with students at Limerick in my Multiculturalism and Political Theory class. I would like to thank multiple generations of them for helping me to understand the theories and puzzles of multiculturalism more clearly, and for showing me new ways to think about the issues they give rise to. I have also benefitted from elongated and recurrent discussions about the issues covered in the later chapters with the members of different (formal and informal) research networks, including the Mobility and Inclusion in Multilingual Europe (MIME) consortium, as well as participants at the Religion and Public Life workshop and its successors.

At different stages of its lifecycle, various anonymous readers gave me very helpful feedback on the project, for which I am very grateful. In particular, Sergi Morales-Gálvez made some helpful suggestions about the penultimate draft and saved me from some blunders. George Owers was a source of sage advice and came up with the title.

Most of all, I thank Catherine, for upending her own life to spend a year away with me whilst I wrote this book, and for everything else.

1

Introduction

This is a book about the normative political theory of multiculturalism. Its subject matter is a set of arguments, theories and recommendations, all of which have been proposed by political theorists during the last thirty years, and all of which, in some way or another, concern how democratic societies should respond to the cultural differences they contain. Like many of the other 'isms' discussed in normative political theory, there is considerable disagreement not only about the merits of multiculturalism, but also, more fundamentally, about what it consists in. Consequently, one thing I will try to bring out in the following chapters is the internal diversity of multicultural political theory, which contains strands drawn from very different traditions, amongst which there are deep tensions and even disagreements.

Over the course of the book, I will not attempt to defend any particular theory of multiculturalism – as one might argue for a radical feminism as opposed to a liberal one, for example, or for an egalitarian form of liberalism over a *laissez-faire* one. Indeed, as will become clear, I am doubtful about whether it really is possible for a single normative theory of multiculturalism to provide appropriate guidance about each of the different issues associated with cultural diversity in contemporary politics and public life. Theories designed in response to differences of nationality or language, for example, are often only tangentially relevant to the situation of religious minorities. With this in mind, I will propose another way to think about multicultural political theory: not as a single theory, but instead as a set of overlapping responses to a series of interrelated, but distinctive, issues.

To support and illustrate this way of characterizing multicultural political theory, I will look carefully at some of the different and specific contexts in which arguments for multiculturalism have been suggested and contested, including ones about the accommodation of religious minorities, about language rights, about political autonomy for national groups, and about immigration and social cohesion. I hope to demonstrate that attending carefully to the complex issues which arise in these very different settings reveals that arguments drawn from a variety of contexts and traditions can be a fertile and instructive source of inspiration for societies confronted by different forms of diversity. Moreover, just as we should not expect to discover a single, cohesive and overarching framework from which to address all of the different issues raised by the politics of diversity, I will argue that multicultural political theory has important limits. For example, a running theme in the book is that it can provide at best a partial and incomplete perspective on the complex moral and political issues involved in the relationship between Indigenous peoples and settler colonial states. In this case, and in others too, multicultural ideas will need to be complemented with additional theoretical resources.

In recent years, there has been something of a backlash against multiculturalism, both in the comparatively calm waters of academic political theory and in the stormier ones of real-world politics. Rumours of multiculturalism's demise, however, have been exaggerated. One reason for this is that some key claims associated with multiculturalism have become so firmly established that it is difficult to imagine them being dislodged. For example, in most democratic societies it is no longer controversial that national minorities are entitled to some form of recognition, that the implementation of public policies should be responsive to differences of language and religion, and that minority religious beliefs and practices should sometimes be accommodated. Of course, the form that recognition, responsiveness and accommodation should take is disputed, but these are issues about how to do multiculturalism, and not about whether it should be done at all. Furthermore, some of the supposed alternatives to multiculturalism, such as policies to promote social cohesion or the emergence of a new agenda of interculturalism, take up themes and ideas already present in multicultural political theory, and are better understood as being continuous with multiculturalism rather than being opposed to or in conflict with it.

In the remainder of this introduction, and before setting out the plan of the book ahead, I will attempt to define, at least in very general terms, what multiculturalism is, and to set out some of the main political claims associated with it.

What is Multiculturalism?

Multiculturalism is a slippery term, not least because it is used both descriptively, to signify the presence of more than one culture, and normatively, to refer to a theory about how political communities should deal with differences of culture and identity. Stuart Hall (2000) suggested a helpful variant of this distinction, distinguishing the adjective 'multicultural' from the noun 'multiculturalism'. Used as an adjective, 'multicultural' refers to 'the social characteristics and problems of governance posed by any society in which different cultural communities live together and attempt to build a common life while retaining something of their "original" identity' (Hall 2000, 209). In this sense, then, 'multicultural' covers a broad range of social phenomena, all of which have to do with the struggles and challenges faced by individual people and their societies when they attempt to live together in diversity. Meanwhile, when used as a noun, 'multiculturalism' refers to 'the strategies and policies adopted to manage and govern the problems of diversity which multicultural societies throw up' (Hall 2000, 209). So, then, it refers to how we respond to, or even attempt to solve, the struggles and challenges of living in a multicultural society.

Although the noun 'multiculturalism' is often used in the singular, including in the title of this book, it would be more accurate to use the plural 'multiculturalisms', since many different strategies, policies, models and theories have been proposed to explain how cultural diversity should be managed and governed. In the following chapters, the methods of normative political theory will be used to examine some of the most plausible candidates, focusing especially on the differences between them. To begin, though, it is worth emphasizing some features that different multicultural political theories share in common, which include the following four. First is a sense of trepidation about the homogenizing tendencies of democratic societies, as implied by the ideal of society as a 'melting pot' into which minorities are expected to assimilate. Second is an anxiety about the propensity of majorities to disregard the fears of minorities about the supposed neutrality and fairness of their shared institutions and procedures. Third is a concern to guard against the marginalization, exclusion and oppression of minority cultural communities. Fourth is a desire to enable members of minority groups to maintain their distinctive identities and practices.

As this list indicates, there is significant convergence amongst multicultural political theorists, aptly summarized by Bhikhu

Parekh's (2000, 1) observation that all multiculturalisms are 'united in resisting the wider society's homogenising or assimilationist thrust based on the belief that there is only one correct, true or normal way to understand or structure the relevant areas of life'. Beyond this shared baseline, however, there is as much disagreement as one would expect to find in any other ideology or political theory. Furthermore, there is another claim that is often attributed to multiculturalism – but which, in fact, is endorsed by very few multicultural political theorists.

This is moral relativism, the controversial thesis that moral standards are not universal, but are relative to particular groups or traditions. Perhaps not coincidentally, cultural differences feature prominently in an influential argument for moral relativism, which starts from the observations that different cultures have different beliefs about morality and that each culture thinks that its own beliefs are correct. From these, it infers that there is no absolute or universal truth about morality and that the moral beliefs of individuals are, in some sense, produced by their cultures. One of the things that makes moral relativism so tempting is a sense that it is both arrogant to judge other cultures and improper to apply one's own values and standards to the practices and beliefs of others. Although it is a thesis about morality, it is often recruited in support of political ends, especially to defend the claim that it would be wrong for people from one culture or society to impose its values on another – for example, by condemning its worldview or interfering with its practices. However, the belief that it is wrong to condemn or interfere with the values or practices of another culture does not follow from moral relativism itself. For if the truth of a moral standard or principle really is relative to its culture, as moral relativists insist, then it is not wrong to do these things, if doing so is consistent with the standards of one's own culture.

The widespread association of multiculturalism with moral relativism can perhaps be explained by the fact that the opposing view, moral universalism, is often thought to be connected to something opposed by all multiculturalists – namely, cultural assimilation. For example, the coercive techniques of assimilation introduced under European colonialism, such as the imposition of the language of the metropole or removing Indigenous children to residential schools, were often rationalized by a belief in the superiority of European values and civilization, a belief that was itself part of a universalist moral worldview. However, the connections between universalism and assimilation are more psychological than conceptual, since moral universalism alone cannot rationalize forced assimilation, and it must also be combined with a sense of certainty on the part of dominant groups about the correctness of their worldview, and a belief in their right to impose it unilaterally.

Furthermore, there are at least two ways in which moral relativism conflicts with some claims commonly endorsed by multiculturalists. First, to the extent that it understands cultures as self-contained wholes, relativism seems to exclude the possibility of mutual learning across cultural differences, as when people from different traditions engage in fruitful intercultural dialogue about morality and values. Indeed, if people cannot judge other cultures and their standards, then nor can they rationally evaluate their ideas and perspectives in order to learn from them. Second, relativism also closes off one important way in which people can exhibit an attitude of respect towards different cultural groups and traditions – namely, by taking their beliefs and practices seriously enough to criticize them. To illustrate this point, philosopher Bernard Williams recounted an anecdote relayed by a Spanish conquistador who travelled with Hernán Cortés to Mexico, and who recorded the sense of horror his fellow soldiers shared upon discovering the Aztec practice of human sacrifice. Williams (1972, 25) thought it would have been 'absurd' to regard their reaction as 'merely parochial or self-righteous', arguing instead that it 'indicated something which their conduct did not always indicate, that they regarded the Indians as men rather than as wild animals'.

So, then, different multiculturalisms share an opposition to cultural assimilation, but do not necessarily endorse moral relativism. Another sense in which the politics and political theory of multiculturalism can be confusing has to do with the different kinds of groups that it focuses on. For instance, people who share similar tastes in music, clothing or sports might justifiably describe themselves as sharing a culture, and they are also a group, but multiculturalists typically do not regard them as a cultural group in the sense they deem relevant. Instead, and this book will follow their lead, they focus on differences of language, nationality and religion. Not only does this exclude differences of lifestyle, but it also means that differences of sexual orientation and gender identity, of social class, or ones relating to disability, do not fall under the purview of multiculturalism. This is stipulative and, admittedly, controversial, not least because some authors include many of these forms of diversity within their analyses of multiculturalism (e.g. Joppke 2017), and because others have developed theories which stress the similarities between them and those of language, nationality and religion (e.g. Young 1990; Galeotti 2002).

Probably the most controversial exclusion from the following chapters is a separate consideration of the place of race and racism in multicultural politics and political theory. Racism has clearly shaped real-world multiculturalism, in both the adjective and noun senses of the word. For instance, a defining feature of the contemporary politics of diversity is Islamophobia, which racializes Muslims, supporting their exclusion as well as making them into targets of suspicion (Modood 2019a). Clearly, it would be impossible to understand the place of Muslims in European or North American society today without considering race. Going back further, racism was central to the history of the countries where multiculturalism is today contested and debated, some of which were founded directly on white supremacy, and all of whom have been moulded by the ongoing legacies of colonialism, itself a racist project. Furthermore, multicultural political theory is a branch of the Western tradition in political thought, which has its own shameful history of excluding people of colour from the status of full personhood (Mills 1997).

So, like many social and political problems confronting us today, the issues addressed by multicultural political theory cannot be easily disentangled from racism. However, there are two reasons for not focusing directly on race in the same way as I will focus on differences of language, nationality and religion. First, arguably at least, race is different from these categories for having hierarchy built into it. Sally Haslanger (2000) makes this point by arguing that races are social rather than biological categories, whereby people are racialized according to perceived physical traits like skin colour and body type, which play a role in justifying their social position as well as how they are viewed and treated. In suggesting that race is distinctive because hierarchy determines its meaning, I do not mean to deny that the social categories of language, nationality and religion also often mark distinctions of superiority and inferiority. Indeed, such dynamics will be a major topic of this book. However, national, religious and linguistic differences can readily be imagined separately from the hierarchies we interpret into them, and this is not the case for race (for a conflicting view, see Jeffers 2019). Second, there is also a danger that treating anti-racism as part of a broader multicultural project will lead us to misdiagnose various social ills, since racism is the failure to acknowledge not just the value of another culture, but rather the humanity of those it victimizes. This point was made forcefully by Kwame Anthony Appiah (1997), who worried that, in the politics of race, talk of cultural differences 'obscures rather than illuminates' because '[i]t is not black culture that the racist disdains, but blacks'.

Alongside these two reasons, one further point worth reiterating is that multicultural political theory is only one strand of political thinking, which must be complemented by other intellectual resources if it is to address complex real-world issues, including resources drawn from the philosophy and political theory of race. The same point applies when it comes to considering the claims of Indigenous people, since any satisfactory account of what justice requires for them will require a reckoning with settler colonialism, a form of political rule based on the seizure and exploitation of territory and the attempted elimination of the original inhabitants, and legitimized by the assumed cultural and racial superiority of Europeans (Wolfe 1999).

Narrowing the focus in the way I propose still leaves a wide range of phenomena. To help make sense of the remaining terrain, Canadian philosopher Will Kymlicka (1995, 11–32), whose work will be examined in detail in chapter 2, has proposed an influential framework that incorporates two distinctions: one between the different kinds of groups to have sought multicultural rights, and another between the different kinds of rights they have sought. The first distinction contrasts national minorities with immigrants. National minorities generally share a language, are geographically concentrated, have a special attachment to a particular territory, and – most importantly – seek to govern themselves. Initially at least, Kymlicka also included Indigenous peoples in this category, implying that groups such as the Sami in Scandinavia, the First Nation and Inuit peoples in Canada, and the Aboriginal and Torres Strait Islander peoples in Australia are entitled to the same kinds of rights as, for example, the Québécois in Canada, the Catalans in Spain, and the Welsh in the United Kingdom. Kymlicka's grounds for amalgamating these groups into a single category is that, unlike immigrants, they were once self-governing communities, who were subsequently incorporated into another state as a result of conquest or colonization.

Meanwhile, immigrants share with these other groups a desire to resist assimilation, but they tend to be much more interested in gaining equal access to the institutions of majority society, as opposed to establishing institutions of their own. As a result, national minorities and immigrants tend to seek different kinds of rights, hence the second distinction Kymlicka draws, between self-government rights and what he calls polyethnic rights. Self-government rights are sought by national minorities, and they are rights to maintain separate political institutions for the purposes of exercising political power over a given territory, for instance in the context of a federal or devolved state. Meanwhile, Kymlicka thinks that immigrants are more interested in polyethnic rights, a rather amorphous category including things such as funding for cultural associations, schools and festivals, as well as exemptions from generally applicable laws. Polyethnic rights are not about maintaining a distinctive society, but instead have to do with establishing fair terms of integration (Kymlicka 1995, 113–15). Their main purpose, according to Kymlicka (1995, 31), is 'to help ethnic groups and religious minorities express their cultural particularity and pride without it hampering their success in the economic and political institutions of the dominant society'. So, like self-government rights, they aim to protect cultural differences, but they do so without giving a group the right to control its own territory, institutions or community.

Kymlicka's overlapping distinctions between national minorities and immigrants, and between self-government rights and polyethnic rights, are a helpful starting point. However, this framework can also be misleading, so should be treated with caution. For one thing, some groups fall awkwardly between the two categories of national minorities and immigrants, including nomadic peoples like the Roma and Travellers in Europe, or religious groups who live apart from mainstream society, such as the Hutterites and Amish in North America. For another, Indigenous peoples are not identical with national minorities, and the two groups make different political demands and have different needs and interests. Furthermore, distinguishing self-government rights from polyethnic rights risks obscuring the fact that national minorities and immigrants often seek very similar things, including forms of recognition and support that fall well short of self-government. Similarly, as will be discussed in chapter 7, it is not only national groups that have sought self-government rights, and some religious groups have called for them too, at least on a partial or limited basis. These groups have sought the transfer of jurisdictional authority to religious courts and tribunals over matters of family law, and for legal powers to enable them to run their own schools, charities and churches without interference.

Furthermore, the association that Kymlicka draws between immigrants and polyethnic rights is problematic in two different senses. First, some of his polyethnic rights are sought by people who are not immigrants. For example, as we shall see in chapter 6, religious accommodations in Europe have been sought by Muslims, Sikhs, Hindus and the members of diverse Christian denominations. Many of the members of these groups are neither immigrants themselves, nor even the children or grandchildren of immigrants. Consequently, either Kymlicka intends immigrants in a catch-all sense, to include everyone who is not included in his other categories, or he must think that religious accommodations for non-immigrants are in some sense different from those for immigrants, falling outside the ambit of multiculturalism. Both of these are implausible. Second, Kymlicka stipulates that the general rationale for the rather ramshackle bundle of policies he clumps together as polyethnic rights is to establish fair terms of integration. However, as will be demonstrated in chapters 4, 6 and 8, a number of different justifications can be given for these measures, which, in addition to the subsidies and exemptions mentioned earlier, also include things as various as affirmative action programmes, supported employment schemes and other labour market interventions, the provision of interpretation and translation services for recent immigrants, and workplace accommodations. If these measures are best justified by appealing to a range of different values, principles and arguments, as I will suggest, and if people who are not immigrants might have a good claim to them, then this calls into question Kymlicka's rationale for gathering them together in the same category.

A final problem with Kymlicka's framework is that it underplays the significance of symbolic forms of recognition, which can be important for national groups as well as for ethnic and religious minorities, and which can play a crucial role in building trust, promoting inclusion and nurturing social ties. For example, a multi-cultural state might invite the representatives of different religions to participate in official state functions, it might recognize its component nations in its flag and anthem, and its officials might apologize for the wrongful treatment of minority groups in the past. All of these things can be crucially important for the success of a multicultural society, but they are difficult to subsume under the headings of polyethnic or self-government rights.

In his subsequent work, Kymlicka has implicitly acknowledged some of these shortcomings, particularly that Indigenous peoples can have different interests from national minorities, that immigrants and national minorities sometimes seek the same policies, that immigrants are interested in their ancestral languages and cultures as well as integration, and that symbolic forms of recognition can be significant. For example, with Keith Banting he has developed a 'multicultural policy index', which identifies a list of measures sought by different kinds of groups (Banting et al. 2006, 56–62). This retains his favoured distinction between immigrant groups and national minorities, but separates out Indigenous peoples as a distinct group in their own right, with unique interests, especially regarding historical claims to land and sovereignty. Furthermore, it acknowledges that national minorities are interested in more than self-government rights; it recognizes the importance of political representation and symbolic/official affirmations for all three groups; and it appreciates that, alongside integration, immigrants are also often interested in retaining ties to their countries of origin, for instance in the form of dual citizenship or language learning for children. Consequently, the index is a significant refinement of, and improvement upon, the framework Kymlicka initially presented in his *Multicultural Citizenship* (1995). However, it still places a great deal of weight on how cultural minorities were incorporated into the state, and this could give rise to the misleading impression that multicultural political theory is basically composed of three discrete domains of enquiry, concerning, respectively, the rights of immigrants, of national minorities, and of Indigenous peoples. But this would obscure the fact that many of the arguments which can be harnessed in support of rights for one of these groups carry over to the situation of the others.

Consequently, instead of sticking rigidly to Kymlicka's distinctions, this book will sketch an alternative map of multicultural political theory, organized around the three main modes of cultural diversity addressed by multiculturalism, which are differences of language, nationality and religion. Two points in particular are worth emphasizing about this approach. First, in prioritizing the mode of diversity, it places less emphasis than does Kymlicka's framework on whether a measure is sought by a national minority or by immigrants. As such, it implies that when we consider how democratic states should deal with linguistic diversity, as we will do in chapter 8, we should discuss immigrant languages in tandem with long-established ones, rather than assuming that these are separate domains of inquiry. This does not preclude coming to the conclusion that only national minorities, and not immigrants, are entitled to have their languages publicly recognized and supported, but it does insist that this conclusion must be argued for, and is not a premise to be assumed, as Kymlicka's framework risks implying. Second, granting priority to the categories of language, nationality and religion does not mean that arguments appropriate for one mode of diversity do not apply elsewhere. So, for instance, when we consider whether religious groups are entitled to institutional autonomy, so as to enable them to run their schools, charities and churches without much state interference – as we will do in chapter 7 – we should freely draw upon arguments that have been given for other religious accommodations, as well as arguments that have been proposed concerning the political autonomy of national minorities.

In addition to avoiding some of the pitfalls that Kymlicka's approach encounters, one further merit of this approach, I believe, is that it better reflects how the political theory of multiculturalism has evolved in recent years. As we shall see in chapters 2 and 3, the major works that continue to define the field – represented here by the writings of Will Kymlicka, Chandran Kukathas, Charles Taylor and Bhikhu Parekh – were comprehensive theories of multiculturalism, with applications across a wide range of issues. Admittedly, some of these spoke more directly to the local preoccupations of their authors, such as the claims of francophone Canadians for Taylor and Kymlicka, and postcolonial immigration in Britain for Parekh. Nevertheless, they supplied general normative principles that could apply to a range of societies and a number of different modes of cultural diversity. Meanwhile, recent work on multiculturalism has tended to be narrower and more focused, concerned with particular issues, such as language rights, religious accommodation or national autonomy. Although this work often draws on theoretical innovations that can be traced to the pioneering work of Kymlicka, Kukathas, Taylor and Parekh, it tends to be less interested in building general theories and more concerned to answer particular puzzles. As a result, multicultural political theory today is increasingly fragmented, up to the point where one might doubt its continuing relevance, at least as a coherent school of thought. In this book I hope to allay that doubt, by drawing attention to the ways in which these apparently separate debates can learn from one another.

Plan

As mentioned already, many of the defining features of multicultural political theory can be traced back to a series of texts produced in the 1990s and the early 2000s. Accordingly, the next two chapters will introduce and assess four leading theories that emerged during this period. These texts were selected both because they reflect the breadth of multicultural political theory, and because each of them continues to shape contemporary responses to cultural diversity.

Chapter 2 concentrates on liberal responses to multiculturalism and seeks to tease out the enduring influence of some ideas drawn from liberalism's early and recent histories. One of these is state neutrality, which initially applied only to religious matters, as reflected in the recommendation to keep church and state separate, but is now sometimes extended as a more general principle of ethnocultural neutrality. The two authors we concentrate on disagree about this extension. The first, Will Kymlicka, argues against it, pointing out that contemporary democratic states already promote the culture of the majority, often unintentionally, such as by using its language, marking its festivals and teaching its literature and history in schools. As a result, members of minority cultures are entitled to seek supports for their own languages, practices and traditions, both to protect them against assimilation and to give them what the majority already gets without asking. Furthermore, Kymlicka provides a powerful philosophical justification for supporting minority cultures in this way, which begins from another idea with a long history in the liberal tradition – namely, that all human beings have an interest in living autonomously. Amongst other things, this means being able to choose and carry out one's own plan of life, selecting goals for oneself and pursuing self-chosen projects, without being directed from the outside. In Kymlicka's hands, this interest provides the basis for a novel argument for minority cultural rights, supported by a connection he draws between culture and autonomy, which says that only against the backdrop of a stable cultural context are people able to make meaningful choices about how to lead their lives. The upshot of this argument is that, in order to protect individual autonomy, minority cultures should sometimes be granted special rights, to enable their members to preserve their distinctive culture and to protect themselves against the homogenizing pressures of majority society.

The second liberal philosopher examined in chapter 2, Chandran Kukathas, argues against these rights and in support of a rigorous form of neutrality. He starts from the observation that autonomy is a far more contentious value than Kymlicka acknowledges, since it is not universally endorsed. Some traditional cultures do not recognize it, and, in any case, Kukathas thinks that a life which is less than fully autonomous can still have value and meaning. Furthermore, promoting autonomy, as Kymlicka recommends, will undermine many traditional ways of life, reshaping them to fit a mould congenial to the temperament of a modern Western liberal, but one that might seem strange and hostile to some minorities. Instead of autonomy, Kukathas believes that the most basic liberal value is toleration, which calls on us to refrain from interfering with other people's practices, traditions and cultures despite disapproving of them. Thus, he controversially argues for a form of multiculturalism that is maximally tolerant, including of practices such as female genital mutilation, ritual scarring and allowing parents to remove their children from school.

Some political theorists believe that liberalism is unable to address the challenges of cultural diversity adequately, and chapter 3 turns to the work of political theorists who have looked to the margins of liberal political theory, and beyond it, to develop new intellectual resources for responding to the challenges of cultural diversity. One of these is recognition, an idea especially associated with Charles Taylor, and the other is dialogue, a leitmotif of Bhikhu Parekh's innovative approach to multiculturalism.

According to Taylor's politics of recognition, achieving an equal and inclusive society will require both the state and its members to recognize and affirm differences of culture. Taylor particularly emphasizes the psychological harms that people are exposed to if their identities are misrecognized, or not recognized at all, as when a religious group is stigmatized or stereotyped in wider society, or when the state refuses to recognize the existence of a particular ethnic group. Although the policy proposals generated by his theory are broadly similar to Kymlicka's, Taylor puts much more emphasis on how the different groups in society perceive one another and on the damaging effects suffered by people through being allocated a subordinate social status.

As he presents it, Taylor's theory is a sympathetic critique of mainstream liberalism, and the effect of his theory is to enlarge liberalism by incorporating additional theoretical resources. Meanwhile, the other thinker discussed in this chapter, Parekh, recommends dispensing with liberalism altogether. According to him, liberalism is not only a political theory, but also a culturally specific worldview, bound up with a particular vision of human life. Appreciation of the fact that liberalism is one worldview amongst others, he thinks, should prompt us to see the importance of stepping beyond it, if we are to manage cultural diversity fairly. One of Parekh's main proposals for achieving this is a distinctive model of intercultural dialogue, in which the representatives of different traditions listen to and learn from one another, with a view to reaching a consensus about how to arrange society, its laws and its institutions. Unlike Kymlicka, Kukathas and Taylor, Parekh does not believe that political theorists themselves can appeal to first principles in order to settle controversial questions about whether particular cultural practices ought to be permitted, or about how institutions in culturally diverse societies should be designed. Instead, these matters must be settled by citizens, after a morally serious and inclusive dialogue.

The next two chapters consider the philosophical and political reception of multiculturalism. Chapter 4 discusses the four most significant philosophical critiques of multiculturalism, two of which concern its egalitarian credentials, and another two its underlying conception of culture. The first egalitarian objection takes aim at the characteristically multicultural idea that people's rights and entitlements should be tied to their culture or identity. Against this, critics argue for a principle of uniform treatment, both on grounds of fairness and in order to discourage competition and conflict amongst social groups. Meanwhile, the other egalitarian objection focuses on the inequalities that arise within cultural groups, and is particularly concerned with the possibility that multiculturalism could be contrary to the interests of women and girls, because its favoured policies will end up supporting patriarchal cultures and practices.

The other two objections concern the philosophical foundations of multiculturalism. According to the essentialist critique, multiculturalism is wedded to an implausible conception of culture, which flattens out differences within cultures and exaggerates those between them. This critique poses a deep challenge since multiculturalists do not just happen to endorse a crude or simplistic conception of culture, but their positive recommendations for society seemingly depend upon such a conception. Finally, the cosmopolitan critique suggests that multiculturalists exaggerate the significance of cultural ties for individuals, pointing out that people manage to construct meaningful lives by moving between different cultures and by drawing on different influences. Accordingly, cosmopolitans argue that multicultural arguments for cultural rights depend on flawed assumptions.

Chapter 5 moves down a register and considers multiculturalism as a public policy orientation, as opposed to an abstract political theory. Taking the recent backlash against multiculturalism as a starting point, it examines the oft-made objection that multiculturalism undermines social cohesion and political stability. In fact, this objection comes in two different guises: sometimes as a claim about the common identity that binds the members of a political community together, and sometimes as a claim about shared values. Although multiculturalists can answer both challenges, they seem to have already lost the battle in the court of public opinion, at least in some European societies. As a result, two alternative public policy approaches have emerged, one insisting on robust civic integration programmes and another going under the title of interculturalism. Although proponents of both have often been passionate critics of multiculturalism, much of what they argue for can be incorporated within a multicultural approach, and indeed has already been called for by leading multicultural political theorists. Thus, I will argue that, at least in the short term, the effects of the backlash against multiculturalism have mostly been cosmetic.

The next three chapters concentrate on the three main forms of cultural diversity – differences of religion, nationality and language. The academic literatures addressing these have become increasingly separate from one another, which is unsurprising given how specialized and fine-grained some of the discussions are. Nevertheless, I will attempt to draw attention to some important areas of overlap, and where scholars working on one issue have learned from debates about one of the others. Furthermore, a recurrent theme in these chapters is the way in which the first generation of multicultural political theory continues to exert a powerful force, influencing – but perhaps also constraining – how political theorists today understand the challenges of religious, national and linguistic diversity.

Chapter 6 examines how two themes from the classical multicultural texts – toleration and recognition – continue to shape discussions amongst liberals and their critics about how democratic societies should accommodate religious diversity. The first half of this chapter concentrates on debates amongst liberal political theorists about religious accommodations, as when laws or employment practices are adjusted in response to religious differences. A difficult challenge for liberal theorists is to identify reasons for accommodating religious practices that do not unduly favour religious beliefs and commitments over non-religious ones, and the most promising solution to this puzzle, I shall suggest, appeals to the value of integrity.

Whilst liberals have been preoccupied with the question of whether particular and controversial practices should be tolerated, other multiculturalists have foregrounded the idea of recognition, exploring the ways in which it supports multicultural inclusion and belonging. In particular, they have criticized liberal political theorists for neglecting important contextual considerations, arguing that issues of religious accommodation should not be settled without paying close attention to the background structure of social relations, and especially inequalities of power and status. Consequently, the second half of the chapter considers two proposals that challenge orthodox liberal views: one for enhancing the public visibility of minority religious identities, and another that promotes multifaith establishment as more suitable for multicultural societies than the separation of church and state.

When it comes to dealing with religious differences, multicultural political theorists have focused primarily on the challenges of securing the full and equal inclusion of religious individuals. More recently, legal and political theorists have addressed the difficulties of accommodating corporate or institutional manifestations of religious diversity, as when churches, religious firms, charities or schools with a religious ethos seek forms of special legal treatment. Chapter 7 takes up this issue and addresses religious forms of self-governance alongside some longstanding puzzles related to national self-determination, topics not usually discussed together. The rationale for doing so is that both are forms of collective autonomy, with significant implications for the distribution of juris-dictional authority. Furthermore, in putting these topics together, I hope to bring out features in each case that might otherwise be ignored. In particular, I suggest that some of the arguments given against granting extensive powers of autonomy to religious associ-ations also contain grounds to be sceptical about self-government rights for national minorities.

To begin, I examine the principle of national self-determination and assess some different arguments that have been given in its support, focusing especially on those endorsed by multiculturalists. For minority nations, the strongest argument for self-government rights appeals to a principle of self-defence, which says that minorities should be empowered to promote their own national cultures and to counter the nation-building projects of the majority. Often, this argument is taken to support some form of devolution or federalism. However, allocating rights over particular territories is not the only way to protect national cultures, and I will suggest that better alter-natives can be imagined. The second half of the chapter turns to the governance of religious associations, exploring some of the different ways in which religious groups have sought special powers to enable them to control their own internal affairs and external relations. Like minority nations, religious associations have sometimes sought to insulate themselves from wider society, though in their case it is not the language or culture of the majority they fear, but its norms and values, as reflected in anti-discrimination laws, for example. After identifying two different frameworks that have recently been developed to explain and evaluate these claims, I suggest that both of them are vulnerable to the egalitarian objections to multiculturalism, discussed in chapter 4.

Chapter 8 considers the topic of linguistic justice, asking whether speakers of minority languages have a right for their language to be used by public institutions, such as in courts, hospitals, schools and in the system of public administration. In other words, should the state promote minority languages – for instance, by granting them official status? Most political theorists who support minority language rights believe that they should be reserved for national minorities, arguing that other language policies are more appropriate for immigrants. These might include, for example, majority language-learning programmes or transitional translation and interpretation services, to ensure that people who cannot yet speak the official language can still avail themselves of their basic rights. This distinction between two different approaches to language policies tracks Kymlicka's distinction between polyethnic rights for immigrants and self-government rights for national minorities. Furthermore, it is also reflected in the practices of actual states, who likewise reserve official recognition and language promotion rights for long-settled languages. However, providing a philosophically satisfactory justification for discriminating in this way is surprisingly difficult, and we shall examine the attempts of some leading multicultural political theorists to do so.

The other topic considered in this chapter concerns how support for different languages ought to be distributed. Historically, democratic states have approached language policies by selecting desirable outcomes, such as preserving a vulnerable language or trying to ensure that everyone is able to speak and understand a shared language. The difficulty with these approaches is that some members of society may not endorse the goals being promoted. Meanwhile, some multicultural political theorists have recently sketched an alternative approach, which is less concerned with bringing about particular linguistic outcomes and instead aims to identify a scheme of underlying language rights that treats everyone fairly. As we shall see, one promising way to do this is to extend equal support to each language spoken in society. However, this still leaves open the thorny question of whether the support given to each language should be determined by its vulnerability, the number of speakers it has, or something else. Some different solutions to this puzzle will be compared and assessed.

One of the main aims of this book, pursued especially in chapters 6 to 8, is to reveal how contemporary debates about language, religion and nationality have been shaped by the classical political theories of multiculturalism, and how these different debates overlap with one another in fruitful and sometimes surprising ways. Another aim, which is developed throughout the book, is to demonstrate that multicultural political theory is not a narrow or stand-alone body of arguments, concerned only with the rights of minorities or the challenges of immigrant integration, but instead involves a number of fundamental debates in political theory, including ones about our most basic political concepts such as freedom, equality and sovereignty.

Finally, one other significant and ongoing theme concerns the limits of multicultural political theory, especially when it comes to Indigenous communities, discussed in chapters 2, 3 and 7. In large part, the political demands of Indigenous communities resemble the standard multicultural policy package for national minorities, including rights of self-government and to cultural preservation, as well as rights for guaranteed representation in parliaments and other public bodies. However, a number of Indigenous scholars have resisted being designated as one cultural minority amongst others, as multicultural political theory often does (Coulthard 2014; Simpson 2014). According to them, orthodox theories of multiculturalism risk obscuring the fundamental grievances of Indigenous peoples, which arise from settler colonialism, and include historical and ongoing land dispossession, the refusal to recognize Indigenous sovereignty, and the attempted destruction of Indigenous people, communities and ways of life (Ivison 2020). The best way for multiculturalists to answer this complaint, I will suggest, is to acknowledge that their own theories not only are incomplete and partial, but also can pull in the wrong direction when applied insensitively, and as a result will often need to be complemented with additional ideas drawn from different intellectual traditions.

2

Liberal Theories of Multiculturalism: Autonomy and Toleration

It makes sense to begin a survey of the political theory of multiculturalism with liberalism. Not only is it the dominant political theory of our times, but it is also central to two intellectual debates that guide and structure this book: one about how liberals ought to respond to cultural diversity; another about whether liberalism is the most appropriate theoretical framework to address the issues raised by multiculturalism. This chapter focuses on liberals themselves, whilst the next will consider liberalism's critics and the alternatives they have proposed.

Liberalism is a rich and multifaceted ideology, and the disagreements amongst liberal political theorists – both about multiculturalism and other topics – are far reaching (on the difficulties of defining liberalism, see Freeden 1996, 2005, and Bell 2014; for surveys of liberalism, see, amongst many others, Gray 1986; Manent 1996; Kelly 2005; Vincent 2010; Ryan 2012; Shorten 2014). This chapter treats liberalism as a body of connected arguments that, amongst other things, aim to provide principled guidance about how the political order should respond to diversity whilst protecting individual freedom. At least as I understand it, liberalism does not have a 'party line' about this but is better understood as a collection of values and principles that, when combined, form a repository of arguments. New additions to this repository sometimes extend earlier ones, but just as often they make the earlier arguments redundant, or call for them to be reconsidered. Thus, whilst some of the arguments constituting the liberal tradition complement one another, there are important tensions and disagreements within it too.

As we shall see, many of the normative arguments that continue to inspire contemporary liberals were first formulated at times and in places where religious differences amongst Christians were the most salient manifestation of diversity. Some political theorists believe that this classical liberal tradition requires only minor modifications to address today's politics of cultural diversity successfully. The work of an influential proponent of this view, Chandran Kukathas, will be examined at the end of this chapter. Meanwhile, other liberal multiculturalists have suggested that arguments developed by liberal political thinkers in previous centuries need to be substantially reconfigured for contemporary politics, especially to account for the moral significance of people's ties to their languages and culture. We look at the work of an important advocate of this approach, Will Kymlicka, later in this chapter.

To set the stage for these theories, the first half of the chapter describes some of the main arguments proposed by liberal thinkers concerning how the state ought to respond to religious and other differences, focusing especially on the contested concepts of freedom, toleration and equality. These central liberal values can be combined to provide powerful justifications for two familiar staples of liberal political morality: religious freedom and the separation of church and state. From the 1970s onwards, it became increasingly common for liberal thinkers to present the principle of state neutrality as a logical extension of this pair. A neutral state is one that neither hinders nor supports different religions, cultures or ways of life, but instead remains neutral amongst them. As we shall see, neutrality remains a controversial feature of liberal political theory, especially within the context of debates about multiculturalism, since it seems to rule out any positive recognition or support for minority cultures. Whilst some liberals, like Kukathas, embrace this implication, others, including Kymlicka, believe that neutrality needs to be complemented – or perhaps even replaced – by other, more difference-sensitive, principles.

Diversity and the Liberal Tradition

Freedom

Freedom is the most important value for many liberal thinkers. For example, the most prominent liberal theory of justice in the twentieth century, John Rawls's (1999) theory of justice as fairness, held that it is permissible to sacrifice one person's freedom only if doing so is necessary to secure the freedom of others. By this, Rawls meant that, although some values may permissibly be traded off against one another, as when a government deliberately limits economic growth for the sake of improving environmental protections, justice requires that freedom must always be maximized, subject only to the constraint that no one has a greater share of it than anyone else.

Although liberal political theorists agree about the special importance of freedom, they reach different conclusions about how to honour its value. Some of these disagreements can be illustrated by considering a famous American court case from 1972, *Wisconsin v. Yoder*. This involved three families, two from the Old Order Amish community and another from the Conservative Amish Mennonite Church, both of which are small Anabaptist sects whose members lead a simple rural life, living apart from mainstream society and without making use of cars, electricity and other modern conveniences. Three children from these families, aged 14 and 15, had completed their elementary schooling, after which their parents failed to enrol them for high school, as was required by law (at the time, the state of Wisconsin required compulsory education up until the age of 16). Upon being convicted and fined, the parents sued the state of Wisconsin for violating the religious freedom that was guaranteed to them under the American Constitution. Their objections to compulsory schooling were complex, but prominent amongst them was the complaint that the values emphasized in public schools, such as self-distinction, competitiveness and scientific accomplishment, were contrary to Amish values like communal solidarity and pacifism, and that exposing Amish children to the values of the public school system would limit the community's ability to transmit its traditional way of life to its adolescent members. Instead of the skills emphasized in public schooling, the parents planned to give their children a practical education, based on traditional domestic and agricultural crafts.

A commitment to maximizing freedom, depending on what we understand by it, might direct us to take opposing views about the parents' demand. On the one hand, some people say that in seeking to force the children to attend school, majority society was trying to impose its own standards upon a reluctant minority. If you believe that this was the case, then you might conclude that freedom requires the Amish to be left alone. For example, Chandran Kukathas (1992, 126) argues that the Amish 'have the right to live by their traditional ways', because they ought to be free to associate on whatever terms they find mutually acceptable. But, on the other hand, some people say that what the parents were seeking was to undermine the freedom of their children, and to prevent them from becoming adults who would be capable of being authors of their own lives. If you believe that this was the case, then you might conclude that freedom requires the children to complete their schooling. For example, according to Will Kymlicka's (1995, 162) description of the case, the Amish removed their children from school in order to limit their knowledge of the wider world, thereby reducing the likelihood of their leaving the community upon reaching maturity.

William Galston (1995, 521) has suggested that disagreements like these are indicative of a deeper division between 'two quite different strands of liberal thought'. The first strand, into which Kymlicka's argument falls, holds that the proper goal of the liberal state is to promote individual autonomy (autonomy in this context refers to a self-directed life). Galston associates this view of liberalism with the Enlightenment, an eighteenth-century European intellectual movement, led by luminaries like Voltaire, Denis Diderot, Jean d'Alembert and Immanuel Kant, all of whom castigated ignorance and superstition as enemies of human freedom and progress. By Galston's account, some contemporary liberals have inherited from these earlier thinkers a view that individual freedom depends upon the capacity for autonomy, and especially the ability to reason and think clearly. Consequently, they tend to believe that removing children from school is unacceptable, because it compromises the development of a child's critical and reflective abilities, which are essential for their freedom, since autonomy depends upon being able to choose for oneself how to live.

The second strand, which is the one that both Kukathas and Galston favour, instead emphasizes toleration and diversity. Beginning from the observation that individuals and groups have extremely different ideas about human life and morality, it continues to say that the state ought to tolerate those different beliefs and their associated ways of life – for instance, by refraining from interfering in the affairs of minorities even when they reject liberal values. Thus, communities like the Amish – who place little value on individual choice and autonomy, and who instead believe that adherence to traditional religious or community values is much more important – should not be required to comply with majoritarian educational norms, since the education system itself is based on values and beliefs that are foreign to the Amish way of life, and might even be destructive of it. From within this strand, it would be unfair for the school system to promote autonomy, since it is only one value amongst others, not universally endorsed. Furthermore, promoting this particular value could stifle diversity in the longer term, encouraging 'a kind of uniformity that exerts pressure on ways of life that do not embrace autonomy' (Galston 1995, 523).

According to Kymlicka (1995, 154), the most basic disagreement between these two strands of thought is 'whether autonomy or tolerance is the fundamental value within liberal theory'. Liberals who treat autonomy as fundamental prioritize ensuring that everyone is able to question and revise their own traditions and customs, whilst those who treat tolerance as fundamental instead prioritize making as much room as possible for different ways of life. This way of carving up the intellectual space occupied by liberal political theory is a helpful starting point. However, it is also potentially misleading, because the disagreements that divide liberals actually cut across a number of different issues. In the following sections, I identify and discuss two of these. The first has to do with toleration – about why and whether it is a virtue, and about how its limits ought to be established. As will be discussed immediately below, some liberals have been reluctant to include toleration amongst the list of liberal virtues, and even those who do include it defend very different views about what forms of toleration are desirable and about what makes particular practices intolerable. Meanwhile, the second issue, which will be discussed in the subsequent section, concerns equality, and has to do with whether or not promoting controversial values like autonomy respects everyone – including those who reject them – as an equal.

Toleration

Toleration is a complex political concept, laden with different meanings that have become attached to it over time. The term is derived from the Latin 'tolerare', which means to bear or to endure something, reflecting the idea that we can only tolerate things we oppose, or disapprove of. Although now closely associated with the liberal tradition, toleration has a much longer history. Indeed, whilst a self-consciously liberal political ideology only took shape in the nineteenth century, toleration gained political significance in Europe three centuries earlier, during the religious wars that followed the Protestant Reformation. At this point in history, toleration was understood primarily as a matter of political expediency, and one historian has concluded that the term was 'mainly used pejoratively' (Walsham 2006, 4–5). It was only later that philosophers began to sketch out some principled rationales for toleration, laying the foundations for the idea that it is a virtue. Alongside earlier writings and practices, these ideas too have fed into the ways in which contemporary liberal political theorists understand the concept. Importantly, as we shall see, these later ideas also contained the germ of an argument that, according to some scholars, conceivably renders toleration obsolete for political theories which emphasize individual rights, such as liberalism. Although most contemporary liberals have been reluctant to embrace this conclusion, many deny that toleration has a fundamental or basic status.

The earlier tradition, which treated toleration as pragmatic means for securing peace, arose out of the shared realization during the Wars of Religion that conflict could be halted only if each side could be convinced that victory was unlikely. Here, toleration meant putting up with one's enemies, in all likelihood reluctantly, and it took an extremely circumscribed form. Indeed, we might even struggle to recognize many of the early practices of toleration as such today. For example, the Treaty of Westphalia (1648), which established a rough-and-ready regime of mutual toleration amongst European kingdoms, incorporated the principle of *cuius regio, eius religio* ('whose realm, his religion'), which was widely understood to be consistent with the suppression of religious dissent and heresy within individual kingdoms.

The subsequent arguments for toleration, proposed during the seventeenth century, put greater emphasis on the freedom to dissent from orthodox or established religion (that is to say, from the official religion of one's country). These were suggested by writers as various as Pierre Bayle, John Locke, John Milton, Baruch Spinoza and Roger Williams. For some of these thinkers, toleration of religious dissent was a virtue because it allowed for the interplay of different ideas, which they understood to be a necessary condition for social and intellectual progress. For example, in his famous essay 'Areopagitica', the poet Milton criticized censorship by suggesting that, when confronted with falsehood, truth would always win out, a suggestion to be developed more comprehensively by John Stuart Mill in the nineteenth century. More typically, however, these authors defended the freedom to dissent from religious orthodoxy for individualist and expressivist reasons, and in so doing began to associate the harm of intolerance with an appreciation of the importance and fragility of individual conscience. For example, Milton argued that censorship was wrong because it undermined an individual's ability to interpret religious truth for himself and to share his beliefs with the world. Similarly, his contemporary Williams (2001, 110), a religious dissenter who had emigrated from England and founded a colony at Rhode Island after being banished from Massachusetts by other Puritans, famously argued that religious persecution assaults human dignity and was a kind of 'soul or spiritual rape'. Locke (2010), too, argued along much the same lines, and in his 'A Letter Concerning Toleration' wrote that governments are not responsible for the religious beliefs of their subjects, and that religious coercion was irrational because genuine religious belief cannot be compelled.

These various arguments had the effect of putting toleration on a much firmer moral foundation. If toleration is justified only for the sake of peace and stability, as the earlier tradition had it, then there is little reason to tolerate those who are weak and unthreatening. Meanwhile, the conscience argument supplies a powerful moral case for tolerating the weak as well as the strong. For, according to it, the necessity of toleration is explained by the fundamental moral demand that people should not suffer the fate of being unable to avoid acting against their deepest beliefs about religion, truth and morality. If one accepts this, then it follows that we have good moral reasons to tolerate those we oppose, grounded in the basic interest that everyone has in being able to live under the guidance of their own conscience.

Over time, the principle that people should not be compelled to act against conscience came to be associated with the idea that people have a right to religious freedom. This right was initially intended to prevent governments from penalizing or persecuting people on the basis of their religious beliefs, something famously secured by the free exercise clause of the First Amendment to the US Constitution, ratified as part of the Bill of Rights in 1791. Rights to religious freedom subsequently become central to twentieth-century human rights doctrines, listed in both the Universal Declaration of Human Rights (Article 18) and the European Convention on Human Rights (Article 9), for example.

The spread of rights-based political moralities has led some contemporary liberals to regard toleration as a derivative, but not a fundamental, value. This is because, for them, liberal political morality already includes foundational value commitments that determine the proper limits of acceptable conduct, making toleration into something produced by the realization of these more basic liberal values. For example, Ronald Dworkin (2011) suggests a particular ideal of dignity, which he calls 'ethical independence', as one of these fundamental values. This entails that individuals be responsible for deciding for themselves how to make something valuable of their lives. As well as implying that people must have a wide degree of discretion over things like religion, sexuality and abortion, ethical independence also means that 'government must never restrict freedom just because it assumes that one way for people to live their lives – one idea about what lives are most worth living just in themselves – is intrinsically better than another' (Dworkin 2013, 130; see also Dworkin 2011, 369). Since respect for ethical independence means protecting personal freedom, Dworkin's preferred society could be described as tolerant. But toleration is something produced by other values, and it has no independent value within his schema.

Whilst views like this are widely endorsed amongst contemporary liberals, others grant toleration a more basic or fundamental value, criticizing theories such as Dworkin's for failing to appreciate the depth and permanence of disagreement over controversial values, including ethical independence. For example, in his later work, John Rawls (1996) argued that people will inevitably and permanently disagree about things such as morality or religion, and that such disagreements are often 'reasonable' – which is to say, not produced by things like prejudice, malice, self-interest or stupidity. Accordingly, a commitment to toleration as a fundamental value means accepting that it would be illegitimate for the state to impose a particular worldview, such as one based on Dworkin's ethical independence, on the rest of society.

Meanwhile, Chandran Kukathas, whose work we will explore in detail later, goes even further than Rawls in trying to restore toleration to the centre of liberal political morality. According to Kukathas (2003, 126), toleration 'checks or counters moral certitude', a necessary virtue given human fallibility. Furthermore, toleration also makes possible the conditions that give human reason its authority. According to him, because there is no definitive method to establish the correctness of our beliefs and convictions, their authority can be established – and even then, only tentatively – by exposing them to a range of criticisms and alternatives. Toleration can secure these conditions, but only if it is unlimited, since there is no common standpoint from which to justifiably exclude any particular criticisms or alternatives.

Equality

As we have seen, contemporary liberals have inherited from earlier writers the idea that individual conscience has a special weight or significance, agreeing that deference is owed to 'the faculty in human beings with which they search for life's ultimate meaning' (Nussbaum 2008, 19). Consequently, regardless of whether they think that toleration qualifies as a fundamental or as merely a derivative value, liberals of all stripes believe that the state has good reasons to tread carefully in certain domains, since it is no small thing to require people to act in ways that could compromise their deepest commitments and beliefs.

In addition to this – and perhaps even more importantly – contemporary liberals are also committed to a principle of equality. As such, they do not simply argue that each person ought to have *enough* freedom of conscience – say, to whatever amount of freedom is secured by the rights and liberties guaranteed by a standard liberal constitution. Rather, they insist that everyone is entitled to *equal* freedom of conscience, such that society's laws and major institutions must respect each person's status as a full and equal member of the political community.

Exactly what this kind of equality requires has been understood to mean different things within the liberal tradition. Probably the most influential answer to this puzzle was suggested by the 'separation of church and state', a phrase used to denote both a historical process and a philosophical doctrine. Historically, separation refers to the gradual detachment of the state from religion, indicating a move towards 'secular' political arrangements and away from religious 'establishment', terms that we will explore in greater detail in chapter 6. Philosophically, it refers *both* to the principle that the state must not promote any version of religion as 'orthodox', and to the principle that the state must not dictate the terms of religious truth to believers themselves. Within the liberal tradition, the idea of separation has increasingly become associated with the idea that religious belief and practice ought to be treated as private – as opposed to public – matters. Thus, for example, Brian Barry (2001a, 24–32) suggests that contemporary liberalism is committed to a 'strategy of privatisation'.

To be sure, not every justification for the separation of church and state depends upon a robust commitment to equality. For example, an early argument for something like it can be found in Locke (2010, 6), who argued that it was important to distinguish 'political and religious matters' and to 'properly define the boundary between church and commonwealth'. For him, the case for separation was based not on a concern for equality, but rather on the respect he believed was properly owed to individual conscience, since it was a way to ensure that neither religious nor political authorities could coercively impose religious orthodoxy. Indeed, in many respects, his was a fundamentally inegalitarian doctrine because he did not extend the logic of toleration to everyone, partially excluding Catholics and atheists.

Later writers recast the case for separation in a distinctively egalitarian form, supplementing Locke's appeal to conscience with the more demanding idea that individuals should not be compelled to contribute to, or otherwise support, religious doctrines or causes they believe to be false. For example, Thomas Jefferson's 'Virginia Statute for Religious Freedom', written in 1777, declared it to be 'sinful and tyrannical' to 'compel a man to furnish contributions of money for the propagation of opinions which he disbelieves' (Jefferson, in Sargent 1997, 69). Not coincidentally, the same idea is reflected in the establishment clause of the First Amendment to the US Constitution, which insists that 'Congress shall make no law respecting an establishment of religion', thereby ruling out recognizing any particular religion as the official or established church. This clause has subsequently been understood to have some quite far-reaching implications, prohibiting things like prayer in public schools, the teaching of faith-based science in public education, and the listing of the Ten Commandments on public buildings such as courthouses (Dworkin 2013, 115).

For good reasons, the egalitarian credentials of the separation principle are now frequently emphasized by liberal political theorists, since establishing a single religion as 'official' would seem to make followers of other religions into second-class citizens (see Laborde 2017 and Lægaard 2017 for a sophisticated analysis of this issue). Notwithstanding this, in practice, many actual liberal democracies have not adopted a strict policy of separation, and, as we shall see in chapter 6, varieties of 'weak establishment', in which one or more religions are granted official recognition, remain common, especially in Western Europe. Further to this, some political theorists from outside the liberal tradition have suggested that separation is not strictly required by equality, since recognizing multiple religions on equal terms is at least a conceivable, and perhaps preferable, alternative (Bader 2007; Bhargava 2015; Modood 2016).

Meanwhile, many contemporary liberal political theorists have criticized the separation of church and state from another direction, suggesting that it only partially fulfils the demands of equality. According to them, liberal equality is properly understood to require a principle of neutrality, in which the state avoids taking sides not only amongst different religions, but also amongst religious believers and atheists, and amongst the different worldviews with which citizens identify. As Dworkin (1985, 191) put it, 'the government must be neutral on what might be called the question of the good life', and 'political decisions must be, so far as is possible, independent of any particular conception of the good life, or of what gives value to life'. Or, in Kymlicka's (1989b, 883) formulation of a similar idea, 'the state should not reward or penalize particular conceptions of the good life but, rather, should provide a neutral framework within which different and potentially conflicting conceptions of the good can be pursued'.

Neutrality is typically contrasted with perfectionism, which is the view that the state ought to promote valuable ways of life. Against this, neutrality instead directs the state to refrain from taking a view about what constitutes living well. As such, it demands more than separation, since neutrality applies to personal and cultural accounts of the good life as well as to religious ones. Beyond this, proponents disagree sharply about exactly what neutrality requires. It is widely accepted that neutrality cannot require that laws, governments and institutions have neutral effects on different ways of life, which would be an impossible ideal to realize (Arneson 2003, 193–4). For example, any set of regulations concerning abortion will privilege some conceptions of the good over others. Moreover, this form of neutrality would also be undesirable, because some basic liberal commitments will predictably lead to non-neutral outcomes (Kymlicka 1989b, 884–5; Rawls 1996, 193). For instance, if religious freedom is understood to include the freedom to proselytize, then over time we would expect some religions to thrive and attract new converts and others to lose members.

Instead of looking at effects, many contemporary liberals have tried to capture the underlying moral ideal of neutrality by focusing on the aims of a policy or its justification. Understood in these ways, a policy might fail to be neutral for one of two reasons. First, because it was designed to advantage or disadvantage a particular view of the good life, as when a particular faith – or religiosity in general – is either suppressed or encouraged. Promoting one conception of the good at the expense of others is, prima facie, unfair. Second, because the policy in question can only be justified by making controversial assumptions about the value of some particular understanding of the good life, as when coercive laws are justified by reference to reasons, values or ideas that are specific to a particular religious or ethical tradition that is not shared by all citizens. Since political power is jointly the property of everyone, assuming the truth of controversial philosophical or ethical views fails to treat everyone with equal respect.

Whichever version of neutrality one prefers, it would clearly be impossible for a liberal state to be neutral about everything. A state would not be recognizably liberal if, for example, it did not take a stand about certain human rights, the dignity of the person, or democracy. Despite what critics of liberalism have sometimes alleged, however, this observation does not render the ideal of liberal neutrality incoherent, or hypocritical, provided that neutrality is understood to apply only amongst divergent conceptions of the good, and not to values which themselves are constitutive of a liberal political order, such as freedom and equality. But for what reason might some values be singled out in this way?

It cannot be that values like freedom and equality are endorsed by every worldview circulating in society, since some people reject them. Nor can it simply be that these are the values which liberals themselves endorse, since this fails to explain why they might rightfully be imposed upon people with non-liberal worldviews. Sometimes it is suggested that worldviews which reject values like freedom and equality do not qualify as conceptions of the good in the first place, since they are based on mistaken ideas about the human good. Thus, the liberal state could be neutral amongst conceptions of the good without being neutral amongst every worldview. But this will no doubt seem arbitrary to those whose deepest beliefs and commitments are relegated in this way.

A more promising solution to this problem has been suggested by a school of political liberals who believe that there are some values which are accepted by most people, because most people are reasonable (Rawls 1996; Quong 2011). On this understanding, to be reasonable is to share in a commitment to society as a fair system of social co-operation amongst free and equal people, and to accept that different people might sincerely and in good faith reach different conclusions about serious moral and political questions. The upshot of this approach is that a liberal state may permissibly insist upon values and principles about which there is reasonable agreement, but must remain neutral regarding matters about which citizens reasonably disagree (for criticisms of this view, see Gaus 2011).

This solution comes at a cost, however, which is that, since many of the values cherished by people who describe themselves as liberal are subject to reasonable disagreement, political liberalism may have to treat much of what is popularly associated with a liberal worldview as only one conception of the good amongst others. Importantly, this arguably includes the ideal of personal autonomy, which as we saw earlier is something that some liberals believe to be an essential ingredient of a good life, and some religions and cultures deny is valuable at all. In short, because people disagree about the value of autonomy, and because this disagreement is 'reasonable', political liberalism recommends that a state committed to treating everyone as an equal must remain neutral about it.

For liberal opponents of neutrality, this is all grist to the mill. For example, if one believes that autonomy really is the fundamental liberal value, and if a commitment to neutrality disqualifies the state from promoting autonomy, then it may seem as if neutrality must give way. Thus, liberal perfectionists like Raz (1986) reject neutrality, and instead say that the state ought to promote autonomy regardless of the beliefs of its members about its value. However, the challenge for this kind of view is to explain how equality can be secured in the absence of neutrality. Meanwhile, there is another reason why some liberals are reluctant to embrace the idea that a commitment to neutrality disqualifies the state from promoting autonomy, which is that one of the most powerful reasons for favouring neutrality in the first place is that people are entitled to equal respect in their capacities to decide for themselves how to live (Mason 1990). Notice, it is the exercise of autonomy that leads to the emergence of different conceptions of the good, and it is because people have a capacity for autonomy that a policy of neutrality would seem to respect them as equals. Thus, for at least some liberals, it seems strange to say that promoting autonomy should be ruled out because it violates the principle of neutrality, if that principle itself relies on an understanding of human beings as having a capacity for autonomy.

Culture and neutrality

Quite apart from these philosophical puzzles, the idea that equality is best secured through neutrality has been particularly controversial in debates about multiculturalism. In this context, it has sometimes been assumed that, since neutrality requires the liberal state neither to promote nor to suppress particular cultures or ways of life, it should be indifferent about their successes and failures, in much the same way as the separation principle seems to require it to be about religions. Thus, the requirement that the liberal state neither favour nor disfavour any particular cultural group has been understood to require it to act as if it is 'difference blind' (Taylor 1994, 62), or to adopt a 'hands-off' approach to cultural identities (Carens 2000, 13–14), or to regard cultural differences with an attitude of 'benign neglect' (Kymlicka 1995, 115). However, critics from both within and beyond the liberal tradition have expressed two related objections to views like these, suggesting that they are neither feasible nor fair.

The feasibility objection was given its classic formulation by Kymlicka (1995, 115), who described the ideal of 'benign neglect' as a 'myth' because governments must make decisions about 'languages, internal boundaries, public holidays, and state symbols', and such decisions 'unavoidably involve recognizing, accommodating, and supporting the needs and identities of particular ethnic and national groups'. Elsewhere, Kymlicka (2001a, 4) refers to the 'myth of the ethnocultural neutrality of the [liberal] state', arguing that a state cannot be entirely indifferent about culture, since political and legal orders always are, and always must be, culturally and symbolically laden, and they cannot avoid advantaging some ways of life at the expense of others.

Meanwhile, the fairness objection says that, since a hands-off approach is impossible, then benign neglect may ultimately be unfair to minority cultures. Kymlicka (2001a, 43) makes this point implicitly, observing that actual liberal democracies are nearly always 'heavily weighted in favour of the majority group', because it is 'the majority's language that is used in public institutions; the majority's holidays that are recognized in the public calendar; the majority's history that is taught in schools, and so on'. Charles Taylor (1994, 43) makes a similar point in more forceful terms, suggesting that, because liberal political institutions and procedures are typically based on 'a reflection of one hegemonic culture', then 'subtle and unconscious' forms of discrimination against minorities may arise if the liberal state proceeds as if it is neutral, when it is in fact not. As will be discussed in the next chapter, Taylor is particularly worried about members of cultural and linguistic minorities, since they are more likely to be denied the institutional supports and privileges that are unreflectively awarded to the majority culture.

Taken together, these two objections suggest that a hands-off interpretation of neutrality might sometimes undermine equality, at least when it comes to differences of culture or language. Nevertheless, one might still believe that neutrality is justified in the special case of religious diversity, since religion would seem to be something that states can avoid recognizing or promoting. However, even this is doubtful, as can be illustrated by considering the 1963 case of *Sherbert* v. *Verner*. This involved Adell Sherbert, a Seventh-Day Adventist working in a textile factory in South Carolina. Sherbert's employers had required her to be available for work on a Saturday, something that she believed she could not in good conscience do, since she thought working on a Saturday to be religiously impermissible. The state took an interest in Sherbert's predicament because it needed to decide whether she was entitled to unemployment compensation, which she would not be had she refused suitable work. Sherbert had not been deliberately victimized by her employer. Indeed, not only did her employer make the same request of her co-workers, but other local employers also imposed similar requirements on their workers too. Rather, her difficulties arose because she observed non-standard Sabbatarian norms, meaning that being available to work on a Saturday would burden her to a greater extent than it would her peers who worshipped on a Sunday. What this case indicates is that majority religious norms, just like majority cultural and linguistic practices, can profoundly shape the background circumstances against which liberal principles are applied. Given this, a difference-blind approach, in which the state studiously ignores religious differences in its application of ostensibly neutral rules and policies, could turn out to be substantively unfair.

Liberals have responded in different ways to the objection that it would be neither feasible nor fair for the state to be neutral about cultural, linguistic and even religious differences. Some suggest that liberal neutrality should be replaced with an alternative principle. For example, Joseph Carens cautions against treating liberal principles as neutral and abstract rules making identical demands on everyone, regardless of their culture, beliefs or identity. Instead, when faced with difficult decisions, we should carry out a 'sensitive balancing of competing claims for recognition and support', taking into account the relevant context, people's particular situations and the historical and cultural context, in order to reach an 'evenhanded' solution (Carens 2000, 12). For example, if we ignore context, then it may appear as if Adell Sherbert was being treated fairly when she was required, like everyone else, to be available for work on a Saturday. But we are likely to reach a very different judgement if we take into account the significance she attached to her religious beliefs, the importance of employment in North American societies, and the historical influence of mainstream Christianity on American under-standings of the working week. Thus, Carens concludes that treating people fairly, in an even-handed manner, may require guaranteeing Sherbert (and others like her) time off to worship on days other than Sunday.

Meanwhile, Alan Patten (2014, 115) has proposed reinterpreting, rather than replacing, the ideal of liberal neutrality, defending a principle of 'neutrality of treatment' whose central claim is that liberal states ought to be equally accommodating of different conceptions of the good, extending equivalent forms of assistance and imposing the same burdens on each. Neutrality of treatment will require different things in different contexts. Whilst the state should sometimes avoid becoming entangled with matters of culture and religion, in other cases it should actively support cultural and religious bodies. Active support can sometimes be provided in a 'generic' way, as when fire and police services are provided to religious institutions, or it might sometimes need to be targeted at particular groups, as for policies to promote or preserve vulnerable languages (Patten 2014, 121).

Patten thinks that providing such targeted supports is consistent
with neutrality of treatment, as long as comparably valuable forms
of support are provided for rival ways of life too.

Both of these proposals amount to roughly the same conclusion –
namely, that equal treatment under conditions of cultural diversity
may sometimes require difference-sensitive policies, such as forms
of recognition or accommodation to address specifically the needs
and interests of cultural minorities, and that such policies ought to
be carefully tailored in light of the relevant context and to ensure
fairness for all. In the end, whether such policies amount to a
deviation from liberal neutrality, as Carens suggests, or are part
of what neutrality of treatment requires, as Patten proposes, is a
secondary issue. Much more pressing is the question of whether such
forms of recognition and accommodation can themselves be justified
in terms acceptable to liberalism, and the remainder of the chapter
will explore two contrasting and influential answers to this question
given by contemporary liberal political theorists.

Autonomy and Cultural Rights

The most influential liberal argument in support of special rights
and accommodations for cultural minorities has been proposed
by Canadian political theorist Will Kymlicka, especially in his
Multicultural Citizenship (1995). His theory belongs to a family of
'liberal culturalist' views, along with those of Yael Tamir (1993),
Joseph Raz (1994), Joseph Carens (2000) and Alan Patten (2014).
These thinkers are united in believing that 'liberal-democratic states
should not only uphold the familiar set of common civil and political
rights of citizenship which are protected in all liberal democracies; they
must also adopt various group-specific rights and policies which are
intended to recognise and accommodate the distinctive identities and
needs of ethnocultural groups' (Kymlicka 2001a, 41). These group-
specific rights and policies include things like financial subsidies for
minority-language schools or cultural activities, guaranteed political
representation, exemptions from generally applicable laws, and
political autonomy. Since their aim is to secure the value of cultural
membership for minorities and to protect them against the threat of
cultural loss, I will refer to them as cultural rights.

According to Kymlicka, the interest served by cultural rights is
shared by all human beings, not only minorities, and it has to do with
exercising one's capacity for autonomy. As noted earlier, this means
being able to pursue projects and plans in accordance with one's

beliefs about what gives value to life, and being able to revise those beliefs and plans over the course of a lifetime. Like other autonomy liberals, Kymlicka thinks that this interest underpins many standard liberal rights and freedoms, such as the major civil and political liberties protecting individual freedoms of choice and association, as well as the social and educational rights ensuring that people can intelligently choose amongst different life plans. Distinctively, Kymlicka (1995, 75) thinks that the same interest can also explain why the liberal state should actively support the attempts of cultural minorities to sustain their distinctive ways of life, since he believes that 'freedom is intimately linked with and dependent on culture'.

Kymlicka's (1995, 83) case for believing that freedom is culture-dependent proceeds from the observation that if people are to form and revise their conceptions of the good, then they will need to have available to them 'a range of meaningful options'. For example, he suggests that living autonomously requires, amongst other things, exposure to a range of possible life plans and the ability to select amongst alternatives. In turn, cultures are crucial for this, because they are 'option generators' (Patten 2014, 93–5), providing us with a 'context of choice' that gives us options about how to lead our lives, as well as the concepts and cultural narratives we need to make sense of those options (Kymlicka 1989a, 166). We can think of cultures as performing two functions: a menu function, by giving us options from which to choose when constructing our life plans; and an interpretive function, enabling us to select amongst those options intelligibly. This interpretive function is crucial, since if we are to make autonomous choices about how to live, then we must have beliefs about which of the available options are valuable, and we can only form such beliefs if we already have some understanding of the meanings our cultures attach to different social practices. Thus, as Kymlicka (1995, 83) summarizes his own thesis: 'freedom involves making choices amongst various options, and our societal culture not only provides these options, but also makes them meaningful to us'.

Notice that Kymlicka has a very specific conception of culture in mind here, which he signals by employing the term 'societal culture'. Many of the groups and ways of life that we might ordinarily describe as 'cultures' are not societal cultures in Kymlicka's sense – such as sports fans, gastronomes or birdwatchers. Even though the members of such groups may be united by strong bonds, shared practices or common outlooks, these are not societal cultures because they do not supply members with a rich enough variety of options across a lifetime. By contrast, Kymlicka (1995, 75) thinks that linguistically distinct nationalities and Indigenous communities are societal cultures, since they play an important role in nourishing the freedom of their members, providing them with 'meaningful ways of life across the range of human activities, including social, educational, religious, recreational, and economic life, encompassing both public and private spheres'. Accordingly, he believes that the viability of societal cultures matters in a basic way for the freedom of members, and in a way that the viability of other and narrower groups and associations does not.

The distinction between 'cultures' in the everyday sense and 'societal cultures' in the special sense helps to bring out an important feature of Kymlicka's argument, which is that his context-of-choice justification for cultural rights does not depend on the strength of a person's emotional or psychological attachments to their cultural practices or identity. Kymlicka is, of course, aware that, as a matter of fact, many people are intensely attached to their own societal cultures. But societal cultures are not distinctive in this respect, since this can also be true of birdwatching associations and sports fans, whose members likewise can take great pride in their group and its achievements, or would suffer a profound loss if their collective activities became unsustainable. Kymlicka is able to explain why societal cultures ought to be publicly supported, even when their members are lukewarm or indifferent about their own culture, whilst birdwatchers or sports fans are not entitled to comparable supports, even if their preferences are much more intense. The difference is that, although birdwatchers and sports fans may very much want to engage in their respective practices, it is only the members of societal cultures who have a freedom-based interest in sustaining a context of choice that provides them with meaningful options.

The context-of-choice argument is vulnerable to a widely discussed objection, which Alan Patten (2014, 75) has aptly labelled the 'particularity problem'. As far as I am aware, this was first noticed by Allen Buchanan (1991, 54), who observed that, according to the context-of-choice argument, 'what is important is that an individual be able to belong to a culture, some culture or other, not that he be able to belong, indefinitely, to any culture'. The normative implications of this objection are significant. For example, John Tomasi (1995, 594) has suggested that Kymlicka's conception of culture 'generates no special rights', since nearly everyone has access to some context of choice or another. Similarly, Avishai Margalit and Moshe Halbertal (1994, 504–5) point out that, by the standards of the context-of-choice argument, the members of an Indigenous community whose culture was 'destroyed by the presence of a white majority in their territory' would have no claim to cultural rights if they 'were able to assimilate, albeit against their will, into the white culture ... because their assimilation into the majority culture guarantees them what is important in a culture from Kymlicka's point of view – the ability to evaluate and choose among various life options'.

Kymlicka (1989a, 166–70) laid the foundations for this objection himself in his first major work, *Liberalism, Community and Culture*, where he suggested that changes to the 'character' of a culture – including changes in the norms, values and institutions of a particular community – do not amount to cultural loss, so long as a cultural 'structure' providing a context of choice remains. He made this claim because, as a liberal, he wanted to protect the freedom of members to modify the character of their own culture. To illustrate the significance of this, he discussed the 'Quiet Revolution' amongst French-speaking Canadians, whose culture was transformed during the 1960s from a traditional, agrarian and religious way of life to a more urbanized and broadly secular one. Although some members may have preferred it had things stayed the same, Kymlicka thinks their interest in freedom was not threatened by this transformation, since throughout the process they retained a cultural 'structure'.

What the 'particularity problem' picks out is that, from the perspective of the context-of-choice argument alone, there seems to be no difference between the situation of a Francophone Canadian who laments modernization and a member of Margalit and Halbertal's Indigenous community who has involuntarily assimilated into the dominant culture. Both individuals regret a process of cultural shift that has nevertheless left them with a good enough context of choice. But many people believe that the members of the Indigenous community were wronged in a way that was not true for the Francophone Canadians. Indeed, Kymlicka agrees, and his writings contain attempts to both modify and supplement his original context-of-choice argument to explain why.

The modification strategy occurs in *Liberalism, Community and Culture*, where Kymlicka (1989a, 167, 169 and 170) occasionally proposes that freedom depends not only on a person having a context of choice, but on them having a 'stable' or 'secure' context of choice. Although he does not explain what exactly he intends these modifiers to signify, a plausible reading is that he believes that autonomy will be compromised when a person's cultural context changes too quickly or dramatically, because rapid transformations will be disorientating and thereby make meaningful choice difficult or impossible. This interpretation conceivably explains the differences between the two examples, since it was only the members of the Indigenous community who found themselves thrown into a deeply different societal culture.

This strategy for shoring up the context-of-choice argument can be supported by considering the often shattering effects culture loss has had on Indigenous peoples. A dramatic illustration of these can be found in philosopher and psychoanalyst Jonathan Lear's *Radical Hope: Ethics in the Face of Cultural Devastation* (2006), where he reflects on the life of Plenty Coups, the last great Crow chief, who led his people through a traumatic transition to life on a reservation, which made his group's traditional way of life, centred on war and hunting, impossible. At least on the face of things, Plenty Coups seemed to accept and even embrace his new situation, continuing as a leader, negotiating with the US government alongside other Crow chiefs, taking up farming, and even winning prizes at agricultural shows. However, in another and perhaps more significant sense, his life – and those of the other Crow – was entirely upended.

Lear (2006, 2) pays special attention to a haunting remark Plenty Coups made towards the end of his life, where he says that, after moving to the reservation, 'nothing happened'. It is certainly possible that, by this, he was simply seeking to convey how dejected the transformation had left his people. Indeed, he also said that after this date, '[t]here was little singing anywhere' and that 'the hearts of my people fell to the ground, and they could not lift them up again' (cited in Lear 2006, 2). However, Lear takes the statement that 'nothing happened' literally and proposes another interpretation, suggesting that when their traditional way of life was halted, history ended for the Crow, because their universe of shared meanings and understandings, which their traditional way of life had sustained, broke down. As Lear sees it, what the Crow lost was not only the possibility of living as they once had done. Rather, everything ceased to make sense or have meaning – 'nothing happened' after this point because nothing of significance was possible.

If something like the account Lear offers is correct, then culture loss for the Crow was not only disorientating and traumatic, but also fatal to their capacity for autonomy. However, it would be too hasty to infer that the autonomy of anyone who directly experiences a similarly rapid and unwelcome cultural transition will be likewise compromised, especially when the differences between cultures are more modest. In particular, many national minorities have cultures that already closely resemble locally dominant majority cultures, such as the Scottish in Britain, the Québécois in Canada, and the Catalans in Spain, for instance. Even if assimilation into the majority would be unwelcome for some of their members, it would hardly have the same effects as it did for the Crow, since they would surely be able to adjust themselves to their new cultural circumstances, creating new and meaningful options from which to construct their lives. Kymlicka (1995, 85) acknowledges as much in his later work, suggesting that people can move between very different cultures without experiencing an injury to their autonomy. Furthermore, he refers to the Quiet Revolution as a 'rapid period of liberalisation', indicating that a societal culture can change quickly and radically without jeopardizing the freedom of its members (Kymlicka 1995, 87). Another and final reason to be cautious about putting too much weight on the idea that people need a 'stable' context of choice is that it risks blurring the distinction Kymlicka drew earlier between the character and structure of a culture. Recall that Kymlicka believes that a culture may operate as a context of choice even when its values, norms and institutions change. But almost any plausible construal of the idea that people need a stable context of choice looks as if it will translate into an injunction to preserve a specific cultural character.

The other strategy Kymlicka (1995, 86) employs to address the particularity problem is to supplement his context-of-choice argument with an additional one about 'reasonable' or 'legitimate' expectations. He first hinted towards this possibility in *Liberalism, Community and Culture*, where he briefly noted a difference between cultural changes that arise 'because of the choices of members' and cultural changes that arise 'in spite of the choices of members' (Kymlicka 1989a, 167). Although this distinction is not fleshed out in any detail, it captures an important dissimilarity between the two cases – namely, that cultural change arose from within for Francophone Canadians, and was something that at least some of them sought, but came about due to external pressures for the Indigenous community, and was something that many members resisted. Kymlicka (1995, 37 and 35) drew a similar distinction in his *Multicultural Citizenship*, suggesting that cultural rights should protect cultures from the 'destabilising impact of [e.g. political and economic] decisions of the larger society' but not from 'internal dissent', such as the decisions of individual members to reject particular cultural traditions or practices.

Another passage in *Multicultural Citizenship* also explains why cultural changes that arise against the wishes of members should concern us. There, Kymlicka (1995, 86) claims that people have a 'legitimate expectation to remain in their culture', and that, as a consequence, 'we should treat access to one's culture as something that people can be expected to want, whatever their more particular conception of the good'. Furthermore, he remarks that '[l]eaving one's culture, whilst possible, is best seen as renouncing something to which one is reasonably entitled', going on to describe this as 'a claim not about the limits of human possibility, but about reasonable expectations' (Kymlicka 1995, 86). Notice that Kymlicka cannot only mean that people have strong preferences about participating in particular cultural traditions or using their own language, since this is likewise true of birdwatchers, gastronomes and sports fans. Rather, it must be that the 'bond' that ties people to their societal cultures is something that should be treated as a kind of basic social or psychological fact. Ultimately, Kymlicka (1995, 90) does not explain what this bond consists in, or why it is so foundational, only speculating that 'the causes of this attachment lie deep in the human condition, tied up with the way that humans as cultural creatures need to make sense of the world'.

So, Kymlicka's considered position is that people are entitled to be protected against cultural loss for two reasons: because everyone has a freedom-based interest in having access to an adequate context of choice, and because continuing enjoyment of one's own culture is something that people can legitimately or reasonably expect. Given that it is the latter reason which explains why people have a right to *their culture*, and not just to *a culture*, it may seem surprising that Kymlicka puts so much emphasis on the autonomy argument. Indeed, some proponents of minority rights have reached broadly similar conclusions to Kymlicka by proceeding immediately to something like his second reason, including Margalit and Halbertal. Like Kymlicka, they believe that the state ought to subsidize and support minority cultures in order to secure an important interest that all people share in common. However, the interest they pick out has to do with a person's 'personality identity'. Because these are shaped by cultures, everyone has an interest in being able 'to preserve the attributes that are seen as central by them and the members of their group' (Margalit and Halbertal 1994, 502), and this will be jeopardized if their culture changes dramatically or against their wishes, as when a traditional way of life becomes unsustainable.

There is, however, a significant difference between Margalit and Halbertal's argument and Kymlicka's, which has to do with the central place of autonomy in Kymlicka's theory. Some cultures frustrate the autonomy interests of members, for instance because they are oppressive, because they restrict the freedom of women and girls, or because they require adherence to strict rules or traditions. If illiberal cultures like these serve the identity interests of members, then by the standards of Margalit and Halbertal's argument they ought to be supported. Hence, Margalit and Halbertal (1994, 506–9) conclude that the Ultra-Orthodox in Israel ought to be given substantial public supports to enable them to preserve their traditional, deeply religious and illiberal, way of life. By contrast, Kymlicka (1995, 95) says that, although 'as a general rule' the liberal state should not prevent illiberal cultures from maintaining their societal culture, it should also 'promote the liberalisation of these cultures'. It is for this reason that Kymlicka argues against exempting the Amish from compulsory schooling. His position here might seem confusing. The Amish arguably have a societal culture by Kymlicka's standards, since they are a distinctive social group whose culture provides its members with an adequate, albeit limited, range of meaningful options. Likewise, the Amish themselves have a reasonable expectation that they be able to continue enjoying their culture. However, Kymlicka's version of liberal culturalism rules out allowing them to remove their younger members from school, since that would prevent them from developing the skills required to critically question and revise their own beliefs. In turn, requiring Amish children to participate in education is a way of promoting the liberalization of their culture.

The significance of autonomy for Kymlicka (1995, 35–44) is further reflected in another distinction he draws about the form cultural rights should take. On the one hand, he cautions against cultural rights that would empower a group to limit the freedom of its members for the sake of religious orthodoxy, cultural purity or group solidarity. Kymlicka (1995, 40) describes policies like these as 'internal restrictions' and he worries that they are often oppressive, as when the Pueblo, a Native American community, undermined the principle of religious freedom by ostracizing members who converted to Christianity, and denied them housing benefits. On the other hand, he is more sympathetic to what he calls 'external protections', which concern relations between groups rather than within them. Although these too can sometimes be unfair – for instance, if they empower one group at the expense of another – Kymlicka is generally supportive of them because they can play a crucial role in supporting equality between different cultures and protecting minorities against majoritarian domination. External protections take a number of different forms, including quotas in electoral systems, subsidizing minority-language media, or funding cultural festivals. However, as discussed in chapter 1, the most important of these are self-government rights, because they ensure that a 'minority cannot be outbid or outvoted by the majority on decisions that are of particular importance to their culture' (Kymlicka 1995, 37–8). These will be the focus of chapter 8.

At the end of the last century, Kymlicka (1998, 143–57) suggested that there was an 'emerging consensus' about liberal culturalism. This judgement was too hasty. As we will see in chapter 4, some liberals oppose multiculturalism and cultural rights, and as we will see in chapter 3, some multiculturalists think that liberalism is the wrong place to start from. Meanwhile, the main multicultural alternative to Kymlicka's theory within the liberal tradition has been proposed by Chandran Kukathas.

The Politics of Indifference

Evocatively, Kukathas (1998, 691) characterizes his own theory as recommending a 'politics of indifference'. This is because he believes that the liberal state should tolerate a great diversity of cultures and ways of life, including illiberal ones, and that minority cultures are not entitled to any special accommodations or supports. Thus, the liberal state should be 'indifferent' in two respects. First, it should leave people alone and resist the temptation to interfere in their traditional cultural practices, allowing them to pursue their own goals and projects, alone or in association with one another. Second, it should also be indifferent about the success or failure of different cultural projects, neither supporting nor discouraging particular enactments of human difference. Consequently, unlike Kymlicka, Kukathas (1998, 692–3) believes that the state should not actively guard against the threat of cultural loss – for instance, by subsidizing vulnerable languages or minority cultural practices – because it is not the role of the liberal state to 'rescue minority groups from their marginalized status in society', and 'from the liberal standpoint', it does not matter if some cultural groups 'are assimilated into the dominant culture of the wider society, or disappear altogether'.

   Although this is a liberal theory, it is very different to Kymlicka's, and there are two basic reasons for this. First, Kukathas and Kymlicka have different understandings of human interests. Like other liberals, they agree that everyone has a basic interest in individual freedom. Kukathas captures this by saying that being unable to do what one thinks is right is one of the worst fates someone can endure. Accordingly, he insists that being able to live in accordance with the demands of conscience is an interest 'shared by the remote Aboriginals of Australia; the fifteenth-century samurai; the Ibo tribesman; the Irish Catholic living in twentieth-century Dublin; the Hasidic Jew in New York; and the Branch Davidian in Texas' (Kukathas 2003, 55). As we have seen, Kymlicka (1995, 81) also thinks there is a universal interest in being able to live according to one's own beliefs, but on top of this he also thinks that each of us has an interest in being able to intelligently question and revise those beliefs. Kukathas (2003, 61) denies the latter claim, arguing that '[i]t is quite possible for the unchosen life to be regarded by the individual living it as worthwhile'. To illustrate this, he discusses a Muslim fisherman from Kelantin in Malaysia, whom Kukathas (2003, 59) supposes lacks the opportunity to intelligently question and revise his beliefs, which have remained, and likely will remain, the same throughout his life. Yet he is comfortable, enjoys love and affection, takes pride in his work and in providing for his children, and justifiably believes that his life has meaning and purpose. Because Kukathas denies that an interest in autonomy is universal, he rejects Kymlicka's autonomy argument for cultural rights. Furthermore, and like Galston, he also points out that promoting autonomy will undermine some traditional ways of life, 'reshaping' them against 'the terms set by their own practices' (Kukathas 1992, 122).

The second basic disagreement between Kymlicka and Kukathas concerns the content and role of liberal values. According to Kukathas (2003, 19), Kymlicka's theory belongs to a distinctive tradition within liberalism that picks out 'a set of values and moral standards' and insists they be upheld across society. Kukathas (2003, 19) criticizes these approaches for not giving moral diversity its due, and for burdening ways of life that do not recognize the values or standards in question, instead recommending that liberals respond to diversity by trying to identify 'principles by which different moral standards may be allowed to exist'. Thus, the problem to be solved is finding acceptable terms of social co-operation for very different, and often conflictual, ways of life.

The central plank in Kukathas's own solution is toleration. Not only does he insist that people must be allowed to live by the lights of their own conscience, but also he criticizes official intolerance of controversial practices for being morally dogmatic, since it does nothing more than convert societal disapproval into legal prohibition. For sure, it is not disapproval *per se* that Kukathas objects to, because some people might feel compelled as a matter of conscience to disapprove of other people's practices. Rather, he objects to making disapproval official, since that involves adopting a standpoint from which to judge a particular practice or conception of the good, something the liberal state must not do.

The conception of toleration Kukathas (2003, 140) opts for is a far-reaching one of 'pure toleration'. This differs significantly from Kymlicka's (1995, 158) 'very specific notion of tolerance' which treats it as a derivative value, subordinate to autonomy, concerned to protect both 'the right of groups not to be persecuted by the state' and the 'right of individuals to dissent from their group'. The latter is essential for Kymlicka, underpinning his wariness about internal restrictions, because otherwise individual autonomy would be vitiated. To motivate support for it, Kymlicka (1992, 35) contrasts his conception of toleration with the 'millet' system of the Ottoman Empire, in which Muslims, Christians and Jews tolerated one another by living separately, in a 'federation of theocracies'. By his account, this was a regime of toleration only in the limited senses that its component groups refrained from interfering in one another's affairs, and religious minorities were mostly left alone by the state. However, individual autonomy was not adequately protected because there was very little scope for individual dissent and self-development within these groups.

Against Kymlicka, Kukathas rejects not only the idea that the liberal state should promote a controversial value such as autonomy, but also the idea that the liberal state should compel groups to tolerate internal dissent. Kukathas (2003, 37) supports the latter claim by pointing out that groups containing dissenters nearly always contain an opposing majority too. Consequently, protecting individual dissenters will often mean requiring the members of that majority to act against, or compromise, their own conscientious convictions. For instance, recall the Christian converts who were ostracized and discriminated against by their fellow Pueblo. On Kymlicka's reading, as seen already, the sanctions imposed on the dissenters were unacceptably strong, since they were tantamount to eliminating their religious freedom, and therefore their autonomy. Meanwhile, Kukathas (2003, 137–8) emphasizes that demanding the majority to tolerate the dissenters was incompatible with their traditional practices. Thus, for him, what was at stake was the freedom of the majority to govern their own affairs according to what they perceived to be the demands of conscience.

The implications of Kukathas's view are radical and controversial. For example, the long list of practices that he has defended include group customs that restrict the opportunities of women to own property and participate in education, child-rearing practices that limit the opportunities of children to prepare for life outside the group, physically harmful operations such as scarring and female genital mutilation, risky initiation rites, animal cruelty, and severe forms of punishment including deprivation and ostracism (Festenstein 2005, 101). Many of these fall into Kymlicka's category of internal restrictions, and Kukathas (1992, 251) acknowledges that his view will allow many groups to constrain severely the freedom of their members: 'Freedom of worship may not be respected; women may have opportunities closed off to them; and the rights of individuals to express themselves may be severely restricted'. In defence of this, he bolsters his appeal to toleration with an additional argument based on the principle of freedom of association.

This argument presses on the observation that, by liberal standards, internal restrictions are not always morally objectionable. For instance, consider the strict rules regulating daily life within monasteries. For most liberals, these are perfectly acceptable, since the members themselves have chosen to forsake a number of freedoms for a higher purpose. Similarly comprehensive and strict regulations also bind the members of most religious traditions. For example, Kukathas (2003, 93) cites the example of the Unification Church, known colloquially as the Moonies, whose members are 'bound by codes that severely restrict their choice of marriage partner, their choice of career, and even their choice of a place – or country – to live'. For some closed religious orders, we might think that what makes internal restrictions acceptable is that the members have chosen to accept them, for instance by taking vows of obedience, poverty and chastity. However, Kukathas (2003, 96) suggests that this need not be the case, and instead proposes a weaker standard, arguing that an association has the authority to bind its members 'for as long as those members recognise as legitimate the terms of their associations, and the authority that upholds them'. In turn, he thinks that the only evidence needed for this is that members have elected not to leave. As he puts it, the 'basis of any association's or community's authority ... [is] the *acquiescence* of its members' (Kukathas 2003, 96).

According to this standard, many groups will have legitimate authority over their members, not only voluntary associations like monastic communities. For example, consider someone born into a particular faith or way of life and who experiences their ensuing membership as unchosen. She has acquiesced to the authority of the group, provided that she may permissibly leave and does not do so. However, acquiescence alone does not explain why particular practices, including internal restrictions, are legitimate, since members might acquiesce to the authority of an association whilst objecting to some of its practices – for instance, if they mark one out as having an inferior status. In response, Kukathas (2003, 99–100) points out that there is a difference between 'agreeing to' something and 'agreeing with' it, and suggests that all that is required for restrictive practices within a community to be legitimate is that members 'agree to' them. Further, people who do not 'agree with' particular internal restrictions always retain the option to exit, thereby repudiating whatever authority the group has over them (Kukathas 2003, 97). Against this, critics have suggested that mere acquiescence sets too low a bar for establishing the legitimacy of an internal restriction, since someone might 'agree to' the norms and practices of a group because of poor self-esteem, a weak sense of self-entitlement, or having inadequate options outside the group (Barry 2001a, 146-54).

Kukathas (2003, 8) depicts his preferred society as an 'archipelago', envisaging a political order made up 'of different communities operating in a sea of mutual toleration', each living out a distinctive view about what makes life meaningful. Because there is no general consensus about morality or the good life, the state must refrain from imposing particular values or moral standards, and must studiously avoid interfering in people's lives in ways that would compel them to act against their consciences. As such, it must not seek to reform illiberal cultures, even if some members of those cultures would like it to do so. Strikingly, although Kukathas's theory condemns the imposition of liberal values on illiberal groups as moral dogmatism, it is comparatively relaxed about those groups themselves, or their leaders, dogmatically imposing an illiberal worldview upon their members, even if this means that vulnerable members find themselves exposed to discrimination or persecution, or with severely limited opportunities for self-development. It is therefore, perhaps, not surprising that liberal-minded critics have condemned his far-reaching conception of toleration as 'a formula for creating a lot of private hells' (Barry 2001a, 143) or a 'mosaic of tyrannies' (Green 1994, 116).

Conclusion

In this chapter we have seen that some liberals recommend that the state adopt a broadly hands-off approach to cultural differences, tolerating a great diversity of minority cultures and their practices, but not supporting or promoting any of them. At the same time, others favour a more hands-on approach – for instance, advocating the protection of vulnerable languages and cultural identities, but sometimes also the promotion of distinctively liberal values within minority cultures too. I have suggested that we can explain the various disagreements amongst contemporary liberal political theorists by situating them within the context of longstanding philosophical disputes about three central liberal values: freedom, toleration and neutrality. Although liberals of all stripes acknowledge these values to be significant, they offer contrasting accounts about what they consist in and what their role is, and these disagreements feed into some very different views about how a liberal state ought to respond to cultural diversity.

It is clear that even those liberal political theorists who are broadly sympathetic to multiculturalism and minority rights disagree about many substantive issues. For example, Kymlicka criticizes Kukathas for failing to appreciate that freedom is a culture-dependent concept, whilst Kukathas accuses Kymlicka of moral dogmatism and of failing to give toleration its proper due. In addition to disagreements like these, many political theorists have also argued that liberalism – properly understood – is incompatible with the kinds of difference-sensitive policies or extensive regimes of toleration that multiculturalists tend to favour. Multiculturalists from outside the liberal tradition have pressed one version of this objection, which we shall examine in chapter 3, arguing that liberal principles provide the wrong theoretical framework from which to address the politics of cultural diversity. Meanwhile, liberal critics of multiculturalism have pressed another version of this objection, which we shall examine in chapter 4, arguing that Kymlicka, Kukathas and others like them go wrong by mistakenly deriving a case for multiculturalism and minority rights from liberal principles.

3

Beyond the Liberal Tradition: Recognition and Dialogue

This chapter explores how political theorists from outside the liberal tradition, or its margins, have questioned liberal approaches to multiculturalism and proposed alternative theoretical frameworks. Although the writings considered draw on different theoretical traditions, one aim will be to emphasize some important commonalities. The most significant of these is the criticism that liberal approaches to multiculturalism are insufficiently egalitarian, and that correcting this will require drawing upon novel conceptual resources. As the title of this chapter indicates, ideas about recognition and dialogue have been central to such proposals. To understand why, it will be helpful to begin by saying something about two shortcomings identified by liberalism's critics.

First, liberalism has been accused of neglecting the background conditions against which its own principles apply, especially the complex dynamics of inclusion and exclusion found in many culturally diverse societies. Liberals too often depict cultural diversity as a form of moral pluralism, constituted by people's different beliefs about morality and the good life. But this way of imagining cultural diversity is reductive since it neglects asymmetries of power and status, instead presenting the primary challenge of multiculturalism as reconciling conflicting belief systems. This leaves liberals unable to comprehend fully some of the most pressing issues faced by multicultural societies, including those which arise because minorities perceive themselves to be marginalized, dominated or excluded on the basis of their identities.

Second, liberalism has also been accused of being misleading for presenting its own principles as neutral and objective, standing above the fray of competing worldviews, doctrines and traditions. But, according to critics, liberalism is one particular worldview amongst others, wedded to distinctive ideas about what makes a human life worthwhile, which are not universally endorsed. As such, it is not only short-sighted but arrogant to posit liberalism as the guiding framework for addressing cultural diversity, since doing so rules out the possibility of mutual learning between liberalism and other intellectual traditions.

This rest of this chapter will explore two approaches to multiculturalism that explicitly challenge the liberal tradition, suggesting ways either to enlarge or to move beyond it. One is the politics of recognition, which says that promoting equality and inclusion requires not only a fair distribution of goods and resources, but also that the state publicly recognize and affirm differences related to things such as language, race, gender, religion, sexuality and disability. Theories of recognition take their intellectual cues from a number of sources, including the German idealist philosopher Hegel and the twentieth-century Frankfurt school of critical theory. Although one motivation for philosophers who appeal to recognition is to reveal the shortcomings of liberal political theory, at least some believe its major demands can be accommodated within a suitably extended liberalism, including Charles Taylor (1994) and Anna Elisabetta Galeotti (2002). After exploring the idea that recognition is a 'vital human need' (Taylor 1994, 26), I will examine some of the main political claims associated with the politics of recognition, including the preservation of vulnerable cultures as well as measures to acknowledge the equal worth of different identities and traditions.

The other approach is intercultural dialogue. It is often difficult and frustrating to reach an understanding between and across cultures because each of us is already immersed within a particular framework of meaning, giving us a vantage point from which it can be difficult to comprehend the value or significance of beliefs and practices rooted in unfamiliar ways of life. Nevertheless, engaging seriously with other cultures and their ideas can benefit us in different ways. As individuals, it 'challenges us intellectually and morally, stretches our imagination, and compels us to recognize the limits of our categories of thought' (Parekh 2000, 167). Moreover, engaging with different ways of life can provide people with an opportunity to reflect on their own cultures and traditions, often providing an impetus to revise and reform practices that no longer satisfy their needs or interests. More controversially, multiculturalists have also suggested that collectively exploring our commonalities and differences offers the prospect of reaching a genuine consensus about how a multicultural society should arrange and regulate its shared institutions.

Recognition

A number of thinkers have argued that the most important contemporary political controversies are not only – or even primarily – about competition over resources, but instead consist in 'struggles for recognition' as individuals and groups seek public affirmation of their identity (Taylor 1994; Tully 1995; Honneth 1996, 2007; Galeotti 2002; Fraser 2008). The demand for recognition typically arises in response to the social influence of majoritarian norms and expectations, which can have the effect of stigmatizing disadvantaged minorities, or pressuring them to conform to dominant social norms, both of which can be oppressive and humiliating. For example, women in patriarchal societies may be treated as sexual objects and find that their experiences are devalued, LGBTQ+ people may be portrayed as deviant and feel unable to express themselves freely, and members of ethnic minorities may feel that they must adjust their behaviour to conform with majority mores. In these cases, and others like them, remedying oppression will require not only extending equal civil, political, economic and social rights, but also affording public respect and recognition to marginalized identities and ways of life. This might be achieved through a variety of measures, including the robust application of anti-discrimination laws, ensuring that minorities are respected and adequately represented in public institutions, and enlarging society's understanding of itself.

The political and philosophical agendas staked out by proponents of the politics of recognition have met with a mixed reaction, ranging from sympathetic scepticism (e.g. Benhabib 2002; Markell 2003; Appiah 2005) to forthright opposition (e.g. Kukathas 1998; Barry 2001a; McNay 2008). This chapter will mostly concentrate on the work of Canadian political theorist Charles Taylor, since he is responsible for developing the most influential account of recognition within the context of debates about multiculturalism. Moreover, he explicitly contrasts his own view with the kinds of theories explored in the previous chapter, which he variously refers to as the 'liberalism of rights' (Taylor 1994, 60) and 'procedural liberalism' (Taylor 1994, 61). Interestingly, Taylor (1994, 62) situates his theory within the liberal tradition, taking himself to espouse a version of liberalism that is less 'rigid' than usual and more 'hospitable' to difference. However, since he is expressly sceptical about many of the central components of liberal political theory, including individualism and neutrality, I treat him as a sympathetic critic, rather than a fully fledged member, of the liberal tradition.

Liberalism's shortcomings

Taylor developed his account of recognition in a now famous essay called 'The Politics of Recognition', first published in 1992. Here, he argued both that recognition of one's identity has become an important human need, and that orthodox liberal political theory could not fully grasp this. Already Taylor had established himself as a leading 'communitarian' critic of liberalism – a school of thought that came to prominence in the 1980s, whose members accused liberalism of neglecting membership, belonging and the role of shared meanings and understandings in supporting democracy (Mulhall and Swift 1996). A characteristic communitarian complaint was that liberal individualism and state neutrality risked inducing isolation, anomie and confusion – fates that could be avoided only by a 'politics of the common good'. As such, unlike many liberals at the time, communitarians believed that fostering greater unity at the level of the nation-state was a legitimate, and indeed desirable, political project. Simultaneously, communitarians also argued that liberal politics threatened some traditional ways of life, calling for various minority rights to protect these vulnerable communities (Van Dyke 1977, 1982).

Taylor's work on recognition extended arguments from his earlier communitarian writings about the limitations of liberal understandings of the self. There, Taylor (1979, 1985) had argued that liberalism assumed a misleadingly atomistic conception of society and its members, imagining the human self to be an autonomous and self-sufficient entity, somehow separable from its projects, goals and defining characteristics, such as language and culture. These themes were rehearsed in his essay on recognition, but now Taylor (1994) drew a contrast between a monological conception of identity formation, which he associated with 'procedural liberalism', and a superior diaological conception. In both formulations of what is basically the same thesis, Taylor accuses liberalism of endorsing a dangerous fiction, and the shifts in terminology can be explained by his different aims in these writings – initially to explain why liberalism was doomed to misunderstand human freedom, and later to make visible the complex dynamics of recognition and misrecognition. Since both arguments are important and complement one another, they will be discussed in turn.

Taylor's earlier writings criticized liberalism for neglecting the ways in which individual identities are constituted by certain 'authoritative horizons'. These horizons come from personal relationships, history and culture, and they both limit and condition the ways in which people are able to understand themselves and interpret the situations they find themselves in. For example, feelings such as fear or shame are not experienced in the same ways and for the same reasons by everyone. Rather, both the feelings themselves and the significances a person attaches to them are bound up with how they comprehend their own situation, and this is shaped by whatever social meanings and conceptual vocabularies are available in that person's historical, cultural, social and linguistic context. The same goes for a person's plans and goals in life, whose meaning and significance cannot be entirely self-generated, but must be at least partially unchosen, inherited from the social and historical worlds they find themselves in. By neglecting this, Taylor (1979, 157) suggests that liberalism contains an empty or characterless vision of human freedom, since, if people had no authoritative horizons, then 'freedom would be a void in which nothing would be worth doing, nothing would deserve to count for anything'. By contrast, Taylor (1985, 197–8) instead defended the 'social thesis', which insists that freedom is always 'situated', in the sense that it depends upon various socially derived enabling conditions. This view was an important influence on Kymlicka's (1989a, 74–99) context-of-choice argument, examined in the previous chapter. However, whilst Kymlicka sought to reconcile the social thesis with liberal principles, Taylor (1989, 160) presented it as a challenge to liberal neutrality, concluding that 'a democratic society needs some commonly recognised definition of the good life'.

In the essay on recognition, Taylor (1994) drew upon a similar critique of liberalism to advance a case for the recognition of minority groups, and especially linguistic minorities. As noted already, Taylor here argued that identities are formed dialogically and not monologically. By this, he meant that human identity is not generated from the inside by self-sufficient individuals, able to choose and discard commitments and projects at will. Rather, identity is shaped and sustained by relationships with others, especially significant (or intimate) others. As such, a person's sense of who they are and their place in the world is always something that is discovered, interpreted and negotiated through dialogue with other people. The dialogical conception of identity formation illuminates some complex political dynamics that arise because we are social creatures, vulnerable to how others perceive us, as the following, widely cited, passage captures:

The thesis is that our identity is partly shaped by recognition or its absence, often by the misrecognition of others, and so a person or group of people can suffer real damage, real distortion, if the people or society around them mirror back to them a confining or demeaning or contemptible picture of themselves. Non recognition can inflict harm, can be a form of oppression, imprisoning someone in a false, distorted and reduced mode of being. (Taylor 1994, 25)

A simple way to grasp what Taylor is getting at is to consider the ways in which individuals or groups may be harmed by how they are represented (or misrepresented) by majority society, as when the members of racially stigmatized groups are portrayed as lazy or criminal, or when women are represented as inferior, or when the members of Indigenous communities are unable to form a coherent sense of self because their history and culture are ignored in the narratives of wider society. If we think of identity-construction in monological terms, as Taylor suggests liberals do, then the insult of being represented in a demeaning way, or of simply being ignored, will only scratch the surface, without doing lasting damage. Meanwhile, if we instead think of identities as being in a constant process of dialogical renegotiation, as Taylor recommends, then we will better appreciate the potentially severe and lasting damage of being misrecognized.

Dignity and difference

Liberalism's shortcomings are not the result of philosophical naïveté but are intimately bound up with a distinctively liberal approach to politics, which Taylor (1994) variously labels the 'politics of equal dignity' (38, 41, 43 44, 50, 51), the 'politics of universal dignity' (39) and 'the politics of equal respect' (60, 61, 68). Found in some of the theories discussed in chapter 2, its origins can be traced to the writings of Immanuel Kant, Mary Wollstonecraft and John Stuart Mill, amongst others. It identifies a particular ideal of dignity as the basis for political morality and associates that ideal with autonomy, understood as the capacity each person has for rational self-direction. Fleshed out as an egalitarian theory of politics, it directs the state to respect the capacities of its members to be authors of their own lives, securing for them an adequate range of rights and freedoms, and remaining neutral amongst the different worldviews they happen to endorse, since to do otherwise would fail to respect everyone as an equal.

The politics of equal dignity has significantly influenced contemporary politics, underpinning a widespread commitment to the idea that legal and constitutional orders ought to allocate an 'identical basket of rights and immunities' to everyone (Taylor 1994, 38). In particular, as Taylor (1994, 43) emphasizes, it directs us to regulate our societies according to 'universal, difference-blind principles' and to ignore the differences between people when allocating things like rights and opportunities. The appeal of these ideas becomes vividly apparent if we consider societies that objectionably fall short of this standard, such as South Africa during the apartheid era. However, Taylor believes they suffer from at least three related shortcomings.

First, although the politics of equal dignity respects the demand for equal recognition, insisting that each person be afforded proper recognition in virtue of their capacity for self-direction, it promises only a partial and incomplete form of recognition, since what are recognized are not people's actual commitments, but rather their capacities to form commitments. This is because the politics of equal dignity is based on an implicitly monological view about identity formation, incorporated right at the centre of the theory, in the claim that people are owed recognition *because* they are autonomous.

Second, and following the lead of scholars such as Iris Marion Young (1989, 1990), Taylor (1994, 62) doubts that 'difference-blind' liberalism 'can offer a neutral ground on which people of all cultures can meet and coexist'. Indeed, he worries that the 'supposedly neutral set of difference-blind principles of the politics of equal dignity' could in fact be 'a reflection of one hegemonic culture', and that upholding it might unfairly force the members of minorities 'into a homogeneous mould that is untrue to them' (Taylor 1994, 43).

Third, Taylor (1994, 60–1) also identifies another sense in which the politics of equal dignity is 'inhospitable to difference', which is that it cannot 'accommodate what the members of distinct societies really aspire to, which is survival'. To illustrate this, he discusses language politics in his native Canada, where successive Quebec governments have taken it to be 'axiomatic' that 'the survival and flourishing of French culture in Quebec is a good', and have actively sought to ensure 'that future generations continue to identify as French-speakers' (Taylor 1994, 58–9). A number of restrictive laws have been implemented in the name of achieving this, including limiting access to English-language schools, requiring larger businesses to operate through the medium of French, and imposing directives concerning language choices on commercial signs. However, from the perspective of the politics of equal dignity, it is difficult to see how these measures could be justified, since in each case individual autonomy is restricted for the sake of promoting a non-neutral collective goal – namely, the preservation of Quebec's distinctive language and culture. Meanwhile, Taylor (1994, 58) takes it to be self-evident that there is a strong moral case for these restrictions and for accepting that society should not be 'neutral between those who value remaining true to the culture of our ancestors and those who might want to cut loose in the name of some individual goal of self-development'. Thus, by his account, the politics of equal dignity is flawed to the extent that it cannot grasp the legitimate aspiration of Francophones to preserve their own way of life indefinitely into the future.

Alongside the politics of equal dignity, Taylor identifies another way in which the demand for equal recognition has been understood – one more hospitable to the demands of minority cultural groups such as Francophones in Canada, and which he labels the 'politics of difference'. Like the politics of equal dignity, which it 'grows organically out of', this is a universalist and egalitarian doctrine (Taylor 1994, 39). However, instead of focusing on characteristics everyone shares, this approach emphasizes each person's need to be recognized for their unique identity. As such, it recommends supports for minorities including various forms of 'differential treatment', such as the provision of special rights and powers to Indigenous peoples, affirmative action policies in education and employment, and rights for linguistic minorities (Taylor 1994, 39, 40, 51–61). These are all standard components of multicultural political theory, endorsed by liberals like Kymlicka too. However, whilst liberals tend to regard these measures as justified exceptions to the norm, Taylor presents them as part of a comprehensive alternative to 'difference-blind' liberalism, with its own logic and justification.

So, both the politics of equal dignity and the politics of difference are forms of recognition politics. In the former case, the recognition each person needs refers to our shared capacity for autonomy. Correspondingly, people are harmed by not being recognized as capable of directing their own lives – say, if they are prevented from making important choices as a result of oppressive laws, or because they inhabit restrictive social roles. Meanwhile, in the latter case, the recognition that each person needs refers to their individuality, uniqueness and distinctiveness. Correspondingly, people are harmed if their particular way of life is not given adequate recognition – say, if it is mocked or marginalized, or if society is indifferent about its erosion.

Instead of autonomy, the politics of difference associates recognition with another ideal, which – following Lionel Trilling – Taylor labels 'authenticity'. At its simplest, this refers to the idea that each individual has a unique identity, an original way of being human, to which she must be true. Unlike the ideal of autonomy, which implies that living a good life is a matter of choosing a path for oneself, authenticity instead associates the good life with listening to one's inner voice or finding the right path for oneself. In his other work, Taylor (1989, 1992) has explored the complexity of this now ubiquitous and distinctively modern idea, attributing its spread to the influence of nineteenth-century Romanticism, as well as the work of eighteenth-century philosopher Jean-Jacques Rousseau. Expressed as an ethical doctrine, authenticity imposes two related demands. First, it directs individuals to live their lives in their own way and to resist the temptation to mould themselves so as to conform better to social expectations. Second, it directs society to acknowledge, publicly, people for who they really are and not require them to hide their identities or to present themselves as something they are not (Taylor 1994, 28–31).

Since authenticity is a characteristic of an identity that is unique and irreplaceable, it may seem to be a thoroughly individualistic notion, making it a curious basis for the politics of difference, which calls for the recognition of collective identities by positively affirming differences related to things such as language, race, gender, religion and sexuality. However, this apparent tension can be overcome by recalling that Taylor construes identity formation as a dialogical process, in which one does not simply discover an identity that is already buried deep inside oneself, or create one's own identity from nothing, but rather negotiates it alongside the others with whom one finds oneself. Languages and cultures play a special role in this process, since they do not merely give us the means to describe the world but are also the filter through which we comprehend it, providing us with the concepts and practices through which we interact with others whilst fashioning our own identities. In this sense, language and culture are constitutive of identity, since it is through them that we acquire the ability to understand who we are. Thus, Taylor appeals to his dialogical conception of identity formation in order to bind together the ideal of authenticity – which refers to being true to oneself and being recognized as such – and the politics of difference – which refers to the positive recognition of group-based differences. This enables him to conclude that recognizing individuals as authentic often also means supporting and publicly affirming the value of their cultures and languages, since these provide the 'webs of interlocution' within which people are (dialogically) formed (Taylor 1989, 36)

Before discussing some criticisms of Taylor's view, it is worth noting an ambiguity in his account of the connections between recognition, dialogue and authenticity, first identified by Patchen Markell (2003, 39–61). On the one hand, when Taylor describes the harms of misrecognition, and especially those which come about when people are ignored or misrepresented, he mostly seems to have a 'cognitive' sense of recognition in mind, in which recognition involves seeing someone for who they authentically are and responding to them appropriately. This understanding of recognition seems to be implicit in Taylor's account of authenticity, which – as Kwame Anthony Appiah (1994, 149) has aptly put it – holds that 'people have the right to be acknowledged publicly as what they really are'. On the other hand, Taylor also uses the term 'recognition' in a 'constitutive' sense, whereby it does not simply involve responding to how things already are, but also involves making the social world. For example, consider a chairperson of a meeting who recognizes someone as a speaker. In doing so, they do not affirm some antecedent state of affairs, but rather create one, since the speaker was not the speaker until she was recognized as such. This sense of recognition seems to be implicit in Taylor's (1994, 34 and 25) account of identity formation, when he remarks that 'my own identity crucially depends on my dialogical relations with others', and when he suggests that misrecognition can have the effect of 'imprisoning someone in a false, distorted and reduced mode of being'.

Not only does Taylor seem to conflate these two different things, but there also seems to be a tension between them, since extending the first 'cognitive' sense of recognition requires that we already know who someone authentically is, whilst the second 'constitutive' sense of recognition reminds us that identities are never fixed or stable but must be continually renegotiated through dialogue. In other words, recognition in the first sense – of recognizing someone for who they truly are – involves a kind of misrecognition in the second sense, since identities are fluid and contingent. But, at the same time, to insist that identities are always in flux and never settled risks depriving people of something Taylor thinks they need, gravely damaging them and their sense of self-worth.

Recognition sceptics

Taylor's politics of recognition has been criticized for making demands that are too modest. Put crudely, his view is that recognition failures can be corrected by convincing dominant groups in society to change their views of subordinate minorities – for instance, by refraining from stigmatizing them and by positively valuing social differences.

However, others have suggested that equality will require considerably more radical transformations. For example, multiculturalist
Bhikhu Parekh (2000, 343) suggests that misrecognition 'can only be
countered by both undertaking a rigorous critique of the dominant
culture and radically restructuring the prevailing inequalities of
economic and political power'. Similarly, socialist Nancy Fraser
argues that the politics of recognition must be accompanied by a
politics of economic redistribution if it is to vindicate its emanci-
patory potential, not because material inequality is just as important
as cultural inequality, but because the two are intertwined (Fraser
and Honneth 2003).

Some of the most forceful critiques in this vein have come from
Indigenous scholars. In a sense this is surprising, since Indigenous
activists have often used the language of recognition to frame their
political demands. For example, in 1975 the Dene Nation, living in
what is now Canada, issued a declaration insisting 'on the right to be
regarded by ourselves and the world as a nation', and characterizing
their struggle as one 'for the recognition of the Dene Nation by the
Government and people of Canada and the peoples and governments
of the world' (quoted in Coulthard 2007, 437). However, despite
the coincidence of terminology, when Indigenous peoples call for
recognition, they typically intend something different from Taylor.
As we have seen, Taylor's struggle for recognition ultimately has to
do with achieving and maintaining self-respect by not being ignored,
demeaned or mischaracterized by others. Meanwhile, the struggles
of Indigenous peoples are primarily political, and only indirectly
about dignity and self-respect. For instance, it was not because of the
psychological harms of misrecognition that the Dene demanded to be
recognized as a nation, and they were not demanding to be seen for
who they truly are, as Taylor's theory would have suggested. Rather,
they sought the privileges associated with nationhood, including
powers to give meaningful effect to what they regarded as their
inherent rights of self-government.

Whilst being denied proper recognition in Taylor's sense potentially undermines a person's sense of self-worth and compromises
their freedom, being denied it in the more bluntly political sense
invoked by the Dene Nation has proven catastrophic, threatening the
very existence of specific Indigenous communities. For example, after
citing various historical practices of the Canadian state, including
land dispossession, the confinement of Indigenous children to
residential schools, and the removal of children from their parents
and communities, Dene scholar Glen Sean Coulthard (2014, 4)
concludes that 'these policies sought to marginalize Indigenous

people and communities with the ultimate goal being our elimination, if not physically, then as cultural, political, and legal peoples distinguishable from the rest of Canadian society'. To be protected against the threat of elimination, in Coulthard's sense, does not require Taylor's (1994, 50) favoured 'regime of reciprocal recognition among equals', but it does require recognition in a more basic sense: of being a nation amongst others and having the corresponding right to govern oneself, so as to enable members to protect their culture and themselves. So, Indigenous struggles for recognition aim for something that is at once both more basic and more radical than Taylor's politics of recognition, since they call into question the legitimacy of settler colonial states.

Although Coulthard takes himself to be arguing against Taylor, the two theories overlap in certain ways. In particular, both agree about the damaging effects of misrecognition for the members of Indigenous communities. For instance, to illustrate the damage done by misrecognition, Taylor (1994, 26) refers to the fact that 'since 1492 Europeans have projected an image of [Indigenous] people as somehow inferior, "uncivilized," and through the force of conquest have often been able to impose this image on the conquered', going on to observe that the internalization of this image 'can inflict a grievous wound, saddling its victims with a crippling self-hatred'. In stronger but similar language, Coulthard (2014, 41–2) also refers to 'the forms of racist recognition driven into the psyches of Indigenous peoples through the institutions of the state, church, schools, and media', and argues that these 'have saddled individuals with low self-esteem, depression, alcohol and drug abuse, and violent behaviours'. However, Coulthard breaks with Taylor by insisting that the latter's favoured form of recognition politics is an inadequate corrective to colonial misrecognition, since it ultimately serves the interests of the colonizer. To make this argument, Coulthard draws on the psychiatrist and anti-colonial scholar and activist Frantz Fanon, who argued that recognition which occurs under conditions of domination and inequality will inevitably be asymmetrical and non-reciprocal, reflecting the interests of the dominant, or hegemonic, party. So, in settler colonial societies, this means that the settler state itself gets to decide on the terms upon which recognition is offered, bestowing it as kind of gift. As a consequence, genuinely mutual recognition is impossible, since it would have the effect of undermining colonial asymmetries of power, and this is not in the interests of state or the majority population, who need the land and resources previously held by Indigenous peoples, but not their recognition (Coulthard 2014, 40). Thus, even when Indigenous communities are granted self-government rights, they are not truly self-determining, since they are not themselves authors of the terms and conditions of their own recognition.

In a striking illustration of how settler societies have used the language of recognition to entrench their own legitimacy, and even to co-opt Indigenous peoples into this project, Coulthard (2014, 105–30) discusses a 2008 official apology made by the Canadian Prime Minister to survivors of the residential school system. As with other similar apologies, this was framed as an attempt to address a historical injustice, with a nod towards reconciliation. On Coulthard's reading, however, the effect of the apology was symbolically to place colonialism in the past, treating it as something from an earlier era, albeit with echoes that can still be heard. Because the reality of colonialism as an ongoing injustice is thereby obscured, so too is the possibility of contesting the legitimacy of the current political order. Instead, the form of recognition manifested in the apology is orientated towards fixing the hurt feelings of Indigenous people themselves, and avoids the question of whether it is the colonial relationship itself – between settler society and Indigenous peoples – that needs to be repaired.

Equal worth

As we have seen, two central demands of Taylor's politics of difference are that recognition sometimes requires differential rather than difference-blind treatment, and that the state ought to support the attempts of cultural minorities to preserve their distinctive identities, languages and ways of life. In addition to these, Taylor (1994, 50) also discusses another, more controversial, demand that might be required in order to achieve 'a regime of reciprocal recognition among equals', which is that society must 'recognise the equal value of different cultures; that we not only let them survive, but acknowledge their worth'. The broad rationale for this is that merely positively affirming the value of marginalized identities will not be enough to secure self-respect, if some identities are nevertheless perceived as superior, since that would be demeaning for those whose culture is marked out as inferior. What seems to be required is the affirmation that all cultures and identities are of equal worth.

An affirmation of this kind is incompatible with the kind of 'hands-off neutrality' endorsed by many liberals, and has been widely rejected by them (e.g. Barry 2001a, 264–79). Meanwhile, the idea has been vigorously contested amongst proponents of the politics of difference. On the one hand, James Tully (1995, 190) strongly endorses it, arguing that:

> Since what a person says and does and the plans he or she formulates and revises are partly characterised by his or her cultural identity, the condition of self-respect is met only in a society in which the cultures of all members are recognised and affirmed by others, both by those who do and those who do not share these cultures.

On the other hand, others reject this demand as incoherent. For example, Axel Honneth suggests that it is contradictory to insist upon the positive evaluation of each culture, because:

> The sort of social esteem that would be entailed in recognising a culture as something valuable is not a public response that could be appealed for or demanded, since it could only arise spontaneously or voluntarily according to standards of evaluative examination ... At best we can here speak only of the readiness to take note of the specific qualities of other cultures such that their value can be reexamined. (Honneth in Fraser and Honneth 2003, 168)

So, Honneth argues that it is impossible to do what Tully wants, positively affirming the value of each tradition and culture, because judgements about value must be sincere and not compelled. Meanwhile, Taylor's own position falls somewhere between these two stools. Like Honneth and unlike Tully, he argues that 'it can't make sense to demand as a matter of right that we come up with a final concluding judgment' about the value of a particular culture (Taylor 1994, 69). Nevertheless, he endorses a weaker version of Tully's proposal, arguing for the 'presumption' that different cultures are of equal value.

Taylor (1994, 66–7) describes this 'presumption' as a 'starting hypothesis', arguing that in the end it must be proven 'concretely in the actual study of the culture'. In the course of a subtle and rich discussion, he develops two different arguments for his view. First, Taylor (1994, 72–3) suggests that it would take a 'supreme arrogance' to assume that a culture with which one is unfamiliar lacks value, or is less valuable than one's own culture, arguing that:

> it is reasonable to suppose that cultures that have provided the horizon of meaning for large numbers of human beings, of diverse characters and temperaments, over a long period of time – that have, in other words, articulated their sense of the good, the holy, the admirable – are almost certain to have something that deserves our admiration

and respect, even it if is accompanied by much that we have to abhor and reject.

Second, Taylor (1994, 68) also appeals to the interest that each of us has in our identity, suggesting that since 'important consequences flow for people's identity from the absence of recognition', then each of us should 'enjoy the presumption that their traditional culture has value'. In other words, it will harm people if others hastily or thoughtlessly presume that their culture lacks value.

At first glance, the second argument may seem to support Tully's formulation better than Taylor's. If one's identity really is compromised when others presume that one's culture lacks value, then surely it will be similarly compromised if others actually affirm that one's culture lacks value, even if they do so after careful consideration. We can perhaps appreciate why Taylor reaches a more cautious conclusion than Tully by considering the issue that motivated his concern with this question, which was the construction of syllabi in university humanities courses. Traditionally, the authors taught in a standard introduction to philosophy or literature course were likely to be mostly dead, white men. For Taylor (1994, 65), the problem with this is 'not, or not mainly, that all students may be missing something important through the exclusion of a certain gender or certain races or cultures', but is instead that 'women and students from the excluded groups are given, either directly or by omission, a demeaning picture of themselves, as though all creativity and worth inhered in males of European provenance'. For Taylor, then, the primary objection to excluding particular identities or perspectives from university curricula is that it potentially undermines the self-esteem of students who share those identities or perspectives. At the same time, however, including them so as to improve the self-esteem of affected students raises a paradox, since it risks sending the signal that 'we' are including 'your' (inferior) authors in the canon (only) in order to make you feel better about your own (inadequate) identity or cultural traditions. Of course, such potentially stigmatizing judgements might be avoided if we follow Tully's recommendation and expressly affirm from the outset that each tradition is of equal value, but to do so without first exploring the basis for making such a judgement would be, according to Taylor (1994, 70), 'an act of breathtaking condescension'.

The more general lesson that comes out of Taylor's analysis of this issue is that we cannot achieve his goal of 'a regime of reciprocal recognition among equals' by presumptively affirming the equal worth of different cultures, but must instead engage in an open-minded attempt to identify the worth or value within different traditions, which we approach with a presumption that they are of value. In this way, we extend a kind of respect to bearers of those identities without patronizing them. However, identifying the worth or value of deeply different cultural traditions is not straightforward, since any attempt to evaluate the products or practices of a particular culture involves judging them against criteria and standards. Since it would be ethnocentric to evaluate non-Western cultural products according to criteria and standards that have evolved within the Western tradition, this raises the puzzle of establishing the appropriate basis for making judgements about cultures that are significantly different from our own, and for which 'we may have only the foggiest idea *ex ante* of in what its valuable contribution might consist' (Taylor 1994, 67).

Taylor's solution to this puzzle is that we must immerse ourselves in the difficult work of trying to understand unfamiliar cultures and their products, and resist the temptation to evaluate them with inappropriate criteria, such as ones drawn from our own culture or heritage. This requirement is partially justified by the respect that we owe to others, which entails presuming that their cultures are of value, even if we cannot immediately perceive what that value consists in. Further, it is also justified for what might be termed fittingness reasons, since the criteria that we use to evaluate a particular cultural object ought to be appropriate to that object and the culture in which it was produced. As Taylor (1994, 67) observes, '[t]o approach, say, a raga with the presumptions of value implicit in the well-tempered clavier would be forever to miss the point'. Immersion in the sense that Taylor recommends will always be limited, since we cannot but experience things from a particular perspective that has already been dialogically formed within a specific context. However, what we should aim for is to 'learn to move in a broader horizon, within which what we have formerly taken for granted as the background to valuation can be situated as one possibility alongside the different background of the formerly unfamiliar culture' (Taylor 1994, 67). As such, we can aspire to what Taylor (1994, 67), following the German philosopher Hans-Georg Gadamer, refers to as a 'fusion of horizons'.

Liberalism, autonomy and authenticity

Taylor situates the struggle for recognition within the context of a conflict between two different forms of politics: an individualistic politics of dignity based on the value of autonomy, and a collectivist politics of difference based on the value of authenticity. Although both are necessary to meet people's 'vital human need' for recognition, they are also often opposed to one another. For example, in the context of Canadian language policy, either we go in the direction of a politics of difference, recognizing Quebec as a distinct society with a right to preserve its identity indefinitely, or we can move in the direction of a politics of dignity, leaving people to make their own choices about language use and acquisition. Any gain for recognition in one sense becomes a loss for it in the other. Although it is clear that in this particular case Taylor favours moving towards the politics of difference, he does not think that the politics of dignity is irrelevant, or a mistake, or that individuals need not be recognized as having a fundamental kind of dignity founded on their capacity for autonomous choice. As a result, his theory struggles to provide principled guidance about how to make trade-offs between individual rights and collective recognition.

Liberals worry that Taylor's sympathy for collectivism leads him sometimes to draw the line in the wrong place. This danger can be illustrated by comparing his position to that of Kymlicka, who, like Taylor, wants the state to support cultural minorities attempting to preserve their distinctive identities, languages and ways of life. Whilst Taylor justifies such measures by appealing to the value of authenticity, Kymlicka – as we saw in chapter 2 – appeals to autonomy and the idea that cultures provide members with 'contexts of choice'. Taylor (1994, 41n) says his approach is preferable since Kymlicka's theory only justifies cultural rights when '*existing* people ... find themselves trapped within a culture under pressure', whilst his can 'justify measures designed to ensure survival through indefinite future generations'. By contrast, liberals worry that Taylor's theory might threaten individual autonomy, since it is seemingly consistent with measures that Kymlicka must oppose, including the preservation of cultures which themselves do not value individual freedom, and the imposition of what Kymlicka called 'internal restrictions'. In response to this, Taylor (1994, 59) recommends that the politics of difference must ultimately be constrained by the politics of dignity, arguing that certain 'fundamental liberties' ought to be 'unassailably entrenched', and that there must be 'adequate safeguards for fundamental rights'. However, his bottom line is some distance below Kymlicka's, since it is fundamental rights and liberties, not individual autonomy, which cultural rights must respect.

At a deeper level, Taylor's sympathy for collectivism arguably also leads him to neglect the possibility that recognizing someone's authentic identity might sometimes require respecting their capacity for autonomy. We can illustrate this by recalling some of his remarks about language policy in Quebec, particularly his suggestion that the state ought to support 'those who value remaining true to the culture of our ancestors' and not those 'who might want to cut loose in the name of some individual goal of self-development' (Taylor 1994, 58). Let us assume, at least for the sake of argument, that the goal of cultural survival does indeed require coercing those who would otherwise decide to alter their, or their children's, linguistic allegiances. Even so, some further reason is required to explain why recognizing one kind of identity (those who wish to remain true to the culture of their ancestors) ought to have priority over recognizing another (those who do not). Taylor's answer to this is that even those who wish to cut loose have nevertheless been constituted by the language and culture in question, and so will be harmed if it is not given adequate recognition. But it is not clear why we should accept this, if people wanting to cut loose deny it. Ultimately, as Brian Barry (2001a, 65) has remarked, it seems as if Taylor's position depends upon an underlying and unappealing thesis about cultural authenticity, containing the idea that 'birth is fate – that simply in virtue of being born into a certain ethnic group one acquires the (potentially enforceable) duty to maintain its "ancestral culture"'.

Both of these difficulties arise for Taylor because he thinks that meeting our need for recognition requires both a politics of dignity and a politics of difference. Meanwhile, the liberal theories of multiculturalism we examined in chapter 2 avoid this trap either by remaining entirely within the terms of the politics of dignity, as Kymlicka does, or by rejecting both of them, as Kukathas does. In chapter 2, we saw that Kukathas associates the politics of dignity with intolerance and moral dogmatism, since he doubts that autonomy really is a universal value. Elsewhere, he also rejects the politics of difference for being dangerously destabilizing. Indeed, in what amounts to a broad critique of recognition politics as such, and not only Taylor's version of it, Kukathas (1998, 693) argues that the liberal state ought to 'resist attempts to put the issue of [cultural] recognition at the centre of political debate'. Responding to claims for recognition is an invitation to civic strife, he argues, since different claims are frequently in conflict with one another or with other political interests. These conflicts are likely to be especially volatile when access to economic and other resources is at stake, as in cases involving disagreements over which groups will benefit from affirmative action policies, or when the character or identity of society as a whole is in question. For example, in a striking illustration of the dangers of cultural recognition, he describes an incident in Australia in 1993, where immigrants from parts of the former Yugoslavia sought recognition as Macedonian. This provoked a challenge from others who likewise regarded themselves as being of Macedonian descent, and who denied the claim made by the initial group. The situation ultimately 'escalated to acts of violence between ethnic communities when the Australian government saw fit to rule on which identification would be officially recognized' (Kukathas 1998, 692). Examples like this, according to Kukathas, teach us that multicultural societies would do well to ignore the demands of the politics of difference as well as the politics of dignity.

Dialogue

Although Taylor is critical of 'procedural liberalism' and the 'liberalism of rights', the net result of his theory is to enlarge the possibilities of a liberal response to cultural diversity without actually moving beyond it. At least for some multiculturalists, this is unsatisfactory, since Taylor's politics of dignity, no less than Kymlicka's liberal culturalism, is ultimately rooted in a particular cultural tradition and worldview, making it an unsuitable basis for a genuinely inclusive politics of multiculturalism. This idea has been pressed in its most sophisticated form by Bhikhu Parekh, a British Asian philosopher whose work is examined here, focusing especially on the book *Rethinking Multiculturalism*, his major contribution to multicultural political thought. Parekh (2000, 13) begins from the premise that, since normative theories of multiculturalism must establish 'the proper terms of relationship between different cultural communities', then 'the norms governing their respective claims, including the principles of justice, cannot be derived from one culture alone'. At first glance, this may seem to resemble the idea of liberal neutrality, which – as we saw in chapter 2 – similarly insists that no particular conception of the good be preferred over others. However, Parekh (2000, 14) rejects liberal neutrality as self-defeating, for he believes that liberalism is already 'a substantive doctrine advocating a specific view of man, society and the world and embedded in and giving rise to a distinct way of life'. In other words, liberal neutrality is not really neutral, since it is arises out of a particular culture. Solving this problem requires shifting 'to a higher level of philosophical abstraction' and, since we cannot transcend our own cultures and worldviews through reflection alone, this will require an 'open and equal dialogue' between different cultural communities (Parekh 2000, 13–14).

Other political theorists have also proposed dialogical and democratic approaches to multiculturalism, including Iris Marion Young (1990, 2000), Seyla Benhabib (2002), Melissa Williams (1998) and Monique Deveaux (2000, 2005). Arguably, these theorists are more attuned than Parekh is to the complex dynamics of democratic politics, and especially the struggles faced by both minority groups and vulnerable group members in exercising democratic voice. However, I focus on Parekh's work here because his account of inter-cultural dialogue is the most theoretically sophisticated attempt to develop a dialogically centred political theory of multiculturalism.

Before assessing Parekh's account of intercultural dialogue, it is worth exploring why he believes that liberalism is an inadequate framework for multicultural societies. Parekh's (2011, 58) basic objection is that '[l]iberalism does not engage in dialogue with other traditions and worldviews because it is certain of its own truth'. In particular, Parekh (2000, 110) suggests that liberalism refuses to 'accept the full force of moral and cultural pluralism' because it fails to 'acknowledge that the good life can be lived in several different ways', and instead assumes that a worthwhile human life must be self-directed and freely chosen. Parekh (1994) traces this 'narrowness' to the nineteenth-century liberal John Stuart Mill, who believed that individuals should determine their own way of life and should aim at constant self-creation. On Parekh's (2000, 44) reading, this means that Mill effectively 'ruled out a wide variety of ways of life, such as the traditional, the community-centred and the religious'. To the extent that contemporary political theories of liberalism follow Mill and include a foundational commitment to the value of autonomy, they too make the mistake of confusing a local, modern and culturally specific value with a universally valid one. This is an error, Parekh thinks, because autonomy is not universally acknowledged as an essential component of the good life. Indeed, it presupposes an 'interiorisation of morality' that is 'essentially Protestant, and played only a limited role in Athens and Rome, medieval Europe, Catholic Christianity and non-western civilizations' (Parekh 2000, 106).

So, like Kukathas – discussed in chapter 2 – Parekh worries that autonomy-centred theories of liberalism are unduly dismissive of worldviews which do not valorize autonomy. However, whilst Kukathas proposes to rescue liberalism from moral dogmatism by replacing autonomy with toleration, Parekh (2000, 111) instead recommends that liberals engage in a 'critical but sympathetic dialogue with other ways of life, now seen not as objects of willing or grudging tolerance but as conversational partners in a common search for a deeper understanding of the nature, potentialities and grandeur of human life'. This does not mean that liberals should give up on the value of autonomy, or cease to advocate measures to support it. Rather, it directs them to acknowledge that their worldview is only one amongst others, all of which must be given due respect if we are to find common principles to regulate shared institutions in a culturally diverse society.

Regulating disputed practices

To illustrate how a dialogical approach to multiculturalism might proceed, Parekh (2000, 264) takes up the puzzle of explaining 'how a multicultural society should decide which minority values and practices to tolerate within what limits', a problem typically arising when society is confronted with minority practices that 'offend against the values of the majority'. Examples of disputed practices found in liberal democracies today include religious methods of slaugh- tering animals, arranged marriages, incest, polygamy, female genital mutilation, ritual scarring and restrictive dress codes. Like Kukathas, Parekh (2000, 264) believes that a society which disallowed all it disapproved of would 'be guilty of moral dogmatism and extreme intolerance', but, unlike Kukathas, he also insists that a multi- cultural society cannot tolerate 'indiscriminately', for 'it has a duty both to raise its voice against morally outrageous practices and to safeguard the integrity of its own moral culture'. The puzzle, then, is to establish whether such disputed practices ought to be permitted or forbidden, and why.

In principle, a society might answer this without resorting to dialogue – for instance, by allowing only those practices which do not violate universal moral values, or which do not harm others. Parekh's grounds for rejecting these proposals are instructive. Although 'universally valid values' exist, these are 'too thin and few to cover all important areas of life', and consequently do not provide sufficiently clear guidance (Parekh 2000, 266). Similarly, there is often sincere disagreement about whether particular disputed practices really are harmful, since, if they are, they tend not to involve physical harm but, rather, 'highly complex notions of emotional, moral and other types of harm' (Parekh 2000, 266). Instead of appealing to universal or objective values, a society might instead ask whether disputed practices are consistent with its own way of life. This is an approach Parekh (2000, 265) has more sympathy for, since he believes that each society 'has a right and a duty to disallow practices that offend against' its 'core or shared values'. However, he doubts that modern diverse societies really do have values that are uniformly and consistently endorsed, since even principles which seem to be widely cherished – such as gender equality and respect for persons – are rejected by many of their members.

Given that we lack a culturally neutral definition of harm, and given that neither universal nor shared values provide definitive solutions to the puzzle of disputed practices, Parekh (2000, 266) concludes that the deep moral disagreements they raise can only be resolved by an 'open-minded and morally serious dialogue with minority spokesmen'. The kind of dialogue he envisages is not an 'open-ended and free-floating' one, concerned to establish whether a particular practice is permissible 'in general' or 'in principle' (Parekh 2000, 267). Rather, it should aim to establish whether a particular practice is acceptable in a particular society. Accordingly, Parekh (2000, 267) insists that dialogue 'start with and centre on the prevailing values, which provide its vocabulary, structure its context, and impose limits on its direction and likely outcome'.

These values, which Parekh (2000, 270) labels 'operative public values', are not a 'crude and non-negotiable standard' against which disputed practices are judged. Instead, they 'provide the context and point of orientation' for subsequent discussions, with dialogue providing the majority with opportunities both to come to terms with unfamiliar practices and 'to take a critical look at its own values and practices' (Parekh 2000, 265 and 267). Operative public values 'represent the shared moral structure of society's public life' (Parekh 2000, 270) and are 'woven into its institutions and practices' (Parekh 2000, 273). Although not everyone shares them, people are familiar with them, generally try to uphold them, and evaluate the behaviour of others according to them. By labelling them 'operative', Parekh intends to convey that they are not only ideas, but widely observed in practice, historically established, and socially repro-duced. Meanwhile, by labelling them 'public', he means that they are already embodied in laws and institutions, and that they regulate the public conduct of citizens. Taken together, operative public values will rarely resemble a well-worked-out moral philosophy. They will not be neatly structured, will often overlap messily with one another, and are subject to varying degrees of public contestation. Nevertheless, all together, they 'form a complex and loosely-knit whole and provide a structured but malleable vocabulary of public discourse' (Parekh 2000, 269).

Although the operative public values of a given society may include universally valid moral values, when considered together they will not be neutral amongst different cultural traditions, but instead embody a distinctive way of life, reflecting a shared history and a partial perspective about what it is to be a human being. Since they are constantly evolving, they must be interpreted by looking to the different levels at which they are articulated. These include the constitution, which establishes society's institutional framework and specifies the fundamental rights and duties of citizenship, and the laws, where the values referred to in the constitution are given fuller expression and worked out in more specific detail. In addition, they also include the norms governing civic relations, where operative public values explain our expectations of one another. Operative public values tend to be thinnest at the constitutional level, and given their distinguishing qualities at the legal and civic levels. For example, many constitutions stipulate that all citizens must be treated equally, but what this actually means is filled out at the other levels – for example, in laws that require men and women be paid the same rates for doing the same work, or when sexist behaviour is informally sanctioned amongst friends and co-workers. Meanwhile, operative public values at the civic level can be nuanced and therefore difficult to navigate, especially for newcomers. To illustrate this, Parekh (2000, 269) describes a group of North African immigrants in Israel who misunderstood local taboos against haggling over bus fares, and a Pakistani professor in the UK who needed to be instructed not to ask his students to do his weekly shopping for him.

Each society has its own operative public values, so we should expect to see different kinds of discussions in different societies about the permissibility of particular practices. Because dialogue has no fixed destination, it will be difficult to predict its outcome. It might encourage a minority to abandon a controversial practice by fostering a debate within that community about its legitimacy. For example, Parekh (2000, 291) suggests that public discussions about the practices of polygamy (having multiple spouses) and polygyny (having multiple wives) might 'go at least some way towards getting [its advocates] to appreciate the value of monogamy'. Alternatively, dialogue might instead encourage majority society to reconsider its own values or its opposition to a practice. For example, Parekh (2000, 273) notes that, whilst the Hindu practices of either scattering the ashes of the dead in rivers or submerging corpses in deep waters initially aroused unease in Britain, wider society came to realize that their objections were ill founded, since the practices did not truly offend against their operative public values.

Dialogue, then, can transform how communities understand both themselves and one another, giving them the opportunity to learn about different traditions and practices, and to reconsider their values and beliefs in light of the arguments and perspectives to which they are exposed. Its benefits extend beyond resolving disputes about controversial cultural practices and might include, for instance, encouraging important civic and intellectual virtues amongst citizens, such as 'mutual respect, civility, open-mindedness, and willingness to be self-critical', as well as an appreciation of 'the contingency and partiality' of their own values and outlooks (Parekh 2011, 76–7). Further, as will be discussed in chapter 5, it can perhaps also help to strengthen a sense of common membership and belonging in multi-cultural societies, both by 'pluralising the dominant culture' (Parekh 2008, 37) and by enabling people from different communities to enter one another's worlds and to see things through one another's eyes, thereby discouraging some of the negative pathologies often found in societies that are divided along ethnic, cultural, linguistic or religious lines.

Defending disputed practices

Dialogue about disputed practices is unlikely to proceed smoothly. Parekh (2000, 272) anticipates that it will often involve 'passages of incomprehension, intransigence, irreconcilable differences', in part because 'moral values cannot be debated and defended in an objective and conclusive manner', but also because 'it is difficult to be wholly detached and open-minded about one's moral values'. To succeed, dialogue must be 'bifocal', addressing the minority practice and its way of life, as well as society's operative public values and its way of life (Parekh 2000, 271). Accordingly, if a majority wishes to disallow a practice, it must give reasons, explaining why the disputed practice offends against its own values and why it holds to those values in the first place. Likewise, if a minority wishes for its practice to be permitted, it must explain why the practice is important and offer a defence of it. A successful defence, according to Parekh, will follow one or more of the following strategies.

First, the minority might seek to defend a disputed practice by establishing that it is 'culturally authoritative' and therefore 'binding' upon its members (Parekh 2000, 272). Importantly, Parekh does not claim this to be a decisive reason in favour of permitting a disputed practice, and he emphasizes that a majority might permissibly withhold toleration if they deem something to be morally unaccep-table. However, he does think that the majority has a stronger reason to tolerate these practices than ones which are mere customs, and this raises two puzzles. How are we to identify when a practice is culturally authoritative? And why should it matter?

Sometimes, it can be established without controversy that a practice is culturally authoritative. For example, surely few would disagree with Parekh's (2000, 249) suggestion that carrying the kirpan (a small dagger) is a 'mandatory symbol' of the Sikh religion and should therefore be understood as a religious requirement. Meanwhile, in other cases, the status of a practice within a community is itself contested. When this occurs, Parekh (2000, 285) cautions against taking the descriptions of advocates at face value, since their motives or reasoning may be 'disingenuous'. For instance, he suggests that, even though defenders of female genital mutilation often claim that 'it is required by their religion or culture and hence is binding on them', they are mistaken to do so, since it is not practised in many Muslim countries, attracts strong opposition where it is practised, is not mentioned in the Koran and referenced only ambiguously in one of the *hadiths* (Parekh 2000, 277).

Even if dialogue yields an agreement about a practice being culturally authoritative, a question remains about why it being so should matter. Parekh's answer to this is nuanced. Since he believes that people are not 'determined' by their cultures and are able to take a 'critical view' of them, he cannot argue that people have no choice but to participate in culturally authoritative practices (Parekh 2000, 157). Rather, the significance of culturally authoritative practices has to do with them being based on 'deeply held moral beliefs' or 'deeply held religious beliefs', such that disallowing them would induce 'a deep sense of moral loss' because they are 'constitutive of the individual's sense of identity and even self-respect' (Parekh 2000, 279, 281 and 241). For example, when discussing Islamic and Jewish dietary laws that require animals to be slaughtered without being stunned first, Parekh (2000, 274) concludes that, even though the practice is 'religiously sanctioned' and 'means much to the two communities', it is not culturally authoritative, since 'it is not integral to the Jewish and Muslim ways of life in the sense that they would suffer profound moral disorientation if it were disallowed'. The implication, then, is that practices which are culturally authoritative are those justified by deep and sincere moral or religious beliefs and about which people would suffer profound moral disorientation or loss if they were disallowed.

If a disputed practice is not culturally authoritative, or if a minority community cannot convince the majority that it is so, then the second strategy they might employ is to emphasize the role it plays in sustaining their community. For example, Parekh (2000, 274) suggests that the Asian practice of arranged marriages might be justified on this basis, since, even though it has no religious basis and is therefore not culturally authoritative, it can be defended on the grounds that it is 'interlocked with other practices, plays an important part in sustaining the Asian way of life, and means a great deal to its adherents'. In particular, Parekh (2000, 275) stresses that it 'makes sense for [Asian] parents to have a say in who their sons and daughters marry', since, from within their worldview, 'individuals are an integral part of their family, and their lives belong not just to them but also to their families'. Consequently, discouraging or even prohibiting arranged marriages would risk altering how parents and their children understand their relationships with one another, thereby compromising their shared way of life.

As with the appeal to cultural authority, Parekh (2000, 272) does not regard this as a decisive reason in favour of toleration, since 'no way of life is sacrosanct' and a majority might conclude that, if the survival of a particular culture depends on practices 'too offensive to be tolerated', then the culture in question must be changed, not society's laws. For example, Parekh (2000, 276) observes that female genital mutilation could in principle be defended on community-sustaining grounds, since, for the communities in which it is practised, 'it is tied up with their other moral and social beliefs and practices and is integral to their way of life'. However, even if it is true that undergoing the procedure saves women and girls from social suspicion, or makes it easier to find a spouse, Parekh (2000, 277) denies that considerations like these outweigh 'the gravity of the harm caused by the practice', concluding that 'the answer lies not in continuing the practice but in judiciously reforming the way of life that makes it necessary'. Meanwhile, he reaches a different conclusion about arranged marriages, since, although he agrees that the practice offends against the value of autonomy, Parekh (2000, 275) also thinks that it would be dogmatic for a majority to impose that distinctively liberal value 'in such culturally crucial matters as marriage', especially since that value is not universally endorsed. Thus, he concludes that the wishes of young Asians should be respected, if they are happy for their parents to choose or to help them choose their spouses.

The community-sustaining defence of controversial cultural practices is importantly different from Kukathas's, examined in chapter 2. Whilst Kukathas believes cultural practices are acceptable so long as the members of a community acquiesce to them, Parekh (2000, 272) stresses that the practice must be 'interlocked with other valuable practices' and be 'central' to a way of life, which would itself be jeopardized if the practice were to be prevented. A significant difficulty for Parekh's more contextual approach is establishing when these conditions obtain, as can be illustrated by reconsidering halal and kosher slaughter practices, where the animal is not stunned prior to slaughter, as is typically required by law. Although Parekh believes that these practices are not 'integral' to Islamic or Jewish ways of life, which implies that they are perhaps not themselves 'central', he does think that they are 'closely tied up with their other beliefs and practices', which suggests that they are 'interlocked with other valuable practices'. Meanwhile, he does not explicitly state whether prohibiting them would jeopardize the respective ways of life, but he does note that Jewish and Muslim communities in Norway willingly consented to a ban on them, which implies that these communities were nevertheless able to sustain themselves (Parekh 2000, 274). So, in this case, despite a disputed practice being 'interlocked with other valuable practices', disallowing it did not seem to undermine the relevant ways of life, meaning that it is ambiguous as to whether the practice can be defended on community-sustaining grounds, as Parekh himself appears to believe.

If a disputed practice is neither culturally authoritative nor community sustaining, the third strategy available to minority communities is 'to step outside their culture and appeal to values the wider society itself subscribes to or can be persuaded to share' (Parekh 2000, 272). This might be done by trying to convince a majority that a practice does not conflict with its operative public values, as was the case for Hindu burial practices in Britain, permitted under the 1989 Water Act. Often, this will involve trying to convince a majority that the disputed practice is relevantly similar to its own practices, as might be the case for halal and kosher slaughter practices. Or perhaps, instead, it will involve trying to convince a majority that permitting the practice is consistent with its own operative public values, properly understood. For instance, although people have aesthetic reasons to oppose the Hindu practice of cremating bodies on funeral pyres, Parekh (2000, 273) thinks they might be willing to allow the practice on the basis that they already believe that matters of taste 'should not be imposed by law'. Alternatively, another strategy is to convince a majority that it has misunderstood a disputed practice, and that it is less objectionable than it seems. For example, sometimes people oppose the hijab for being a proselytizing religious symbol, but after dialogue they might come to appreciate that such fears are not justified (Parekh 2000, 253). Meanwhile, if a practice genuinely does conflict with operative public values, then a majority might be convinced to permit it by reconsidering their own values, or for the sake of enriching society.

Since dialogue about disputed practices will not always yield agreement, Parekh (2000, 272) recommends that operative public values should prevail when a majority remains unconvinced about a particular practice, offering three reasons for minorities to 'gracefully accept' its decision. First, because allowing a practice that diverges radically from society's operative public values could cause moral and social disorientation, since these values are woven into society's way of life and its institutional structure. Second, because, although society has an obligation to accommodate minorities and their ways of life, this should not come at the cost of sacrificing its own way of life. Third, because minorities, and especially immigrants, are unfamiliar with the majority's way of life and so should defer to its judgement in contentious matters.

Pluralist universalism

Parekh's model of intercultural dialogue aspires to be a viable alternative to liberalism without falling into the trap of moral relativism. Moral relativism, recall, is the view that the truth of moral judgements is relative to the traditions, convictions or practices of a group of persons (including, for example, cultural groups). Its proponents tend to believe that criticizing the morality of another culture is not only pointless but disrespectful, since each culture is entitled to its own way of life. By contrast, Parekh's dialogical approach assumes the possibility of productive moral exchange and learning across cultural differences, and he insists that, although we must not seek to mould different cultures in our own image, respect for others should not 'prevent us from criticising their choices and ways of life' (Parekh 2000, 176–7). Further, Parekh (2000, 127) also criticizes relativism for being sociologically naïve in assuming that each 'culture is a tightly integrated and self-contained whole [which] can be neatly individuated'. Instead, Parekh (2000, 163) insists that cultures are almost always 'multiculturally constituted' and 'inescapably influenced' by one another – ideas considered further in chapter 4.

Parekh (2011, 72–4) calls his own approach pluralist universalism: pluralist because different cultures 'value different forms of excellence, moral sensibilities, virtues, capacities, dispositions, and expectations of life', but universal because at least 'some moral values can be shown to have universal validity'. In order to qualify as universal a value need not be accepted by every culture or ethical tradition. Instead, its validity can be established through either abstract philosophical reflection or dialogue, the latter of which is preferable since listening to different experiences and sensibilities 'ensures that we appreciate human beings in all their richness' (Parekh 2000, 128). Parekh grants universal values a special status in intercultural dialogue, even when they are not accepted by all participants. For example, he suggests that polygyny ought to be disallowed, in part because it 'violates the principle of the equality of the sexes', which is a 'rationally defensible universal value' (Parekh 2000, 284). However, these values cannot decisively settle all complex political questions, since they are 'inevitably general and vague' and can be interpreted in different ways (Parekh 2011, 73). Consequently, multicultural societies must turn for guidance to their operative public values, which already underpin their way of life and are woven into its laws, norms and constitution.

In seeking to combine pluralism and universalism, Parekh's theory is vulnerable to criticisms from two opposing directions. First, some liberals object that it not universal enough, since giving priority to operative public values makes it biased towards the status quo (Barry 2001b; Phillips 2007, 166). Historically, many societies have been based on norms and standards that conflicted with universal moral values, including racist and patriarchal societies. Although dialogue offers a mechanism for vulnerable members of society to register their grievances about oppressive norms and standards, there is no guarantee that the majority will revise or replace them. As we have seen, when it comes to disputed practices, Parekh maintains that if a majority is unconvinced by the minority's case, then its own interpretation of the operative public values should prevail. However, this seems to allow for the possibility of majoritarian domination, since it permits the suppression of minority practices which do not themselves violate any universal moral values, on the basis that they are perceived to violate society's operative public values, which themselves might conflict with universal moral values.

Second, Parekh's theory is also vulnerable to the criticism that it is too universal, perhaps even implicitly biased towards the very same liberal morality it ostensibly disavows. This is because Parekh (2000, 340) observes that the kind of intercultural dialogue he envisages requires 'certain institutional preconditions' and calls for particular 'political virtues'. Since these are the basis for dialogue, they cannot be established or justified dialogically, but must instead constitute a kind of universalist core at the foundation of Parekh's theory. Noticeably, they include much that would not look out of place within the kind of liberal universalism which Parekh (2000, 340) wants to avoid, including 'freedom of expression ... participatory public spaces, equal rights, a responsive and popularly accountable structure of authority ... empowerment of citizens ... mutual respect and concern [and] tolerance'. Although none of these institutions or virtues is exclusively liberal, and many of them are endorsed by a variety of ethical and cultural worldviews, it is also true that many of them are not currently accepted universally. Consequently, underpinning Parekh's theory are some substantial and controversial universalist commitments, meaning that, despite appearances, his theory is perhaps rather more universalist than it is pluralist.

Conclusion

Whilst Kymlicka and Kukathas believe that the liberal tradition already contains the intellectual resources multiculturalism requires, Taylor and Parekh challenge this assumption in different ways. Taylor is sceptical about some of liberalism's central tenets, including neutrality and individualism, and he worries that liberal political theory tends to obscure some of the most important dynamics in contemporary political life. Crucially, he thinks that meeting the 'vital human need' for recognition will sometimes involve supporting collective identities, even at the expense of individual autonomy, putting him either at the margins of the liberal tradition or outside it altogether.

Like Kymlicka and Kukathas, Taylor thinks that questions about minority rights and recognition are ultimately to be settled by political theorists themselves, reflecting upon, interpreting and applying different values and principles. By contrast, Parekh proposes a dialogical approach to multiculturalism, in which society must settle difficult and contested questions about its own regulation by engaging in an 'open-minded and morally serious dialogue' amongst different cultural communities. Parekh's approach is based on a far more thoroughgoing critique of liberalism than Taylor's, and he insists that liberal principles supply only one perspective amongst others, all of which deserve to be heard. Although some of the values endorsed by liberals are genuinely universal, some are not, and instead reflect the lifestyle and culture of dominant social groups. Hence, he concludes that it is both arrogant and narrow minded to assume that liberal principles ought to provide the framework to address multicultural controversies.

A central theme in both Parekh's and Taylor's writings is the importance of engaging seriously with unfamiliar practices, beliefs and ways of life, since doing so not only enlarges one's own universe but also is a necessary condition for both recognition and mutual understanding. Neither author underestimates the difficulties of comprehending unfamiliar cultures, or their beliefs and practices.

Although both philosophers are careful to disavow moral relativism, or the related idea that all ways of life are of equal value or worth, they are also sensitive to the dangers of evaluating different practices and beliefs according to inappropriate criteria, such as those drawn from our own culture. Accordingly, they draw attention to something that is perhaps underemphasized by liberal political theorists – namely, the important role played by the virtues of humility and open-mindedness in multicultural societies.

4

Philosophical Criticisms of Multiculturalism

Just as multicultural policies have attracted scepticism and even hostility from politicians and the general public, so too have multicultural political theories been criticized by philosophers. This chapter considers four such criticisms, whilst the following one shifts register, turning to the contentious political reception of multicultural theories and policies.

As for any political theory, philosophical criticisms of multiculturalism come from more and less sympathetic sources. Some of the most serious objections come from other multiculturalists, such as Parekh's complaint that liberal theories of multiculturalism are biased towards individualistic values and ways of life, considered in chapter 3. Disagreements like these, although heated, are basically amongst 'insiders' – which is to say, amongst philosophers who take different views about the exact form their common project ought to take. Meanwhile, the four objections considered in this chapter come from 'outsiders' – which is to say, from philosophers sceptical about that very project. For different reasons, these thinkers believe that multicultural political theory is based on faulty premises or risks taking society in a dangerously mistaken direction. As will become clear, these objections overlap in complex and interesting ways. Importantly, one should not assume that all of them apply to each of the thinkers considered in chapters 2 and 3, since they were formulated in specific contexts and for particular purposes.

The first, egalitarian, objection was forcefully, if polemically, articulated by Brian Barry (2001a) in his *Culture and Equality*, which argued that multiculturalism risked undoing hard-won progressive victories. In particular, Barry worried that multiculturalism threatened the principle of equality before the law by calling for various forms of special treatment for cultural and religious minorities. The second, feminist, objection also draws on the idea that multicultural politics are contrary to the norm of equal treatment, and was first expressed in a provocative essay by Susan Okin (1998). She criticized multiculturalists for focusing too much on the relationships *between* cultural groups and not enough on those *within* cultural groups, leading them to neglect the risks of extending supports to patriarchal cultures.

Whilst the first two objections primarily focus on the political programmes endorsed by multiculturalists, the other two address its underlying philosophical assumptions. The third, essentialist, objection was mentioned in the writings of both Barry and Okin, but it was given a more complete articulation by Anne Phillips (2007) and Seyla Benhabib (2002). In different ways, these authors suggest that multiculturalism is based on a misleadingly group-based conception of culture, which exaggerates the differences between cultures, ignores those within them, and as a result 'essentializes' the identities and practices of particular cultures, treating them as singular and bounded entities. Not only does this mean that multicultural theories are often sociologically impoverished, because they are based on static and naïve models of culture itself, but also that they can be politically dangerous, giving solace to those who would seek to impose an 'authentic' cultural identity on members. The final, cosmopolitan, objection also concerns the conception of culture endorsed by multiculturalists, taking aim at the idea that people need to remain rooted in a particular culture in order to flourish or live a worthwhile life. This objection was articulated vigorously by Jeremy Waldron (1995, 2000), who also criticized multiculturalism for attempting to shield cultural minorities from the realities of modernity and globalization.

The Egalitarian Critique

In his spirited critique of multicultural politics and political theory, Barry (2001a, 325) argued that the policies proposed by multiculturalists were dangerously misconceived, and that the articulation and dissemination of multicultural ideas diverts attention away from more pressing forms of oppression and injustice. He regarded the emergence of multiculturalism as an especially unwelcome development for liberal political theory, since, like Kukathas, he believed that liberalism already contains a satisfactory response to cultural pluralism. However, Barry's egalitarian brand of liberalism differs significantly from the *laissez-faire* version favoured by Kukathas. Indeed, Barry (2001a, 132–3) argues that Kukathas's own theory hardly qualifies as liberal, since it fails to appreciate a 'defining feature' of liberalism, which is that 'there are certain rights against oppression, exploitation and injury to which every single human being is entitled to lay claim, and that appeals to "cultural diversity" and pluralism under no circumstances trump the value of basic liberal rights'.

The liberalism endorsed by Barry was essentially a child of the Enlightenment, sharing with it an emphasis on the norms of equal citizenship and legal uniformity. Multiculturalism posed a challenge to this, he thought, because it owed a significant debt to the Counter-Enlightenment, a term popularized by the historian Isaiah Berlin to refer to a body of reactionary political thinking that took shape during the late eighteenth and nineteenth centuries, especially in the writings of conservative thinkers such as Joseph de Maistre, Edmund Burke and Georg Hegel. These philosophers opposed the universalistic rationalism of the Enlightenment, as had been manifested, for instance, in the establishment of a uniform system of legal administration during the French Revolution. This system replaced the patchwork of privileges and special arrangements that had characterized the *ancien régime* and to which Counter-Enlightenment thinkers wanted to return. As Barry (2001a, 10) presents things, contemporary multiculturalists are willing heirs to this anti-liberal and anti-egalitarian strand of political thought, since they too aim to create 'a mass of anomalies and special cases'.

Barry is quite right to say that many multiculturalists are sceptical about legal and political uniformity. For example, Parekh (2000, 179 and 181–2) describes a 'dominant' model of the modern state in which 'citizens are homogenized and related to the state in an identical manner, enjoying equal status and possessing identical rights and obligations'. For Barry (2001a, 10), the widespread dispersal of this model was a significant and thoroughly laudable historical achievement, since 'uniformity of treatment is the enemy of privilege'. By contrast, Parekh (2000, 185) worries that uniformity of treatment 'can become an instrument of injustice and oppression'. Strikingly, Barry and Parekh appeal to the same value – equality – in order to celebrate and condemn, respectively, the principle of uniform treatment. Parekh (2000, 240), like other multiculturalists, insists that '[e]qual rights do not mean identical rights', since 'human beings are at once both similar and different' and people 'with different cultural backgrounds and needs might require different rights to enjoy equality'. Thus, he believes that uniform treatment is 'morally problematic' and can become 'an ideological device to mould humankind in a certain direction' (Parekh 2000, 240). Meanwhile, Barry (2001a, 262) reaches the opposite conclusion, insisting that equality requires giving each person the same rights and freedoms, since everyone has roughly similar interests and 'human beings are virtually identical as they come from the hands of nature'.

The most influential expression of Barry's insistence on the primacy of uniform treatment is his case against the rule-and-exemption approach, a phrase he popularized to refer to the practice of exempting religious and other minorities from laws that conflict with their customs, practices or beliefs. Multiculturalists are, for the most part at least, sympathetic to these accommodations, examined in more detail in chapter 6, since they worry that the uniform application of laws may sometimes be unfair to, or excessively burdensome for, minorities. Examples include the exemptions from motorcycle helmet and weapons laws that allow Sikh men to wear turbans and carry kirpans, and the exemption from the requirement that animals be stunned prior to slaughter which enables Jews and Muslims to follow their respective religious dietary laws.

According to Barry (2001a, 43, 48 and 62), an exemption from a generally applicable law is justified as a matter of principle if, and only if, the following three conditions obtain: if there is a good case for a particular rule; if there is a reason to exempt some people from that rule; and if this reason pertains to some people but not everyone. Barry believes these rarely occur simultaneously, proposing what one commentator calls the 'pincer' argument against exemptions (Greenawalt 2008, 305). According to it, 'either the case for the law (or some version of it) is strong enough to rule out exemptions, or the case that can be made for the exemptions is strong enough to suggest that there should be no law anyway' (Barry 2001a, 39). So, for example, either we should accept that reducing head injuries to motorcyclists is a valid objective for public policy, in which case Sikhs – like everyone else – must wear crash helmets, or, if we allow Sikhs to decide for themselves whether riding without a helmet is an acceptable risk, then we should extend this same freedom to everyone else.

In addition to the pincer argument, Barry also responds to two different arguments for exemptions appealing to the value of equality. The first is that exemptions eliminate the unfairness of religious believers being especially burdened by particular laws – that is to say, more burdened than the typical person is. For example, the legal requirement that animals be stunned prior to slaughter is distinctively burdensome for Jews and Muslims, since only their dietary laws are incompatible with it. Likewise, the requirement that motorcyclists wear protective headgear is distinctively burdensome for Sikh men, since doing so is impossible if they are to wear a turban. In response, Barry (2001a, 34) argues that legal rules standardly burden some people more than others and that '[t]his is simply how things are'. He thinks there is no reason to think that differential burdens as such are unfair, reminding us that we tend to be untroubled by fast drivers being dismayed by reductions in the speed limit or smokers being frustrated by smoking bans. The mere fact that a law burdens some people more than others, Barry concludes, is not a sufficient reason to deviate from the norm of uniform treatment.

The second argument is more subtle, and it is that exemptions are sometimes justified in the name of equality of opportunity, in order to compensate people for unchosen disadvantages arising from their distinctive cultural practices or religious beliefs (see, e.g., Taylor 1994, 60–1; Kymlicka 1995, 114–15; Parekh 2000, 241). For example, consider the rule making it mandatory to wear protective headgear when working on a building site. Arguably, this regulation denies Sikh men, who wear turbans, an opportunity everyone else has – namely, to work in the construction industry. Thus, in order to equalize opportunities, Sikhs ought to be granted an exemption from the rule.

The interpretation of equality of opportunity underpinning this argument is controversial, since the unequal opportunities in question are arguably as much the result of the beliefs and practices of Sikhs as of the particular legal rule. Indeed, it might seem as if a law requiring workers to wear protective headgear does not itself prevent Sikh men from working on building sites. Rather, if Sikhs consider themselves to be unable to work on building sites, it is because of their belief that they must wear turbans and their corresponding refusal to wear hard hats.

In response to this, some multiculturalists have proposed more nuanced understandings of what it is to have an 'opportunity', thereby hoping to demonstrate why an exemption-less hard-hat law will deny Sikh men an opportunity that everyone else has. For example, Parekh distinguishes between having an opportunity to do something and something being a mere possibility, arguing that wearing a hard hat is a possibility but not an opportunity for most Sikh men. This is because opportunities, according to Parekh (2000, 241), are 'subject-dependent', in the sense that a person must have 'the capacity, the cultural disposition, or the necessary cultural knowledge to take advantage' of them. Since Sikh men lack the cultural disposition to wear a hard hat, the uniform application of a regulation requiring hard hats would leave them with fewer opportunities than everyone else. Accordingly, Parekh concludes that an exemption is justified for the sake of equal opportunities.

Barry (2001a, 37) is withering about Parekh's view, suggesting that it 'destroys the meaning of the word opportunity' because a person's having the opportunity to do something does not depend on their beliefs but is 'an objective state of affairs'. A better explanation of examples like the Sikh builder, according to Barry (2001a, 40–6), is that Sikhs who refuse to wear hard hats have an 'expensive taste', since their preference to wear a turban comes at the cost of foreclosing opportunities that require wearing hard hats. Barry (2001a, 40) generalizes this point and concludes that the costs arising from a person's own 'moral convictions or religious beliefs' are neither unjust nor unfair, so need not be compensated for with exemptions. In other words, since wearing a hard hat is a possibility for a Sikh man, a rule which makes them mandatory for construction workers does not undermine equality of opportunity, because any disadvantages for Sikhs are their own responsibility.

How convincing is Barry's expensive tastes argument? His view is that religious beliefs are relevantly like preferences, in the sense that individuals should bear the costs of satisfying them. For example, suppose that I like sunsets and you like opera. Equality of opportunity does not require me to give you some of what I have so that you can enjoy the opera as often as I can enjoy sunsets, since we are both responsible for meeting the costs of satisfying our own preferences. For Barry, a Sikh who is unable to work on a building site because of his religious convictions is similarly responsible for the costs arising from his beliefs. He has no complaint in justice about feeling unable to work on building sites, since he has the same opportunity as everyone else to do so.

Meanwhile, an alternative view has been proposed by Jonathan Quong, who suggests that there is an unequal opportunity in cases like these, but not the one Parekh identified. The opportunity Quong (2006, 62) has in mind is not simply that of working on a building site but, rather, that of combining one's 'religious pursuits with basic civic opportunities like employment and education'. To illustrate his view, Quong (2006, 626) gives the example of Jeff and Jonah, who would both like to become police officers. Each man has similar abilities and ambitions but different religious beliefs: Jeff is a liberal Protestant, and Jonah is an Orthodox Jew. Current police regulations require officers to be available to work on the weekends, but, since Jonah is unwilling to work on his Sabbath, he is unable to serve in the police force. By the standards of Barry's theory, both have equal opportunities, since working on weekends is a possibility for Jonah, even if he is unwilling to avail of it. Meanwhile, Quong suggests that the two have unequal opportunities, since Jeff can combine his religious beliefs with his chosen career whilst Jonah cannot. Equality, then, requires accommodating Jonah's religious practices.

So, in summary, Barry's thesis that exemptions violate the principle of equal treatment can be resisted in one of two ways. First, Parekh distinguishes between opportunities and possibilities, insisting that a person's being able to do something is not the same as their having a meaningful opportunity to do that thing. Second, Quong argues that equalizing opportunities sometimes requires ensuring that people can combine particular opportunities, such as adhering to the fundamentals of their faith whilst accessing employment or educational opportunities. Whilst Parekh's view relies on a controversial understanding of what it is to have an opportunity, Quong's requires that we specify the kind of opportunities that people should be able to combine with their religious beliefs. If either view is convincing, then Barry has failed to demonstrate that the rule-and-exemption approach is incompatible with equal treatment.

The Feminist Critique

At around the same time as Barry developed his egalitarian critique of multiculturalism, a number of feminist political theorists were questioning whether cultural rights could sometimes be detrimental to the interests of women and girls. For instance, in the opening passage of her *Multicultural Jurisdictions*, Ayelet Shachar (2001, 2–3) observed that:

> Multicultural accommodation presents a problem ... when pro-identity group policies aimed at levelling the playing field between minority communities and the wider society unwittingly allow systematic maltreatment of individuals within the accommodated group – an impact which in certain cases is so severe that it can nullify these individuals' citizenship rights. Under such conditions, well-meaning accommodation by the state may leave members of minority groups vulnerable to severe injustice within the group, and may, in effect, work to reinforce some of the most hierarchical elements of a culture.

Shachar and other feminists had observed that, although the foundational texts of multicultural political theory were highly sensitive to inequalities *between* cultural groups, they said little about inequalities *within* groups. And whilst the status of minority communities and the viability of minority cultures are important, so too are power relations within groups, particularly given the ubiquity of patriarchy within majority and minority cultures alike. Especially important are the frequent pressures on women, especially mothers, to uphold cultural traditions and to preserve minority ways of life. Feminist scholars argued that when multicultural theories neglect these things, they risk overlooking – and perhaps condoning or even contributing to – significant forms of oppression within groups.

The vigorous debates about the relationship between feminism and multiculturalism were initiated by Susan Okin's (1998) landmark article 'Feminism and Multiculturalism: Some Tensions'. This was later revised and republished under the more provocative title 'Is Multiculturalism Bad for Women?' (Okin 1999). Although Okin (2005) later said that there is 'no simple answer' to this question, many of her readers took her to be arguing for an unqualified 'yes' (e.g. Kukathas 2001), even accusing her of doing so with 'militant insensitivity' (Benhabib 2002, 100). Few essays in recent political theory have generated such an intense and often polemical critical response.

In her original essay, Okin's stated aim was to identify and describe some points of tension between gender equality and at least some of the rights called for by multiculturalists. Her central thesis was that cultural rights are often not in the best interests of girls and women, since someone's place within their culture is likely to be at least as important as the viability of that culture for their self-respect, dignity or capacity for autonomy. Consequently, even if there are powerful arguments for cultural rights, such as those proposed by multiculturalists, special care must first be taken to investigate inequalities within groups seeking such rights, especially inequalities between the sexes. Furthermore, these inequalities are difficult to discern because they are typically found in the private domain of family life, which is also the place where cultural identities are transmitted and sustained.

At least two normative recommendations follow from Okin's analysis. First, given that gendered forms of oppression are often connected to cultural identities, cultural rights – i.e. rights to preserve and promote a given culture – will often be contrary to the interests of women and girls. As Okin (1999, 12) puts it, 'group rights are potentially, and in many cases actually, antifeminist'. Second, and more provocatively – given that nearly all cultures are sexist, and some minority cultures especially so – then their members 'may be *much* better off, from a liberal point of view, if the culture into which they were born were either gradually to become extinct (as its members become integrated into the surrounding culture) or, preferably, to be encouraged or supported to substantially alter itself so as to reinforce the equality, rather than the inequality, of women' (Okin 1998, 680, emphasis in original).

A striking example Okin used in her essay concerned Ultra-Orthodox Jews in Israel. As a community and as individuals, this group benefits from the kinds of rights that multiculturalists typically favour. For instance, they receive significant financial subsidies from wider society, and individual members are exempted from various civic obligations, including military service. According to some multiculturalists, such special treatment is necessary for the group to preserve its distinctive identity, and justified because of the strong interests that group members have in preserving that identity (e.g. Margalit and Halbertal 1994). Meanwhile, Okin points out that, because many of the group's practices violate liberal norms, including gender equality, granting special rights will not necessarily advance the interests of female members. Indeed, by her account, Ultra-Orthodox women and girls might be better off leaving the group and assimilating into mainstream Israeli society.

By Okin's reckoning, multiculturalist sympathy for the Ultra-Orthodox confirms their indifference to the content of minority group practices, which, in the case of the Ultra-Orthodox, include what Okin (1998, 673) describes as 'blatant sex discrimination' and 'the lifelong repression' of girls' 'freedom to dress, play, move, and even sing, because of their status within the culture as "dangerous sexual objects"'. If multiculturalists were instead more willing to investigate the internal life of the groups they support, then they would realize that cultural rights are often contrary to the interests of women. For instance, as Okin emphasizes, because the primary role of women within the Ultra-Orthodox community is to facilitate the religious scholarship of men, both financially and domestically, their subordinate status is hardly conducive towards promoting self-respect or a sense of equal worth.

Liberal multiculturalists like those examined in chapter 2 have two different responses to this line of argument, neither of which satisfies Okin. First, following Kukathas, one might question the assumption that cultural rights for illiberal and patriarchal cultures are contrary to the interests of female group members. Indeed – conceivably, at least – female members of traditional and illiberal minorities might endorse the customs and beliefs that Okin criticizes. Kukathas's theory, recall, emphasizes toleration, and his preferred tolerant state does not pass judgement on the content of a culture or its practices. Thus, provided that members are willing to accept their treatment, he thinks that a group has the right to be 'left alone', and wider society should not interfere. Against this, Okin (2002) objects to how Kukathas operationalizes the idea of consent. True, if women really did consent to sexist group practices, then a liberal state would have a powerful reason to tolerate those practices. However, Kukathas thinks that the liberal state should tolerate sexist practices provided that women acquiesce to them – for instance, by not leaving their group – and this is a significantly lower bar. But it seems implausible that acquiescence could do the same normative work as consent, given that acquiescence to oppressive practices can be caused by a lack of power or self-esteem, or by being socialized into accepting a subordinate status and, correspondingly, having a weak sense of self-entitlement. Consequently, Okin concludes that, by the lights of the moral foundations of Kukathas's own theory, minority groups such as the Ultra-Orthodox do not really have a right to be 'left alone', because we cannot be sure that their members really do accept their treatment.

Second, one might instead follow Kymlicka, who agrees with Okin that cultural rights should not be extended to patriarchal and illiberal groups. Kymlicka argues that societal cultures ought to be protected by cultural rights when, and because, they support the autonomy of members by providing them with a context of choice. Like Okin, he is much concerned with the internal character of minority communities, and he notes that closed or discriminatory cultures cannot support individuals in developing their capacity for autonomy. On his account, it is crucial that individuals have the freedom and capacity to question and revise the traditional practices of their community, should they come to see them as no longer worthy of their allegiance, since 'to inhibit people from questioning their inherited social roles can condemn them to unsatisfying, even oppressive lives' (Kymlicka 1995, 92). Consequently, just as he opposes an exemption to allow Amish parents to remove their children from school early, he should also disallow cultural rights for groups like the Ultra-Orthodox, at least if Okin's account of their culture and practices is accurate.

Given that Kymlicka and Okin seem to agree on the substantive issues, one might wonder whether Okin was justified when she accused multiculturalists of not paying enough attention to the content of minority cultures. Indeed, Kymlicka (1999) made exactly this point in his response to Okin, emphasizing that his theory – like hers – rules out cultural rights for illiberal minorities. Meanwhile, Okin (1998, 678) argued that Kymlicka fails to take the tension between liberal multiculturalism and feminism seriously enough, since if he really believed that groups which violate the norm of gender equality should be denied cultural rights, then he would have to acknowledge that very few groups are entitled to such rights in the first place, and this is something he never does:

> There are many cultures that, though they may not impose their beliefs or practices on others, and though they may appear to respect the basic civil and political liberties of women and girls, do not in practice, especially in the private sphere, treat them with anything like the same concern and respect as men and boys, or allow them to enjoy the same freedoms. As I have suggested, discrimination against and control of the freedom of females, to a greater or lesser extent, is practiced by virtually all cultures, past and present, but especially by strictly religious ones and those in the present that look to the past – to ancient texts or revered traditions – for guidelines or rules about how to live in the contemporary world.

According to Okin, when Kymlicka works out the implications of his own theory and attempts to apply it to real-world cases, he tends to neglect hidden and private forms of sex discrimination. For example, within many societal cultures, unpaid domestic labour is divided unequally between the genders, women are expected to defer to men, relations between the genders are marked by status and economic inequalities, pervasive and discriminatory standards of beauty and grooming apply to women but not men, and female educational attainment is less highly regarded than male educational attainment. Consequently, even if a societal culture does contribute to a person's autonomy, as Kymlicka thinks, in practice nearly all societal cultures undermine the self-respect and self-esteem of women, and so should not be candidates for liberal multicultural rights.

To a significant extent, the disagreement between Okin and Kymlicka seems to boil down to Okin's (1998, 667) controversial claim that 'most cultures have as one of their principal aims the control of women by men'. As a result, she not only opposes cultural rights, but also argues that it would often be better for women if their culture were to become extinct (at least if the option of cultural reform is not available). One reason to be troubled by Okin's position is that it seemingly relies upon a simplistic, monolithic and essentialist conception of culture itself, a complaint often levelled at multiculturalists themselves, to be examined in the next section. Another reason is the relatively low significance she grants to the interests that women might perceive themselves to have in their own cultures.

In the wake of Okin's critique, a number of theories of multicultural feminism were developed. These authors reject the crude binary of either-multiculturalism-or-feminism and instead proceed from the assumption that many women have significant interests in both preserving *and* reforming their cultures. For these thinkers, because cultures are malleable, not fixed or static, patriarchal cultural practices can be contested and patriarchal cultural norms can be re-interpreted. Consequently, the aim of a feminist political theory of multiculturalism is to find ways to empower women to do this, either through democratic means (Benhabib 2002; Deveaux 2006) or through creative legal-constitutional mechanisms (Shachar 2001). Although these theories were self-consciously developed as alternatives to Okin's less hospitable approach, in the end she arguably reaches much the same conclusion (Okin 1998, 684; 2005, 72–5).

The Essentialist Critique

The essentialist critique of multiculturalism concerns how multi-cultural political theory conceives of culture. Its proponents accuse multiculturalists of essentializing the identities and practices of minority cultures by emphasizing the differences between cultures at the expense of those within them, treating cultures as bounded and relatively homogeneous entities, and consequently neglecting cultural fluidity and hybridity. In turn, these errors are attributed to the multiculturalist tendency to associate particular cultures with particular properties or characteristics, as when the members of a given culture are said to share a distinctive belief or worldview, or when a particular practice is said to be constitutive of a group's identity. Although claims like these often have a superficial plausi-bility, they rarely withstand careful scrutiny. Considered reflection typically reveals the belief or practice in question is not actually shared by every member of the culture, and that not only is there variation amongst members, but often the beliefs or practices are not really distinctive to the group in the first place.

According to those who press this objection, essentialism renders multicultural political theory descriptively false by virtue of committing it to an implausible and naïve conception of culture. Further, and more importantly, essentialism also makes multiculturalism normatively flawed: multicultural policies are counterproductive *because* they are based on essentializing assump-tions. Despite intending to expand the freedom of minorities, multiculturalism constrains the members of minority cultural groups. For example, Anne Phillips (2007, 14) writes that multi-culturalism 'exaggerates the internal unity of cultures, solidifies differences that are currently more fluid, and makes people from other cultures seem more exotic and distinct than they really are'. As a result, she thinks that multicultural policies might turn out to be more of a 'cultural straitjacket' than a 'cultural liberator', potentially forcing the members of minority groups 'into a regime of authenticity, denying them the chance to cross cultural borders, borrow cultural influences, and to define and redefine themselves' (Phillips 2007, 14). Similarly, Nancy Fraser (2001, 24) also worries that multiculturalism 'puts moral pressure on individual members to conform to group culture' and often imposes 'a single, drastically simplified group identity, which denies the complexity of people's lives, the multiplicity of their identifications and the cross-pulls of their various affiliations'. Similar fears have also been articulated outside the realms of political theory. For instance, an early version of this critique can be found in an essay by the anthropologist Terence Turner (1993, 412), who worried that multiculturalism 'risks reifying cultures as separate entities by overemphasising the internal homogeneity of cultures in terms that potentially legitimise repressive demands for cultural conformity'.

As these examples indicate, the essentialist critique is often framed in rather general terms, as an objection to multiculturalism *per se*, rather than as a critique of any particular theory. Consequently, it can be difficult to discern whether and why any particular theory really is guilty as charged. Helpfully, Seyla Benhabib has illustrated how the arguments of two different multiculturalists – Charles Taylor and Will Kymlicka – seemingly lead them into the trap of essentialism. Interestingly, although she thinks that both philosophers endorse a 'reductionist sociology of culture', which (mistakenly) regards cultures as 'clearly delineable wholes [that are] congruent with population groups', she argues that they arrive at the same 'faulty epistemic premises' by different routes (Benhabib 2002, 4).

In Taylor's case, Benhabib suggests that the problem of essentialism arises because of the close connection in his theory between the recognition of individual identity and collective forms of oppression and marginalization. As discussed in chapter 3, the normative impetus behind Taylor's theory is that a person's identity is shaped by recognition, misrecognition or the absence of recognition, the latter two of which can distort or damage the formation of the self. Although the harms associated with mis- and non-recognition are experienced by individuals, and not groups, Taylor suggests that they are often connected to collective experiences, such as how one's group is perceived in wider society. So, for example, he emphasizes that being part of a socially unpopular group may compromise one's self-esteem or even induce self-hatred, and that being part of a group which is denied equal political rights may undermine one's self-respect.

It is this close connection that Taylor perceives between culture, identity and recognition which gives rise to the suspicion that his theory might rely on an essentialist conception of culture. Meanwhile, the normative recommendations he proposes seem to confirm the diagnosis. Recall that Taylor believes that achieving the proper recognition of each person's individual, authentic and unique identity may require policies to promote or stabilize collective identities, such as policies to help Quebec retain its distinctive culture. Benhabib (2002, 52) suggests this mistakenly assumes that 'individual authentic self-expression' runs 'in tandem' with the recognition of collective identities, when in reality multicultural and group-based policies will not always enhance individual recognition and may even frustrate the freedom of group members.

Meanwhile, Benhabib (2002, 67) attributes the problem of essentialism in Kymlicka's theory to his 'remarkably static and preservationist' account of culture. As discussed in chapter 2, the normative impetus behind Kymlicka's (1995, 76) theory is that individuals require stable 'societal cultures' if they are to exercise their autonomy, since these 'provide members with meaningful ways of life across the full range of human activities'. When it comes to allocating cultural rights, as will be discussed in chapter 7, Kymlicka (1995, 80) restricts them to groups exhibiting certain objective criteria – including being territorially concentrated, sharing a language and having a way of life that is institutionally embodied – on the grounds that only groups with these characteristics are likely to be able to maintain their culture. However, as Benhabib notes, this implies that it is because a group exhibits these objective characteristics that its societal culture should be preserved. In turn, Benhabib thinks this further implies that political movements representing minority nations ought to be supported regardless of the content of their specific political goals, so long as they represent societal cultures with the required objective features. But, as she points out, this is surely too quick: before reaching a judgement about whether to support a minority in its quest for cultural rights, we should first study its political platform – for instance, by asking whether democracy, gender equality and the rights of other minorities will be respected (Benhabib 2002, 65).

How convincing are Benhabib's objections? One thing to note is that it is surely unfair to describe Kymlicka's account of culture as 'remarkably static', since he evidently believes that cultures are malleable and change over time. Not only does he insist that illiberal cultures are liberalizable, but Kymlicka (1995, 87–8, 104 and 184) repeatedly returns to the example of Quebec's 'Quiet Revolution' to illustrate how people can rapidly and dramatically transform their own culture. Perhaps, however, this is to miss the point of Benhabib's critique, since her concern about essentialism is ultimately normative, not anthropological or sociological. In particular, she thinks that implementing multicultural political theories such as those of Kymlicka and Taylor will have the effect of frustrating people who want to transform their own cultures, and disempowering those who are struggling against cultural constraints (Benhabib 2002, 66–7). She attributes this to an underlying model of 'mosaic multiculturalism', which regards cultures as separate entities, like the pieces of a mosaic (Benhabib 2002, 8). For Benhabib (2002, 68), this model inevitably 'yields illiberal consequences' – for instance, by pointing towards the need to 'police' the boundaries between cultural identities, thereby legitimizing 'culture-controlling elites', and privileging the 'continuity and preservation of cultures over time as opposed to their reinvention, reappropriation, and even subversion'.

However, it is not clear that liberal theories of multiculturalism must embrace the illiberal normative implications of mosaic multiculturalism. For one thing, as discussed in chapter 2, Kymlicka distinguishes between 'internal restrictions' and 'external protections' precisely so as to ensure that cultural rights do not suppress individual freedom in the way Benhabib fears. Unless Benhabib can demonstrate that this distinction is illusory, or that Kymlicka's theory entails internal restrictions as well as external protections, then her critique has no bearing on his theory. Furthermore, as Kymlicka (2015a, 221–9) himself has pointed out, unless Benhabib's view is that *all* claims to cultural recognition and support are illegitimate, then her position must in the end amount to one very similar to his own since, like her, he believes that liberal democratic norms must constrain the recognition of collective identities. Recall that she does not rule out supporting cultural rights, but only insists that doing so should not be at the expense of minority rights, democracy and gender equality. In this regard, her theory seems to reach much the same conclusions as Kymlicka's.

So, then, the essentialist critique is unconvincing in at least one respect, since a normative theory of multiculturalism can incorporate safeguards to protect individual freedom. However, there is perhaps a deeper truth to it, which Alan Patten (2014, 38–45) has labelled the 'dilemma of essentialism'. This arises because non-essentialist conceptions of culture, despite being empirically more realistic, seem to be unsuitable for the purposes of multicultural political theory. If cultures are conceptualized as heterogeneous rather than homogeneous, as fluid and contested rather than static, and as messy and overlapping rather than as pieces of a mosaic, then it will be difficult for political theorists to advance arguments in support of cultural rights, since neither the subject nor object of those rights will be readily apparent. For example, consider the case for preserving minority cultural distinctiveness, such as by empowering minorities against the homogenizing pressures of majority culture. The arguments given by political theorists in support of this typically rely upon the (essentializing) assumptions that cultures really are distinct and that each human group has its own – perhaps 'authentic' – way of life. Dropping these assumptions seemingly undermines the normative force of much multicultural political theory – why should we want special measures to preserve cultural distinctiveness if cultures are not really distinctive after all? Moreover, it makes it difficult to see how multicultural policies are supposed to work, since, if cultures are not distinct, then how can we implement policies to maintain their distinctiveness, and who should be the beneficiaries of those policies?

Patten's (2014, 39) dilemma, then, is that '*either* culture is understood in an "essentialist" way, in which case multiculturalism is empirically and morally flawed; *or* culture is understood in a nonessentialist way, but then the concept no longer supplies multiculturalism with the means of making the empirical judgments and normative claims that matter to it'. The obvious solution is to formulate a non-essentialist conception of culture that is nevertheless adequate for the purposes of multicultural political theory. However, doing so has proven challenging, and even multicultural political theorists who formally denounce essentialism have been accused of implicitly relying upon it.

This difficulty can be illustrated by considering the work of two multiculturalists who have been accused of falling into the grasp of essentialism despite being highly sensitive to it. First is Iris Marion Young (1990, 2000), who developed one of the most theoretically sophisticated justifications for special group representation rights. These rights promote the inclusion of oppressed groups by ensuring that their perspectives are represented – for instance, by reserving seats for them in legislatures or by implementing similar measures in state and civil society bodies. In advocating for these, Young does not make the crudely essentializing assumption that a single group member can stand for the group as a whole, and she is careful to avoid the implication that all members of an oppressed group share the same interests or opinions. Nevertheless, Alison Jaggar has suggested that her model of group representation cannot entirely evade the problem of essentialism, since implementing it in practice will require determining which groups require representation and who should represent them. As such, on Jaggar's (1999, 314) reading, Young's model ends up being unable to avoid 'an essentialized and naturalized conception of groups as internally homogeneous, clearly bounded, mutually exclusive, and maintaining specific determinate interests'. Jaggar's objection, then, is not that Young depends on essentialist ideas when justifying special representation rights, but that group representation itself is an essentializing practice, which could conceivably have the kinds of damaging political effects Benhabib feared if, say, elites within a group are able to use it to pursue a narrow agenda or to dominate vulnerable group members.

Second is James Tully, whose book *Strange Multiplicity* begins with a forthright critique of essentialism. Here, Tully (1995, 10) expressly rejects what he refers to as the 'billiard ball' conception of culture, which is his preferred term for the view that Jaggar attributed to Young, and Benhabib attributes to Taylor and Kymlicka – namely, that cultures are 'separate, bounded and internally uniform'. However, according to Brian Barry (2001a, 256–61; and 2002, 284–7), Tully ends up endorsing a different belief that is also characteristically essentialist, which is that certain cultural groups have an authentic way of life – i.e., a set of practices and beliefs to which they must be true. To illustrate this, Barry refers to Tully's assessment of the Canadian 'Sparrow Case', which concerned the rights of the Musqueam nation to fish in its traditional waters, despite a fishing ban having been imposed in the interests of conservation. On Tully's (1995, 172) reading, the courts were right to allow the Musqueam to continue fishing, since 'fishing a specific body of coastal water is constitutive of [their] cultural identity'. But, as Barry points out, this will qualify as a reason to defer to the wishes of the Musqueam only if we make the essentializing assumption that being unable to fish in a particular body of water would prevent the Musqueam from being themselves, or living authentically. For Barry, this means that Tully ends up with a conception of culture that is no less monolithic and essentializing than the other multiculturalists he criticizes.

So, in summary, the objection that multicultural political theories threaten individual freedom because they are based on essentialist conceptions of culture is unconvincing, because multicultural theories can easily incorporate safeguards to protect individual freedom. Meanwhile, the deeper objection, which is that a viable multicultural political theory must endorse, at some level, an essentialized (and hence mistaken) conception of culture, is harder to overcome.

The Cosmopolitan Critique

The word 'cosmopolitan' comes to us from Ancient Greece and it has two sources: *kosmos*, which refers to the world or universe, and *politês*, which denotes a citizen. A cosmopolitan, then, is literally a citizen of the world. In the context of debates about multiculturalism, cosmopolitanism stands for the belief that human beings can flourish by drawing on, and experimenting with, ideas from many different cultures (Scheffler 2001; Caney 2010). It is a view about human well-being or flourishing, which says that people can, and perhaps should, construct their lives from many different cultural sources. Importantly, cosmopolitans such as Jeremy Waldron (1995, 99) believe that a life lived in a 'kaleidoscope of cultures' is no less authentic or meaningful than one attempting to remain true to an ancestral culture. As a result, they reject an idea often associated with multiculturalism – namely, that human beings need to remain loyal to or rooted within a particular culture or community in order to enjoy an autonomous, meaningful or dignified life.

Waldron (2000, 228) offers the following (self-referential) example to illustrate a cosmopolitan 'approach to lifestyle':

> [A] person who lives in California, but came there from Oxford via Edinburgh, and came in turn to Oxford from the other side of the world, the southwestern corner of the Pacific Ocean, whither his English and Irish ancestors emigrated in the mid-nineteenth century ... [S]omeone who did not associate his identity with any secure sense of place, someone who did not take his cultural identity to be defined by any bounded subset of the cultural resources available in the world. He did not take his identity as ... compromised when he studied Greek, ate Chinese, wore clothes made in Korea, worshipped with the Book of Common Prayer, listened to arias by Verdi sung by a Maori diva on Japanese equipment, gave lectures in Buenos Aires, followed Israeli politics, or practiced Buddhist meditation techniques.

Perhaps surprisingly, the life depicted here seems to encapsulate what many people have in mind when they consider the benefits of living in a globalized and culturally diverse society, and so it may seem strange to invoke these ideas in an argument against multicultural political theory. Indeed, Robert Goodin (2006) has described a theory of 'polyglot' multiculturalism, which says that multicultural societies are desirable precisely because they expand and deepen the range of options available to their members in the way Waldron describes. According to this, the 'great virtue of multiculturalism is that it provides a broad smorgasbord of mix-and-match options from which to choose' (Goodin 2006, 295). Similarly, the earliest use of the term 'multicultural' seems to be very close to Waldron's vision of cosmopolitanism. According to historian Rita Chin (2017, 8), this was in the title of an American novel, *Lance: A Story about Multicultural Men*, written by Edward F. Haskell and published in 1941. The eponymous multicultural men, like Waldron's cosmopolitans, had allegiances to humanity at large, not a particular group or nation. For Haskell, multiculturalism signified an outlook in diametric opposition to national chauvinism and prejudice.

However, contemporary theories of multiculturalism, such as Taylor's and Kymlicka's, are different, since they both affirm something that Waldron denies – namely, that people have fundamental interests in preserving their cultures of origin. For Kymlicka, this is because cultural memberships provide people with a context of choice that makes individual autonomy possible, whilst for Taylor it is because recognition, including recognition of one's cultural identity, is a vital human need. Against these, Waldron instead argues that the very possibility of a cosmopolitan way of life indicates that people do not depend on their ancestral cultures. Indeed, as he observes, since people manage to flourish by constructing their identity from a wide variety of cultural sources, this suggests that immersion in a single culture cannot be a necessary precondition for achieving a coherent sense of self, or for having available the kinds of choices that make a good life possible. As Waldron (1995, 99–100) puts it, a 'freewheeling cosmopolitan life, lived in a kaleidoscope of cultures, is both possible and fulfilling ... rich and creative, and with no more unhappiness than one expects to find anywhere in human existence'. Consequently, it cannot be true that 'people need their rootedness in the particular culture in which they and their ancestors were reared in the way that they need food, clothing and shelter' (Waldron 1995, 100).

According to Waldron, then, the possibility of a cosmopolitan way of life undercuts the kinds of arguments for cultural rights made by Kymlicka and Taylor. His view, in short, is that, whilst 'we need cultural meanings', we do not need 'homogeneous cultural frameworks'; or, put another way, although human beings are cultural creatures, they do not require 'cultural integrity' (Waldron 1995, 108). In response, Kymlicka (1995, 86) has suggested that Waldron exaggerates the ease with which people move between cultures. According to him, moving between cultures is typically far more difficult and disorientating than Waldron implies, and in some cases it may be impossible for someone to integrate fully into a new culture if it is deeply different from their culture of origin. Waldron underestimates these challenges, Kymlicka suggests, because of the kinds of examples he relies upon. For example, Waldron (1995, 108) portrays an 'Irish-American who eats Chinese food and reads her child Grimm's Fairy Tales' as living in a kaleidoscope of cultures. However, Kymlicka thinks it more accurate to say that this person is really enjoying the diverse opportunities offered by a single diverse societal culture – anglophone American society. Further, even when it is possible to leave one's ancestral culture and build a new life in a different cultural context, Kymlicka insists that people should not be expected to do so, since 'the choice to leave one's culture can be seen as analogous to the choice to take a vow of poverty and enter a religious order'. Thus, as discussed in chapter 2, he concludes that '[l]eaving one's culture, while possible, is best seen as renouncing something to which one is reasonably entitled' (Kymlicka 1995, 86).

In addition to arguing that people do not really *need* their cultures – or at least not in the sense that protective multiculturalists such as Kymlicka and Taylor sometimes suggest – cosmopolitans also propose a radical interpretation of authenticity. Waldron's cosmopolitan, recall, constructs his life from snatches of different cultural fragments, embraces complexity and fluidity, and 'refuses to think of himself as defined by his location or his ancestry or his citizenship or his language' (Waldron 1995, 95). According to him, this kind of 'hybrid lifestyle' is 'the only appropriate response to the modern world in which we live', and those who would instead prefer to live immersed in a traditional culture are not living in 'the real world'. To be immersed in a traditional culture 'might be a fascinating anthropological experiment, but it involves an artificial dislocation from what actually is going on in the world'. This is because the 'real world' is one 'formed by technology and trade; by economic, religious, and political imperialism and their offspring; by mass migration and the dispersion of cultural influences' (Waldron 1995, 100).

Waldron's claim here is striking, inverting an accusation typically levelled at cosmopolitans. This accusation can be found, for example, in conservative political theorist Roger Scruton's (1982, 100) depiction of the cosmopolitan as a 'parasite, who depends on the quotidian lives of others to create the various local flavours and identities in which he dabbles'. A different version of it can also be found in Taylor's (1992, 58) expressed sympathy for people who value 'remaining true to the culture of our ancestors', as opposed to those who wish to 'cut loose in the name of some individual goal of self-development'. Both of these thinkers, albeit in different ways, associate authenticity with fidelity to a particular way of life, and criticize those who want to 'cut loose' from their ancestral culture or 'dabble' in other ways of life. Whilst Scruton suggests that dabblers take advantage of those whose cultures they appropriate, Taylor implies that those who cut loose fail to do their part in helping to sustain a shared ancestral culture.

By contrast, Waldron argues that it is those who wish to remain within their ancestral culture, as Scruton and Taylor recommend, who take advantage of others. As he puts it:

> From a cosmopolitan point of view, immersion in the traditions of a particular community in the modern world is like living in Disneyland and thinking that one's surroundings epitomize what it is for a culture really to exist. Worse still, it is like demanding the funds to live in Disneyland and the protection of modern society for the boundaries of Disneyland, while still managing to convince oneself that what happens inside Disneyland is all there is to an adequate and fulfilling life. (Waldron 1995, 101)

There are two related aspects to Waldron's objection. First, he criticizes the ideal of authenticity found in the writings of both conservatives and multiculturalists, instead arguing that an authentic engagement with the modern world means embracing the hybridity and complexity that has arisen as a result of globalization. Second, because he endorses this different conception of authenticity, he also rejects the multiculturalist thesis that outsiders have duties of justice to support the attempts of minorities to preserve their cultures.

Cosmopolitanism about culture has two further characteristics worth emphasizing. First is its distinctive – and anti-essentialist – conception of culture. On the cosmopolitan account, cultures themselves are neither stable nor delineable, and the cultural life of a society is messy, dynamic and constantly in flux. For cosmopolitans, cultural pluralism has less to do with the group-based differences emphasized by multiculturalists and more to do with a person's internal life. In other words, pluralism is not something that arises *between* people, but is rather found in what Waldron (1995, 94) described as 'the chaotic coexistence of projects, pursuits, ideas, images, and snatches of culture *within* an individual'. Although this understanding of culture differs significantly from those of Kymlicka and Taylor, it is perhaps compatible with another kind of multiculturalism. Indeed, Joppke and Lukes (1999) have referred to a 'hodgepodge' theory of multiculturalism, which emphasizes cultural hybridity, fusion and the mixing of influences, and which they contrast with Benhabib's 'mosaic' model of multiculturalism.

Second is its broadly aesthetic appreciation of culture, which emphasizes borrowing, hybridity and fusion to explain cultural innovation and change. This is illustrated, for example, in Kwame Anthony Appiah's criticisms of people who would prefer to keep cultures pure and untainted in the name of a mistaken ideal of authenticity. Instead of 'cultural purity', Appiah (2006, 111–13) celebrates something that he calls 'cultural contamination', which refers to the complex ways in which people creatively reimagine and repurpose disparate cultural influences to forge new possibilities. Similarly, Waldron began his first essay on cosmopolitanism by quoting from the writer Salman Rushdie, who was subject to a fatwā calling for his assassination as a result of publishing a novel, *The Satanic Verses*. Rushdie had argued that, whilst his critics believed that 'intermingling with a different culture will inevitably weaken and ruin their own', his own work instead celebrated 'hybridity, impurity, intermingling, the transformation that comes of the new and unexpected combinations of human beings, cultures, ideas, politics, movies, songs' (Rushdie, quoted in Waldron 1995, 93).

The cosmopolitan celebration of hybridity and fusion is exhilarating and powerful. However, cosmopolitan innovation might come with a hefty price tag. For one thing, cosmopolitanism in practice may end up having less to do with spontaneous creativity and more to do with spreading a bland uniformity. For instance, consider the ways in which globalization has deepened the hegemony of the English language at the expense of multilingualism. Similarly, to many of its critics, cosmopolitanism is associated with Americanization (Brennan 1997), imperialism (Pagden 2000) and elitism (Pinsky 2002). Furthermore, encouraging hybridity and innovation by modifying longstanding cultural traditions, or allowing ways of life to decline, could have catastrophic effects if cosmopolitanism threatens not only outdated ideas or practices, but also entire ways of being in and making sense of the world.

Conclusion

Political theorists have criticized multiculturalism for undermining the ideal of equality and for its reliance upon faulty philosophical premises. The first objection, that equality requires uniform treatment as opposed to the regime of exemptions and special treatment recommended by multiculturalists, is not decisive. In particular, multiculturalists can convincingly respond to it by either calling into question the blunt conception of opportunity used by their critics, or by arguing that a society of equals must ensure that someone's background does not preclude their participating in important civic opportunities.

The second objection was that multiculturalism can undermine the interests of vulnerable group members, including women and girls. This presses most forcefully against those theories which give priority to toleration, as well as those which are not firmly committed to an underlying scheme of liberal rights and freedoms. Meanwhile, as a number of feminist scholars have argued, it is crucial not to lose sight of the fact that, like men, women have interests in their cultures, and so, instead of setting cultural rights aside, it may be better to search for democratic solutions to the tensions between feminism and multiculturalism.

The third objection, that multicultural political theory is committed to an essentialist conception of culture, has often been unfairly inflated. For one thing, multicultural political theorists generally do not insist that cultures have a static or unchanging essence, or that every culture can be neatly separated from all the others. However, the real challenge of this critique is twofold. First is the worry that multiculturalism has undesirable normative consequences, since it risks imprisoning people in a cultural identity that, although officially recognized as authentic, is not one they regard as true to themselves. The solution to this, as we saw, is to insist on robust safeguards for individual freedom, so that cultural rights do not have the essentializing effects their critics fear. Second, meanwhile, is the worry that multiculturalism relies upon an essentialist conception of culture, and that correcting this will jeopardize the various arguments for cultural rights that have been offered. Assessing this worry requires asking whether a non-essentialist conception of culture can be harnessed in support of cultural rights. Although this cannot be ruled out in principle, nor should the challenge be underestimated, and it is noticeable that some of the most sophisticated attempts to develop such a theory to date have not been entirely successful.

The fourth objection says that multiculturalism is redundant, since people can lead dignified, autonomous and flourishing lives by experimenting with ideas drawn from different cultures and traditions, and so do not need their cultural memberships in the sense that multiculturalists sometimes imply. The cosmopolitan critique succeeds to the extent that it complicates the connections multiculturalists sometimes draw between cultures and individual well-being. However, it is perhaps better to think of this critique as pointing towards an alternative form of multiculturalism, rather than as rejecting it outright. In particular, cosmopolitanism enlarges the one-dimensional conception of authenticity sometimes invoked by multiculturalists, by demonstrating the possibility of an authentic and meaningful hybridized lifestyle.

5

Diversity, Cohesion and Integration

Multiculturalism has acquired negative connotations in many European societies, facing a much discussed 'backlash' due to its association with a logic of separation (Grillo 2007; Vertovec and Wessendorf 2010). For instance, during 2010 and 2011, the leaders of Western Europe's three largest countries issued separate statements that reflected a shared unease about multiculturalism. These began with German Chancellor Angela Merkel's declaration that multiculturalism had been 'an absolute failure', followed by British Prime Minister David Cameron's pledge to replace 'state multiculturalism' with an assimilationist doctrine of 'muscular liberalism', and concluding with French President Nicolas Sarkozy's suggestion that France had 'been too concerned about the identity of the new arrivals and not enough about the country receiving them' (for accounts of these interventions, see Bowen 2011; Chin 2017). All three echoed conclusions reached a few years earlier by the authors of the Council of Europe's White Paper on Intercultural Dialogue, which reported that multiculturalism had fostered 'communal segregation and mutual incomprehension', was based on moral relativism and a rigidly essentialist conception of culture, and threatened individual rights, especially of women (Council of Europe 2008, 19).

Social scientists are divided over whether the backlash against multiculturalism at the level of public discourse has been accompanied by a genuine 'retreat' from it as a public policy orientation (Joppke 2004). The first part of this chapter will address this issue by examining some policies recently recommended as alternatives to multiculturalism. I will suggest that these innovations can be reconciled with a multicultural framework and that multicultural ideas remain relevant and influential, even if they now come in different guises. Then, the second part of the chapter probes further into the reasons underlying the backlash against multiculturalism, exploring the worry that multiculturalism threatens social cohesion.

Multiculturalism and its Alternatives

Except as 'the proverbial punching bag', the term 'multiculturalism' is rarely found in official statements or policy documents today (Levrau and Loobuyck 2018). The United Kingdom offers an instructive example of its waning political fortunes. In the UK, the highpoint of official multiculturalism was the publication of the Report of the Commission on the Future of Multi-Ethnic Britain, at the turn of the millennium. Chaired by Bhikhu Parekh, its recommendations reflected many of the themes discussed in chapter 3, including the proposal to reconfigure British national identity as a more inclusive 'community of communities' (CMEB 2000). Within a year, however, another official report pointed in the opposing direction, attributing rioting in towns in the north of England to the 'parallel lives' led by white and Asian populations (Cantle 2001). Scepticism about multi-culturalism's effects on social cohesion deepened in the aftermath of the 2005 London bombings, when the chair of the Commission for Racial Equality, Trevor Phillips, publicly (and controversially) warned that multiculturalism had allowed Islamic extremism to go unchecked, declaring that Britain was 'sleepwalking into segre-gation' (Chin 2017, 280). Following this lead, official reports by the Commission on Integration and Community Cohesion, published in 2006 and 2007, intentionally avoided the term 'multiculturalism', which by then had become irretrievably associated with separation and inequality in the public imagination (Joppke 2017, 51). From here, it was a short step to David Cameron's (2011) public repudi-ation of 'state multiculturalism', which he justified by claiming that it had 'encouraged different cultures to live separate lives, apart from each other and apart from the mainstream'.

Similar narratives about multiculturalism's political trajectory could be told for other European countries (see, e.g., Triandafyllidou, Modood and Meer 2012, and Chin 2017). However, despite its declining fortunes in the various courts of public opinion, there is evidence to suggest that multiculturalism has held its ground as a public policy orientation. For instance, using their policy index discussed in the introduction, Banting and Kymlicka (2013, 579) have argued that, although some European countries have rolled back on multiculturalism, this is not the 'dominant pattern' and '[t]he larger picture in Europe is one of stability and expansion of multicultural policies'. Similarly, not long after Cameron's pledge to abandon 'state multiculturalism', Varun Uberoi and Tariq Modood (2013) argued that multiculturalism had actually deepened in Britain, emphasizing the additional supports made available for minority faith schools and strengthened anti-discrimination laws. Admittedly, evidence regarding the subsequent period is more nuanced, and Arjun Tremblay (2019) suggests that British multiculturalism experienced a combination of retreat and survival in different policy domains between 2010 and 2017, an outcome that nevertheless reflects surprising resilience in the face of right-wing opposition to multiculturalism in both government and the media.

Assessing whether, as a matter of fact, multicultural policies really are in decline in different parts of the world is beyond the scope of this book (for a thorough explanation of this issue, see Joppke 2017). Nevertheless, it is worth noting that the backlash against it is primarily a European phenomenon. For example, it has not been replicated in Canada, where multiculturalism retains popular support (for one attempt to explain why, see Miller 2018). Furthermore, opposition to multiculturalism even within Europe has arguably been more a phenomenon of political rhetoric than policy reality. For instance, commenting on the European scene in general, Steven Vertovec and Susanne Wessendorf (2010, 21) observed that 'policies and programmes once deemed "multicultural" continue everywhere', albeit under new descriptions.

The remainder of this section explores this thesis further, suggesting that the two most prominent alternatives to multiculturalism are not actually in conflict with it, as is often suggested, but are better understood either as continuations of multicultural policies in a new form or as broadly compatible with it. First are loyalty oaths, citizenship tests and civic integration programmes for newcomers, often introduced by governments responding to public concerns about immigration. In different ways, these aim to promote social unity and to strengthen national identity, and for this reason are often juxtaposed with multiculturalism, as reflected in one scholar's characterization of them as 'a renovated version of assimilation' (Zapata-Barrero 2017, 1). However, when appropriately designed, they are compatible with multiculturalism, and in some countries have been understood as being integral to it. Second is the proposal to replace multiculturalism with something called 'interculturalism', typically made by diversity-friendly scholars and policy makers

(Bouchard 2011; Cantle 2012). Although interculturalists themselves have been keen to stress the distinctiveness of their approach, many of their ideas belong to the broad family of multicultural political theories, rather than in opposition to them.

Civic integration programmes aim to familiarize immigrants with the language, history, culture and institutions of their new society, perhaps also testing them on their knowledge of these things, and perhaps also requiring them to sign integration contracts or pledge oaths of loyalty. They have spread rapidly in Europe in the last few years and have recently been described as its 'dominant policy of immigrant integration in the new millennium' (Joppke 2017, 60). Some scholars believe they conflict with multiculturalism. Liav Orgad (2015), for example, refers to them as a form of (majoritarian) 'cultural defence'. Meanwhile, others think they might be compatible with multiculturalism and respect for cultural diversity. For instance, Sara Goodman (2014, 35 and 16) characterizes them as 'nation-building in the least "national" way imaginable', arguing that they can 'empower individuals to act independently in their host society', 'foster cohesion' and 'imbue newcomers with a sense of belonging'.

Certainly, it is possible for particular civic integration programmes to conflict with multiculturalism, especially if they are perceived to express hostility towards specific groups. A notorious example of this was a test briefly used in the German state of Baden-Württemberg, widely understood to be directed towards Muslims, which asked questions such as 'Do you find it acceptable for a man to lock up his wife or daughter to prevent her from shaming him in public?' 'Would you have difficulty with a woman in authority?' and "What would you do if your son announced he was homosexual and wanted to live with his boyfriend?' (Chin 2017, 229). Similarly, particular civic integration programmes have also been criticized for being intrusive, and shaming immigrants into adjusting their behaviour and attitudes. For instance, Orgad (2015, 102) discusses a residency test designed to be taken by migrants planning to move to Holland. This asked applicants what 'Zara' should do if the director of the retirement home in which she works walks into the coffee room (apparently, instead of waiting for him to speak to her, or continuing to work and waving at him, the Dutch thing to do is to shake his hand and tell him her name).

These examples both concern the form of particular programmes, and not civic integration itself. Multiculturalists would have strong grounds to be wary about civic integration programmes in general if, as Orgad (2015, 116–17) intimates, those programmes were to consistently emphasize the 'ways of life, traditions and values' of the 'native-born population', and did nothing to reassure immigrants about their place in society and the value of their own values and traditions. However, Goodman (2014, 32) has argued that civic integration programmes do not, generally speaking, require newcomers to sacrifice their 'home culture or traditions'. Consequently, and unlike Orgad, she regards them as attempts to 'establish common values and knowledge that can support cultural diversity, not to subsume multiculturalism' (Goodman 2014, 258). Experience outside Europe seemingly supports Goodman's position, since civic integration has long been a feature of immigration policy in Canada, one of multiculturalism's strongholds (Banting 2014). Indeed, Christian Joppke (2013, 3) has suggested that there is something distinctive about 'the coercive and punitive tone in some of Europe's new citizenship tests and loyalty requirements', suggesting that the tests used elsewhere are more inclusive. Furthermore, even Orgad (2015, 7) acknowledges that civic integration programmes 'do not mark a return to policies of forced assimilation'. What this indicates, in summary, is that, although the dispersal of exclusionary and intrusive civic integration programmes may qualify as evidence of multiculturalism's retreat in Europe, we should not hastily conclude that these programmes must be incompatible with multiculturalism, since they can be (re-)designed and implemented in diversity-sensitive ways to form part of a multicultural integration policy.

The relationship between interculturalism and multiculturalism has provoked similar debate. On the one hand, some advocates of interculturalism view it as a rehabilitated form of multiculturalism. Ricard Zapata-Barrero (2016, 54), for instance, says it offers a 'lifeline' to multiculturalism. Meanwhile, Ted Cantle (2016, 133) disagrees, insisting that interculturalism is 'an entirely different conceptual and policy framework' for how 'to live with diversity'. On the other hand, some multiculturalists think lessons can be learned from interculturalism (Parekh 2016), whilst others believe that interculturalism adds little to multiculturalism (Modood 2017a, 2018) and even risks playing into the hands of xenophobes by exaggerating the latter's shortcomings (Kymlicka 2016).

Adjudicating amongst these alternatives is complicated by the fact that interculturalism is an inchoate theory coming in at least two varieties – European and Québécois (Cantle 2016, 140; Joppke 2018). Each of these responds to different considerations; the worry that multiculturalism has encouraged separation and is based on moral relativism in Europe, and the worry that immigration could threaten the position of the French language in Quebec. Since there is no single interculturalism, it cannot be concluded that interculturalism as a whole is compatible with multiculturalism. However, what can be demonstrated is that the characteristic ideas found in its two main variants can be placed within the broad family of multicultural political theories.

More than anything else, the positive vision of European interculturalism is about building social cohesion and trust by promoting intercultural contact (Council of Europe 2008; Cantle 2008, 2012, 2016; Zapata-Barrero 2016, 2017). In one sense, this extends an idea found in Parekh's (2000, 167) version of multiculturalism, which also stresses the benefits of engaging across cultural differences, pointing out that dialogue can 'expand each [participant's] horizon of thought and alert each other to new forms of human enrichment'. What makes interculturalism distinctive, however, is the special place it gives to everyday or street-level intercultural interactions, as opposed to dialogue in formal or official settings. Drawing on contact theory from the field of social psychology, interculturalists argue that regular face-to-face interaction, at least under favourable and broadly egalitarian conditions, can reduce prejudice and induce positive changes in attitude (Cantle 2008, 115–16; 2012, 104). Furthermore, promoting interaction between people from different backgrounds, but with shared interests or goals, can help to 'build bridges' (Zapata-Barrero 2016, 57) and promote mutual understanding and trust (Cantle 2012, 102–3). Thus, interculturalists encourage policy makers to remove barriers to interaction in local and everyday shared spaces, such as neighbourhoods, workplaces, community gardens, schools, shops, festivals, playgrounds, libraries and other public amenities.

Because it emphasizes the local and the everyday, interculturalism has direct implications for areas of public policy that multiculturalists have largely neglected, such as urban planning. Broadly speaking, there is no reason why multiculturalists should not welcome these proposals, which complement and extend their own theories. However, multiculturalism does have two salutary lessons for this aspect of European interculturalism. First, if minorities experience intercultural interaction as hostile, or feel pressurized into adopting a defensive posture, then it is unlikely to induce positive transformations in attitudes (Merry 2013, 32–3). Thus, not just any intercultural interaction will do, since interaction must occur under the right kinds of conditions to build trust and reduce prejudice, and these are best secured by bread-and-butter multicultural policies aiming to tackle minority discrimination and marginalization. Second, the hostility to segregation that characterizes many interculturalist writings should be tempered by the fact that minorities sometimes have understandable reasons to seek space apart from majority society. For instance, as Parekh (2019, 172) observes, even when minorities are 'keen to participate in the collective life, it is not uncommon for them to feel nervous, diffident, overwhelmed by the all-pervasive majority culture'. Again, if interactions are to promote positive changes in people's attitudes, then some forms of multicultural 'separation' may sometimes be necessary.

Let me now turn to interculturalism in Quebec, which has been centrally concerned 'to reconcile ethnocultural diversity with the continuity of the French-speaking core' (Bouchard and Taylor 2008, 19). The tension between these two arises from the fear that immigrants in Quebec whose first language is neither French nor English will tend to 'gravitate linguistically' towards the minority anglophone population, given the precariousness of the French language in Canada and North America (Gagnon and Iacovino 2004, 29). Thus, unchecked multiculturalism could threaten Quebec's identity as a distinctive francophone society. In response, the solution proposed by the leading Quebec interculturalist, Gérard Bouchard (2011, 451), is to grant the majority culture 'ad hoc (or contextual) precedence'. As Bouchard (2016, 85–6) conceives it, this involves not only acting to maintain French as the common public language, but also prioritizing the majority culture in other spheres, such as by emphasizing 'the majority narrative' in the educational curriculum.

As was the case for European interculturalism, Bouchard's approach builds on arguments already advanced by multiculturalists, who likewise believe that the state should sometimes take active measures to ensure the continuity of vulnerable cultural identities. The crucial difference, of course, is that multiculturalists emphasize the anxieties of minorities, generally assuming that the majority culture can 'take care of itself' (Margalit and Halbertal 1994, 492). Bouchard's (2011, 445) innovation was to notice that members of 'foundational' majorities are also – and perhaps increasingly – anxious about their 'values, language, memory and identity', so they too might seek cultural rights.

The similarities between this form of interculturalism and the multiculturalism it intends to supplant have also been noticed by Bouchard's critics. For instance, a leading European interculturalist, Cantle (2016, 140), accuses Bouchard of endorsing the same 'defensive form of identity management' that both thinkers associate with multiculturalism. Furthermore, Cantle (2012, 204) also suggests that Bouchard's theory has inherited the same flawed 'static conception of culture' from multiculturalism, a charge discussed in chapter 4. However – arguably, at least – these accusations are unfair to both

Bouchard and multiculturalism, since requiring immigrants to learn and use the French language need not consign people to rigid cultural identities. Indeed, as Bouchard (2015, 35) points out, establishing French as the public language is compatible with simultaneously insisting that the language reflect Quebec's growing cultural diversity, be open to the rich variety of different 'traditions, contributions and interventions', and be 'spoken in many voices'.

Meanwhile, Bouchard's theory faces another and more serious problem that potentially does render it incompatible with some theories of multiculturalism – namely, liberal ones. This is that his principle of 'ad hoc (or contextual) precedence' is indeterminate and potentially oppressive. To be fair, Bouchard (2011, 452) is careful to stipulate that it would be 'out of the question' to understand majority precedence as a 'general legal principle', since that would 'lead to the creation of two classes of citizens' and 'open the door to abuses of power'. Nevertheless, Bouchard (2011, 451) does insist that 'seniority' and 'history' dictate that the identity interests of majorities have priority over those of minorities, offering only anecdotal and tentative grounds for distinguishing 'legitimate' from 'abusive' manifestations of majority precedence. The dangers of this ambivalence can be illustrated by considering restrictions on the building of mosques and minarets in historically Christian societies. For sure, Bouchard (2016, 86) himself recommends against such a ban, at least in Quebec. However, his preferred identity-sustaining majority precedence argument has elsewhere been used to support a ban in Switzerland, both in academic writing (e.g. Miller 2016) and in public discourse (see Baycan and Gianni 2019, for an account of how these arguments were employed in the 2009 Swiss referendum). The problem is that Bouchard's own principles can reasonably be interpreted in favour of a conclusion he himself rejects.

So, in summary, the central components of both European and Quebec interculturalisms extend and complement arguments first developed by multicultural political theorists. For that reason, they are best understood as potential members of the broad family of multicultural political theories, and not as alternatives to multiculturalism. Different strands of interculturalism and multiculturalism are often in tension with one another, but, as we saw in chapters 2 and 3, this is also true for the traditional multicultural theories. Nevertheless, much like the spread of civic integration programmes, the positioning of interculturalism as supplanting multiculturalism reflects a wider disquiet about the latter, now discredited in the eyes of many policy makers and the general public, as a result of its perceived ambivalence about social cohesion and political unity. The following section will suggest that, despite its widespread dispersal, this charge is misplaced.

Solidarity, Values and Cohesion

As we have seen, a persistent and influential criticism of multiculturalism in European public discourse is that it undermines social cohesion. This objection comes in at least two forms: one says that multiculturalism has negative effects on social solidarity and threatens people's positive identification with their political communities; the other says that multiculturalism jeopardizes shared values and that the presence of incompatible worldviews undermines political stability. Often, and regrettably, these two objections are run together in both public discourse and scholarship. However, in practice, they often come apart. For instance, consider Muslims in Britain, frequently at the centre of public debates about social cohesion in the country. Considered collectively, Muslims have moral beliefs that in some respects are quite distinct from those of the majority population, especially regarding matters of gender and sexuality (Joppke 2015, 156–9). Nevertheless, they also have high levels of positive attachment and are 'more likely to be both patriotic and optimistic about Britain than are the white British community' (Wind-Cowie and Gregory 2011, 41; see also Meer and Modood 2015). Meanwhile, almost exactly the opposite applies to minority nations such as the Catalans, Québécois or Scottish, some of whose members feel little positive attachment to the neighbouring or majority identity, despite sharing many values in common with its members. Consequently, in order to clarify when multiculturalism is, and is not, a threat to social cohesion, it is worth distinguishing between these different objections before exploring what multicultural political theorists have had to say about each of them.

Solidarity in the multicultural state

According to Brian Barry (2001a, 83), multiculturalism risks leaving society with a hollowed-out national identity, so weakened as to be 'incapable of providing the foundation of common identity that is needed for the stability and justice of liberal democratic politics'. Barry (2001a, 300) insists that citizens need this foundation because progressive and democratic politics require members who feel as if they 'belong to a single society and share a common fate'. Meanwhile, by positively affirming cultural differences and promoting minority identities, multiculturalism could undermine the common identity which motivates solidarity, instead encouraging groups to compete against one another for recognition and support. As a result, Barry (2001a, 325) concludes that multiculturalism not only 'diverts political effort away from universalistic [egalitarian] goals', but also threatens to 'destroy the conditions for putting together a coalition in favour of across-the-board equalisation of opportunities and resources'.

The same worry also underlies something that Kymlicka (2015b, 1) terms the 'progressive's dilemma', which is 'the fear that there is a trade-off between being pro-immigrant and being pro-welfare state' (see also Van Parijs 2004). There is now an extensive empirical literature about whether immigration and ethnic diversity undermine popular support for redistributive policies and a robust welfare state. Its results are ambiguous, with one recent survey reporting that 'the evidence is mixed at best' (Stichnoth and Van der Straeten 2013, 380), and another observing that 'there are nearly as many studies rejecting the negative effects of diversity as arguing for them' (Schaeffer 2014, 4). Nevertheless, the idea that solidarity is in decline, and that immigration and multiculturalism may be to blame for this, has a firm grip on the imaginations of both scholars and politicians.

As a result, it should not be surprising that concerns about solidarity also animate many multicultural political theorists. For instance, Parekh (2000, 343) refers to the importance of not 'weakening the ... precious identity of shared citizenship', and Kymlicka (1995, 174–6) emphasizes the importance of public-spiritedness and solidarity. However, these thinkers, and other multiculturalists, diverge from Barry in three ways. First, multiculturalists insist that solidarity must not come at the cost of assimilation. This is reflected, for instance, in Parekh's (2000, 343) observation that multicultural societies face the formidable task of 'reconciling the legitimate demands of unity and diversity, achieving political unity without cultural uniformity, being inclusive without being assimilationist, cultivating among ... citizens a common sense of belonging while respecting their legitimate cultural differences, and cherishing plural cultural identities'. Second, multiculturalists reject zero-sum assumptions about political identities, whereby stronger minority identities lead to weaker national or state-wide political identities, and vice versa. Instead, they argue that strong minority identities must be counterbalanced by a similarly strong emotional pull from an inclusive and multiculturalized national identity (see, e.g., Modood 2013, 138).

Third, whilst Barry assumes that only a singular common identity can underpin solidarity, multiculturalists have developed

pluralistic models of political membership, or what Clayton
Chin (2019, 730–2) refers to as theories of 'differentiated unity'.
These combine the ideas that citizenship need not be a uniform
or unitary phenomenon, and that people can share a political
membership without necessarily having the same cultural identity.
For instance, Keith Banting and Will Kymlicka (2017, 31) have
argued for a 'solidarity-promoting multiculturalism', in which
society self-consciously develops an understanding of itself as multicultural and thereby encourages immigrants and other minorities
to 'express their culture and identity as modes of participating and
contributing to the national society'. Something like this has also
long been a constituent part of the multicultural ideal in Canada,
in which minorities are incorporated into wider society through
their communities. For instance, Charles Taylor (1993, 182) writes
that '[f]or Quebeckers and for most French Canadians, the way of
being a Canadian (for those who still want to be) is by belonging
to a constituent element of Canada, *la nation québécoise*, or
canadienne-française'.

Instead of common identity, the central concept in multicultural
models of solidarity is belonging. For instance, Parekh (2000, 263)
puts this value on a par with equality and social harmony, and his
sometime collaborator Tariq Modood (2017a, fn. 11) describes it as
even 'more central' than justice. For Parekh (2000, 342), belonging
has psychological as well as political aspects – it is 'about being
accepted and feeling welcome' and can be contrasted with feeling
like an outsider, for instance because one is demeaned or dismissed
by wider society. Other accounts put more emphasis on feeling
at home in one's society and with its institutions and practices
(Mason 2000, 127–32). In either case, achieving a sense of common
belonging will typically be a socially transformative and reciprocal
'two way process', making demands on the majority community as
well as minorities themselves (Kymlicka 1995, 96; Parekh 2005, 10;
Modood 2013, 44). For example, immigrants may need to adjust
themselves to their new home, committing to it and acquiring the
competences required to navigate it, whilst the majority may need to
establish protections against discrimination, ensure that minorities
are represented in major institutions, and redesign public spaces to
reflect and normalize diversity. Crucially, the success of this reciprocal process will depend on majorities and minorities feeling 'at
ease with themselves and with each other', since if either group 'feel
threatened, besieged, fearful of losing their culture, they [will] turn
inward [and become] defensive and intolerant' (Parekh 2008, 87 and
94–5).

In a similar vein, Kymlicka (1995, 176–81) has also drawn attention to the ways in which multicultural policies can strengthen belonging, and thereby solidarity, praising polyethnic and special representation rights for addressing exclusion and promoting the integration of immigrants. He especially highlights the ways in which these rights do not aim at separation – as multiculturalism's critics often imply – but instead have to do with empowering minorities to participate in the wider society, including in its social life, labour markets and politics. Furthermore, other scholars have also noted that participation itself, especially in core activities such as politics, can strengthen membership and belonging. For example, James Tully (2008, 180) suggests that successful democratic participation can nurture 'a sense of identification with the larger society' by supporting 'a sense that one is acknowledged and respected by others'.

Most multicultural accounts of belonging and membership focus primarily on immigrants and their children, with occasional references to national and religious minorities too. Less often considered are Indigenous peoples, for whom models of solidarity-promoting multiculturalism or differentiated unity may be a more ambivalent prospect. On the positive side of the ledger, Joseph Carens (2000, 177–99) points out that these models are a clear improvement on unitary conceptions of political membership, since Indigenous communities are more likely to feel a positive attachment to the wider political community if it makes space for their collective self-determination and if their representatives are treated with respect – conditions that have frequently been violated in the past. Indeed, it would be naïve to expect Indigenous peoples to identify with, and feel as if they belong to, a unitary state whose institutions and officials they have good reasons to distrust, and whose history, culture and values they do not recognize as their own.

Meanwhile, on the negative side of the ledger, the members of Indigenous communities have reasons to be wary about even differentiated forms of unity, if democratic entanglement with the settler state carries the risk of assimilation. For example, Dale Turner (2006) points out that dialogue and mutual understanding between Indigenous and settler communities are difficult because they are divided by radically different worldviews and massive power disparities. In practice, Indigenous intellectuals and political activists have little choice but to engage with the hegemonic legal and political discourses of the state, hoping to challenge and remould the categories and concepts that make up these discourses so as to better reflect Indigenous interests. But moving between different intellectual cultures means that activists and intellectuals risk losing touch with their own communities and their own distinctive ways of thinking and acting. As Turner (2006, 114) puts it, democratic engagement often induces anxiety because 'the problem of assimilation is always close at hand'. Not only is this regrettable at an individual level, but also it is a political loss, since Indigenous activists may find themselves unwittingly advancing a worldview – to themselves, to the other members of their communities and to settler society – that is contrary to their own real interests.

So, in summary, multiculturalists have responded to concerns about solidarity by proposing models of differentiated-unity and solidarity-promoting multiculturalism, and by putting the concept of belonging at the centre of their analyses, in place of Barry's focus on common identities. Many different strategies can be used to promote a shared sense of belonging, including the kinds of policies called for by multiculturalists to secure what Kymlicka (1995) calls 'fair terms of integration'. However, even differentiated models of unity may be too much for some minorities, including Indigenous peoples wary of the threat of assimilation.

Shared values and political stability

The other objection about multiculturalism's effects on social cohesion concerns values rather than identities, and is that societies cannot accommodate too diverse a range of worldviews and perspectives because political stability depends upon citizens sharing common values and principles. As multiculturalists themselves emphasize, different religious and cultural traditions have contrasting, and sometimes incompatible, ways of making sense of the world and explaining what gives meaning and value to life. Whilst multiculturalists tend to celebrate the benefits of communicating across differences, their critics worry that, when the gaps between worldviews are especially deep, either it will be impossible for society to agree on basic political values, or any consensus reached will be too thin to attract the lasting support of citizens from different backgrounds. For instance, consider the divisions between religious traditionalists and progressive liberals. As discussed in chapter 2, it is unrealistic to expect both sides to agree about the value of, say, autonomy, or even about the basic rights and freedoms to which people are entitled.

One response, endorsed by some multiculturalists, is to deny that deep and intractable disagreements about values threaten political stability, provided that the different groups who make up society are able to find pragmatic and mutually acceptable compromises over political institutions and procedures (Kukathas 2003; Horton 2006, 2010, 2011; Levy 2007). However, this view is controversial, and many other political theorists believe that at least some consensus about values is necessary for lasting political stability. For instance, two of the leading figures in recent political theory – John Rawls (1996) and Jürgen Habermas (1996, 1998) – both argued that the members of a political community must agree, at least in a broad sense, on a set of fundamental values and principles, and in particular on those which are to be reflected in the constitution or basic law.

Another possible response is that the shared values objection rests on an exaggeration, since the most politically salient cultural differences are rarely about values or principles at all. As will be demonstrated in chapters 6, 7 and 8, few of the issues confronting multicultural societies today have much to do with conflicting worldviews. For instance, there is no more disagreement about values between anglophone and francophone Canadians, or between the different national groups in Spain or Belgium, than there is within each respective community. Furthermore, and as we saw in chapter 4, the sociology of multiculturalism is typically far more complex than the simple equation of cultural and value pluralism suggests. Although Indigenous peoples, and groups such as the Amish in the United States or the Hutterites in Canada, sometimes have distinctive worldviews that diverge significantly from those of the majority, these are the exception rather than the norm. More often, value pluralism is expressed internally, within individuals and cultural groups, rather than between them.

Nevertheless, even if value disagreements are not the driving force behind most cultural conflicts, it remains true that multicultural societies will often contain people with different worldviews, perspectives and outlooks, who profoundly disagree about fundamental moral issues. Some of these disagreements are ones that citizens must learn to live with, since they are to be expected in a free society, are likely to be permanent, and concern matters of great importance in people's lives, such as the different views people have about sexuality and marriage. Ensuring that people are willing to tolerate one another's beliefs and practices about matters like these is thus a key challenge for multicultural societies, especially their education systems (Shorten 2010a). Meanwhile, both liberals and multiculturalists have stressed the importance of reaching a consensus in other domains, including about the place of values such as toleration, and of doing so without unduly threatening the different religious and ethical belief systems of their citizens.

As discussed in chapter 2, the leading liberal view, articulated by Rawls (1996), recommends that citizens aim to reach an 'overlapping consensus' about a narrow range of political principles (i.e. principles to shape the basic structure of their society, including its constitutional order). In a similar fashion, Parekh also argues that society must be based upon a shared body of values concerning how people are to live together. However, Parekh's (2019, 191) view has a wider scope, since he thinks we need shared values not only about our major social and political institutions, but also for 'normal social interactions with neighbours, strangers, colleagues, fellow members of organisations, etc.'. Although this makes his view more demanding, in another sense it is more relaxed since, unlike Rawls, Parekh (2019, 191) thinks that people can share values even when they 'interpret, relate and prioritise them differently'. For example, the value of equality means different things to liberals, libertarians, social democrats and socialists, and these different traditions balance equality against liberty in different ways. These are significant and substantive disagreements, but they do not really matter for the purposes of political stability, according to Parekh (2019, 192), since '[s]haring values does not involve complete agreement on their interpretation and importance. All it means is that we accept them as values, feel their pull, and broadly agree on the relative importance of at least the most basic of them.'

Notwithstanding these differences, both thinkers agree on the basic point – namely, that some form of value consensus is required for political stability. Here, however, the value pluralism challenge returns with a vengeance – what is to be done when consensus is not forthcoming? Many contemporary liberal democracies, for example, contain both a significant number of people who reject otherwise widely accepted norms about gender equality, and also a much smaller number of people – including religious fundamentalists, for example – who reject democratic and liberal values *tout court*.

Parekh's (2019, 192) solution to this is to say that society 'may legitimately require all citizens to respect' the common values that are embedded in its public culture and major institutions. Importantly, respect does not entail endorsement. So, for example, he says that British people who do not 'share or believe' in the values of liberalism or democracy can nevertheless be expected to 'respect' them, 'partly out of respect for the overwhelming number of their fellow-citizens who deeply cherish them, and partly because these values are an integral part of the community's moral and political structure to which they are bound as its citizens' (Parekh 2019, 200–1). Rawls, meanwhile, is much less interested in securing the respect of such citizens and more concerned about preventing the spread of doctrines that might undermine the normative stability of society. So, for example, he notes that there will always be views which reject democratic freedoms, and goes on to observe that this gives us 'the practical task of containing them – like war and disease – so that they do not overturn political justice' (Rawls 1996, 64, fn. 19).

Regardless of the details of Parekh's duty of respect, or Rawls's strategy of containment, these examples illustrate that if value consensus – in some form or another – is a necessary condition for stability, then something will need to be done about people who are unable or unwilling to accept the values of wider society. Further, it may be difficult to do so without compromising on the principles of toleration or equal respect, which themselves are often thought to be core values for liberal democratic states. Nevertheless, given that it is a mistake to crudely equate value and cultural forms of pluralism, the extent to which these challenges are connected to the politics of multiculturalism specifically should not be exaggerated. Indeed, liberal societies would still have to confront them even if they entirely gave up on multiculturalism as a public policy.

Conclusion

This chapter examined some of the effects and issues surrounding the recent public backlash against multiculturalism. Arguably, hostility towards multiculturalism has been manifested more at the level of political rhetoric than in public policies themselves, and there is only limited evidence of a genuine retreat from multiculturalism as a public policy orientation. Furthermore, the most prominent supposed alternatives to multiculturalism, civic integration programmes and interculturalism, are substantially compatible with it.

Multiculturalism's unpopularity is mostly due to its association with a logic of separation and the resulting fear that it will undermine social cohesion. Distinguishing between two different ways in which this charge has been formulated reveals that multicultural political theorists have already developed sophisticated and plausible responses to it. First, they have proposed innovative models of belonging and differentiated unity to explain how culturally diverse political communities can nourish the psychological ties of affection underpinning social solidarity. Second, they have demonstrated that cultural diversity as such need not jeopardize shared values, and that political stability does not depend upon people from different religious and cultural traditions agreeing about everything.

Nevertheless, there are significant challenges that many multicultural societies will need to confront, if they are to remain cohesive and stable, including how to respond to people who reject their fundamental values or who are deeply alienated from its institutions, as is sometimes the case for Indigenous communities.

6

Beliefs and Identities: Tolerating Religious Practices and Recognizing Religious Differences

Many issues and controversies discussed under the banner of multiculturalism are directly or indirectly about religion. For instance, as discussed in chapter 2, a landmark legal case that influenced the emergence of multicultural political theory was *Wisconsin v. Yoder* (1972), which concerned a conflict between Amish religious traditions and compulsory education requirements in the state of Wisconsin. Similarly, some of the first dividing lines to open up between multiculturalists and their critics concerned the accommodation of religious practices, including halal and kosher slaughter by Muslims and Jews, as well as the different legal issues connected to the obligations for Sikh men to carry a kirpan and wear a turban. Recent years have seen the spread of further and similar controversies, concerning things as various as religious clothing like Islamic headscarves, the public funding of religious schools, the display of religious symbols in public institutions, the building of mosques and minarets, the limits of free speech and religious offence, and religiously motivated discrimination on grounds of sexual orientation or gender identity.

Since there is no single normative theory of multiculturalism, it should not be surprising that multiculturalists do not have a party line on these, or indeed on any of the difficult issues confronting multifaith societies today. Furthermore, whilst religious differences are prominent in some multicultural theories, such as Parekh's, others mention them only sporadically. Strikingly, Kymlicka (in Jewkes and Grégoire 2016, 396) has recently acknowledged that religion was a 'glaring' omission from his *Multicultural Citizenship*, pleading that when he wrote the book, 'the issue of religious difference and religious accommodation was not at the heart of the debate about multiculturalism'. Nevertheless, multicultural political theory has profoundly influenced how these issues are now understood and discussed, both within the confines of academic political theory and in public discourse more generally. In particular, some of concepts at the centre of multicultural political theory are now routinely employed in discussions about religion in contemporary democratic societies. This chapter focuses on the most important two of these: toleration and recognition.

Following the distinction drawn earlier in this book, the chapter proceeds in two stages, initially discussing arguments drawn from the liberal tradition before turning to ones that challenge and aim to move beyond it. Within the liberal tradition, religious diversity raises difficult questions about toleration and its limits – for instance, regarding legal exemptions and religious accommodations for minority beliefs and practices. Meanwhile, multiculturalists from the margins of the liberal tradition, or beyond it, have suggested that today's politics of religious diversity is as much about identities as about beliefs and practices. Thus, they have asked whether, and when, multicultural inclusion requires public recognition and support for minority religious identities.

Liberalism, Toleration and Accommodation

Members of a particular faith community benefit from an accommodation when things like laws, employment practices or social norms are adjusted in light of their distinctive beliefs or practices. Examples include releasing Sikh men from the requirement to wear a motorcycle helmet, providing halal and kosher meal options in prisons and schools, and relaxing uniform requirements for religious employees, so that women can wear headscarves and men can wear beards or turbans, for instance. Because they involve principled forbearance, accommodations are sometimes characterized as forms of toleration (Jones 2015; Bardon and Ceva 2018). As Martha Nussbaum (2008, 21) puts it, they give beneficiaries a 'break', usually by making judgements or applying regulations in a way that is sensitive to religious differences. However, accommodating religion in this way is controversial because, as Peter Jones (2015, 549) notes, it 'typically requires people to make a sacrifice or endure an inconvenience for the sake of beliefs they do not share'. Indeed, some critics have argued against religious accommodations on the grounds that they entail an unfair form of burden-shifting (Jones 1994; Arneson 2010; Leiter 2013).

For example, allowing Sikh men to ride motorcycles without helmets creates burdens for healthcare systems and workers, and providing meal options to satisfy different religious dietary rules is costly for caterers and may leave other diners with fewer options. After describing some different religious accommodations, this section discusses some arguments offered in support of them by liberal political theorists.

Varieties of accommodation

Political theorists writing about religious accommodations have focused mostly on statutory legal exemptions written directly into primary legislation. Although now closely associated with multi-culturalism, some frequently discussed exemptions are of a much earlier vintage. For example, the exemption releasing Jews and Muslims in Britain from the requirement to stun animals prior to slaughter, therefore allowing for the production and consumption of halal and kosher meat, was first provided for in the 1933 Slaughter of Animals Act (Poulter 1998, 134). Earlier still, the 1916 Military Service Act contained an exemption from military conscription on grounds of conscientious objection, something called for by Quakers especially. A few years later in the US, the 1919 National Prohibition (or 'Volstead') Act accommodated Jews and Catholics by exempting them from laws banning the sale of alcohol, allowing them to use wine for religious purposes (Levy 2000, 128).

Because legal exemptions permit some people to do something that everyone else is prohibited from doing, they nearly always concern practices that are in some sense objectionable, such as carrying a knife in public, failing to wear protective headgear, or slaughtering animals without stunning them first. These practices are no less objectionable for being performed for religious reasons, and so it may seem as if the rule-and-exemption strategy will inevitably express a kind of official censure about the actions it nevertheless permits. Indeed, Bhikhu Parekh (2000, 279) welcomes this implication, and for this reason recommends an exemption allowing (adult) female genital mutilation in exceptional circum-stances, arguing that it is good for society to convey a message that it generally disapproves of the practice. However, even if exemp-tions do communicate official disapproval, most liberals cannot count this as part of their justification for them, since the doctrine of neutrality precludes negative appraisals of lawful actions by the state. Furthermore, many exemptions – like accommodations more generally – are justified by a concern to vindicate people's rights to religious freedom, and exercising rights is hardly something that a liberal state can officially condemn.

Other accommodations are not written into primary legislation but are the product of courtroom decisions. Whilst, in the United States, these are usually about the free exercise clause of the First Amendment, in Europe they typically concern Article 9 of the European Convention on Human Rights, which protects the freedom to manifest one's religion or beliefs. Cases involving the latter have touched on a wide range of issues, including whether elected politicians should be required to take an explicitly Christian oath (*Buscarini and Others* v. *San Marino*, 1999), a request by an English Muslim schoolgirl to attend school wearing a jilbab (*Begum* v. *Denbigh High School*, 2004), a request by a Christian employee to wear a visible religious symbol (*Eweida* v. *United Kingdom*, 2013), and a request by a Hindu to be cremated on an open funeral pyre (*Ghai* v. *Newcastle City Council*, 2010).

Importantly, neither the free exercise clause nor Article 9 provides for an absolute right to religious freedom. In the US, it is permissible to burden religious practices for the sake of a compelling state interest, whilst in Europe the freedom to manifest one's religion or beliefs can be limited by interests in public safety, public order, health, morals and the rights and freedoms of others. Because these categories are rather elastic, they sometimes provoke controversy. For instance, the European Court of Human Rights ruled that the French ban on the full-face veil, criticized by many for discriminating against Muslim women, was justified in order to uphold the principle of living together – le *'vivre ensemble'* – which it construed as an element of protecting the rights and freedoms of others (*SAS* v. *France*, 2014). Likewise, and more than twenty years earlier, the US Supreme Court insisted that there was a compelling state interest in discouraging the use of hallucinogens, and so refused to grant to members of the Native American Church permission to ingest peyote for religious purposes (*Employment Division* v. *Smith*, 1990). This decision was controversial, amongst other reasons, because of the legal exemption that had much earlier been provided for Jews and Catholics regarding prohibition.

One context in which religious accommodations have proven especially controversial is employment law. For instance, in 2008, a UK employment tribunal found that the owner of a 'funky, spunky and urban' hairdressing salon had indirectly discriminated against Muslim women by having a policy that required employees to make their own hair visible to showcase the salon's styling (*Noah* v. *Desrosiers*, 2008). The employer was required to accommodate

Muslim religious practices by altering her policies. In a comparable case in the US, the Newark police department's policy of requiring its officers to appear clean-shaven was struck down after it was challenged by two Muslim police officers, who objected to the fact that the policy provided for exemptions on medical but not religious grounds (*Fraternal Order of Police* v. *City of New York*, 1999).

Notwithstanding these examples, courts in both Europe and the US have been reluctant to characterize practices that disadvantage religious employees as discriminatory. For instance, recall Adell Sherbert, discussed in chapter 2, who, the US courts concluded, did not have a legal right to refuse paid employment on a Saturday, her Sabbath (*Sherbert* v. *Verner*, 1963). The English courts reached a similar conclusion fifteen years later, when they denied the request of a Muslim school teacher who wished to attend Friday prayers without giving up his full-time employment contract (*Ahmad* v. *Inner London Education Authority*, 1978). More recently still, the request of a Christian registrar of births, deaths and marriages in London for permission not to officiate at the civil partnership ceremonies of gays and lesbians was also denied (*Lillian Ladele* v. *London Borough of Islington*, 2008).

Finally, religious accommodations arise not only in primary legislation or judicial rulings, but also in the formal policies of institutions and at the informal level of social norms. For instance, a factory might provide a Muslim prayer room, or a public swimming pool might offer women-only swim times in deference to Islamic modesty norms. Meanwhile, at the level of social norms, religious accommodations might take the form of encouraging people to change their behaviour or expectations in light of an appreciation of religious differences. For example, Christoph Baumgartner (2019) has suggested that Europeans should accommodate Muslims who prefer not to shake hands with members of the opposite sex by encouraging the use of alternative greetings, especially in professional settings.

Arguing for accommodations

As discussed in chapter 4, a powerful argument for accommodations is based on equality of opportunity. According to this, special legal treatment is justified if it is necessary to enable beneficiaries to do something that everyone else can already do, such as work on a building site, serve as a police officer, ride a motorcycle or eat meat. Although associated with Parekh (2000), this approach is broadly consistent with Kymlicka's (1995) own characterization of religious accommodations as polyethnic rights – i.e. as rough-and-ready mechanisms to promote the inclusion or equality of minorities – and versions of it have also been proposed by other liberals (e.g. Miller 2002; Quong 2006; Shorten 2010b; Patten 2017). However, in addition to the serious philosophical difficulties it runs into, discussed already, the equality-of-opportunity argument only applies to a narrow range of accommodations. For instance, equality of opportunity is unlikely to be advanced by allowing Quakers an exemption from military service or Sikhs to carry kirpans. At the very least, then, it will need to be supplemented by another argument.

Within contemporary liberalism, the other main approach is to grant legal protections to a special category of conscientious beliefs and practices. At the foundation of this view is what Alan Patten (2016) labels the 'no burden' principle, which says that the state should not burden people by preventing them from acting according to their convictions. Something like it has been endorsed by Kent Greenawalt (2008, 315), who writes that 'the state wrongs people if it trespasses on [a] deep-seated conviction without a more substantial need', and by Martha Nussbaum (2008, 138), who further argues that it is unfair for someone to be 'prevented from abiding by the dictates of [their] conscience when others are not so burdened'. Although arguments derived from the no burden principle come in many different forms, its liberal proponents have increasingly converged on two points of consensus: first, that some religious commitments are indeed special, in a sense that distinguishes them from mere preferences and explains why they deserve legal protection, but, second, that they are not unique for being special, since some non-religious commitments also deserve legal protection on analogous grounds (Laborde 2017, 43; Bardon and Ceva 2018). Consequently, the principle is now often used to support accommodations for adherents of non-religious worldviews, such as ethical veganism, pacifism or environmentalism, as well as for religious believers.

The family of arguments based on the no burden principle has been criticized from both sides. First, some commentators insist that religion truly is unique – for instance, because only it has a distinctive kind of transcendental value (e.g. McConnell 1985; Laycock 1990; Koppelman 2006, 2017). These authors reject the idea that non-religious commitments are analogous to religious ones, and so they also reject the view that things like ethical veganism, pacifism or environmentalism also deserve accommodations. Admittedly, this objection is not fatal to the case for accommodations, but, rather, narrows the range of potential beneficiaries. However, few liberals can accept this restriction, since they are generally committed to a form of neutrality that disallows privileging religious beliefs and practices specifically.

Meanwhile, the second objection is potentially fatal, and must be answered for the no burden case for accommodations to get off the ground. According to it, deeply held convictions, whether religious or not, do not deserve special protections at all, since there is no consistent way to distinguish these beliefs and commitments from ordinary preferences (Dworkin 2013, 124–36; Balint 2017, 73–5). Just as liberal neutrality rules out privileging religious beliefs over non-religious ones, so too must it condemn any attempt to prioritize a wider set of accommodation-deserving commitments over mere preferences. For example, whilst discussing the lawfulness of ingesting peyote, Ronald Dworkin (2013, 125–6) suggests that, although it might be an important ritual for some Native Americans, there are no neutral grounds to favour their demand for special treatment ahead of claims for the same legal privilege from followers of Aldous Huxley, or from people who simply want to get high. Similarly, Peter Balint (2017, 73) worries that it would violate neutrality to accommodate a Sikh police officer who wishes to wear a turban in place of the prescribed headgear, but not his fashion-conscious colleague, who simply prefers to wear a more stylish uniform.

Evidence for the fact that many contemporary liberals are troubled by this objection can be found in their efforts to show that supporting accommodations for things like Islamic headscarves and Sikh turbans does not also commit them to supporting accommodations for wearers of chicken suits, baseball caps or clown hats (Nussbaum 2008, 169; Maclure and Taylor 2011, 77; Laborde 2017, 199–200). To maintain their position, pro-accommodation liberals must identify a neutral means for picking out the practices or beliefs that deserve special legal protection, and one promising answer starts from the idea of conscience. As discussed in chapter 2, being true to one's conscientious convictions is something that everyone, religious or not, seems to agree is important. Furthermore, as the example of conscientious objections to compulsory military service indicates, it is already widely accepted that adherents of both religious and non-religious worldviews can have reasons of conscience that put them in conflict with the law (as found, for instance, in *United States* v. *Seeger*, 1965, in which the court held that a belief in God was not necessary to qualify for conscientious objector status).

Arguments from conscience have been developed by a number of liberal thinkers (e.g. Nussbaum 2008; May 2017). In Jocelyn Maclure and Charles Taylor's (2011, 75) widely discussed proposal, the purpose of legal accommodations is to respect a person's 'core convictions', or what they refer to as their 'meaning-giving beliefs and commitments'. So, for example, they argue that an employer should respond sympathetically to a request to leave early from a Jewish worker who wants to respect Shabbat, but not from someone who simply wants to beat the traffic. Both have a preference, but – *contra* Dworkin and Balint – the former is more significant than the latter, since it is related to a conviction of conscience, and therefore bound up with a person's meaning-giving beliefs and commitments. In turn, meaning-giving beliefs and commitments are significant because of the role they play in a person's moral identity. Hence, we tend to experience them as obligations, such that honouring them is essential to our self-respect, and failing to do so is associated with betraying oneself or straying from the path one has chosen, a point Maclure and Taylor (2011, 77) illustrate by characterizing a conscientious vegetarian forced to eat meat as suffering a kind of 'moral harm'. Importantly, just as a person's meaning-giving beliefs and commitments need not be bound up with a particular faith, nor do they need to be underpinned by a coherent or integrated worldview, such as one might expect to find in theology or moral philosophy textbooks. Indeed, Maclure and Taylor (2011, 94) suggest that it is perhaps more common for people's value systems today to be 'fluid' and 'eclectic'. Furthermore, they insist that it is for individuals themselves to decide whether a given commitment truly is meaning-giving, and, when it comes to accommodations, what matters is what someone themselves takes their conscientious duties to be, and not what their co-religionists or religious authorities declare (Maclure and Taylor 2011, 81–4).

Meanwhile, Cécile Laborde (2017, 66–7) suggests that, although this argument is promising, it has a significant shortcoming, which is that it cannot explain why the liberal state should accommodate religious rituals that are not 'strictly speaking duties of conscience', such as Catholics observing Lent, attending Mass or refraining from eating meat on a Friday, or Muslims observing Ramadan, reciting prayers or wearing a hijab. According to Laborde (2017, 67), since people do not typically perform these 'acts of habitual, collective religious devotion' for reasons of conscience, then by the lights of Maclure and Taylor's argument they are not worthy of special legal protection. This shortcoming arises, she thinks, because Maclure and Taylor's view relies on an individualized and Protestant view of religion emphasizing inner experience, and which, as a result, neglects the social, habitual and communal aspects of religious experience.

At least on the face of things, this objection appears mistaken, since Maclure and Taylor (2011) do argue for accommodating some of the practices that Laborde lists, and other ones that look as if they belong on it, including the Jewish duty to observe Shabbat (p. 79) and the Muslim practice of veiling (p. 77). However, Laborde's objection is not really that Maclure and Taylor themselves are too frugal about accommodations. Rather, it is that their argument must indulge in a fiction, misinterpreting habitual religious practices as Protestant duties of conscience, if it is to justify the corresponding accommodations.

Reformulated in this way, her objection is plausible, but potentially answerable. Maclure and Taylor's (2011, 77) appeal to conscience is based on the idea that being required to act against one's preferences can sometimes be a moral harm, and they explain the harm in question by associating it with having compromised one's 'sense of integrity'. Now it is true, as Laborde (2017, 67) suggests, that some religious practices are not experienced by religious believers themselves as duties of conscience, but instead arise from a sense of wanting to remain 'faithful to relationships of community ... that are central to [people's] lives'. But this does not mean that Maclure and Taylor's argument cannot recognize why those practices ought to be accommodated, as long as their argument is reinterpreted as being fundamentally about integrity. Either someone experiences participating in certain rituals alongside others to be meaning-giving and central to her own integrity, in which case Maclure and Taylor's argument should support an accommodation. Or, if someone does not, then an accommodation need not be extended.

So, then, Maclure and Taylor's argument can be rescued from Laborde's objection by placing integrity, rather than conscience, at its foundations. However, perhaps it might be better to start directly with this idea, since, like conscience, integrity is something that is valued by both religious and non-religious people (Bou-Habib 2006, 119). This is what Laborde (2017, 197–258) herself does in her own theory, which effectively replaces Maclure and Taylor's category of meaning-giving beliefs and commitments with a broader one of 'integrity-protecting commitments'. Like Maclure and Taylor's category, integrity-protecting commitments (or IPCs) matter because sacrificing them will induce 'feelings of remorse, shame or guilt' (Laborde 2017, 204). Distinctively, however, they include both duties of conscience derived from one's religion, culture or community (obligation-IPCs) *and* commitments and practices related to one's culture or way of life (identity-IPCs). Though the former category is intentionally broad, it is the latter one that fills the gap Laborde identifies in Maclure and Taylor's theory.

According to Laborde, identity-IPCs are significant since, even though the practices they refer to are not experienced as obligatory in the strictest sense, people nevertheless value them for providing meaning and connection with others, and because they form part of a thick web of ethical and social meanings. Laborde's distinction between obligation-IPCs and identity-IPCs resembles Parekh's distinction between culturally authoritative practices and community-sustaining ones, discussed in chapter 3. Indeed, like Parekh, Laborde (2017, 217 and 222–5) thinks that burdens on obligation-IPCs are generally more severe than burdens on identity-IPCs, and thus require a stronger justification, since it is worse to be unable to fulfil one's obligations than it is to be disadvantaged when it comes to participating in practices and activities with a looser connection to one's culture or community. Unlike Parekh, however, and in common with Maclure and Taylor, Laborde (2017, 63) favours a subjective conception of obligations and commitments – individuals themselves are the final authority on which IPCs they have and their relative significances.

Perhaps surprisingly, when it comes to justifying accommodations, it is obligation-IPCs, and not identity-IPCs, that Laborde thinks will usually be relevant. Further, her argument about these is very similar to Maclure and Taylor's. According to it, an accommodation is justified when someone incurs a burden on one of their obligation-IPCs, and when that burden is disproportionately severe, considering the aims served by the law in question and the likely effects that an accommodation will have upon others. So, for example, Muslim police officers should be exempted from regulations requiring them to appear clean-shaven because this rule severely burdens one of their obligation-IPCs, because this burden outweighs the aims advanced by the policy, and because the exemption will not be costly for others. Contrastingly, an accommodation would not be justified, according to Laborde, if the policy in question served highly significant ends, or if exempting people from it would shift significant costs onto others.

Meanwhile, Laborde's (2017, 229–38) more distinctive thesis is that identity-IPCs are also relevant to assessing claims about some accommodations, in particular when people are burdened as a result of 'majority biases' within social institutions. To illustrate this, she discusses Iftikhar Ahmad, a Muslim school teacher in London who wished to attend his mosque on a Friday, during school hours (Laborde 2017, 231; other instructive discussions of this case include Jones 1994; Bou-Habib 2006; and Seglow 2017). Ahmad was disadvantaged by comparison with other teachers, who were able to uphold their comparable commitments (to pray weekly, with others, at a recognized place of worship) whilst also working full-time, an important social opportunity. The case for accommodating him, Laborde argues, does not depend on whether attending his mosque is a strict matter of religious obligation or due to conscientious conviction. Rather, it is explained by something like Quong's equality-of-opportunity argument, discussed in chapter 3. Thus, Laborde (2017, 231) concludes that, without an accommodation, Ahmad would be 'denied the opportunity to be a teacher in a state school as a Muslim – a significant infringement of equality'.

Laborde's integrity argument is striking for being both broad and comprehensive, features that are manifested in four different ways. First, like other liberals, she does not restrict accommodations to specifically religious commitments and practices, but also allows for accommodating their non-religious equivalents. Second, she understands integrity to encompass matters of identity as well as ones of conscience, thereby opening the door to a wide range of potential accommodations. Third, because the significance of a person's IPCs is determined subjectively, accommodations are not restricted to practices with a clear authority in scripture or tradition, as was the case for Parekh's argument, examined in chapter 3. Fourth, she combines an expanded conscience-based argument for accommodations with an equality-of-opportunity argument, refined and rehabilitated via the concept of majority bias.

Recognition and Inclusion

As we have seen, the standard liberal multiculturalist response to religious diversity focuses on particular and controversial practices, asking whether and why they ought to be tolerated. Meanwhile, some other multiculturalists have criticized this approach, not because they object to the kinds of exemptions and accommodations endorsed by liberals, but because these do not go far enough. The primary shortcoming of conventional liberal theories, according to these critics, comes from their insistence on treating religion as a private matter, which leaves liberalism unable to grasp the full political significance of religion.

This section examines two ways in which this thesis has been developed, each of which draws on themes first encountered in chapter 3. First, Anna Elisabetta Galeotti applies a theory of recognition that draws upon, but significantly modifies, the one developed by Charles Taylor. Galeotti argues for a difference-sensitive form of liberal neutrality, which promotes inclusion by giving the identities of stigmatized minorities public visibility. Second, we will then examine some recent challenges to the liberal ideal of secularism – in the first instance, by examining some revisions to that ideal from within the liberal tradition, and then by looking at Tariq Modood's proposal for a more thoroughgoingly multicultural ideal of secularism, which extends some proposals that had earlier been made by Bhikhu Parekh. Crucially, both Galeotti and Modood appeal to the idea that full inclusion will sometimes require that one's religious identity be appropriately recognized.

Recognition, difference and visibility

In her *Toleration as Recognition*, Galeotti (2002) sets out to develop a theory to correct some of the deficiencies she associates with the conventional liberal model. That model, on her account, promises to secure equal freedom of conscience by combining state neutrality with a sharp division between private and political matters. Consequently, as discussed already, religions are treated as another worldview or belief system amongst others, deserving of neither especially favourable, nor especially punitive, treatment. At the same time, a person's religious beliefs and practices are treated like their sexual preferences and literary tastes – as private matters that ought to be tolerated, provided they harm no one else.

Galeotti's (2002, 53–84) critique picks out three features of the liberal model for attention. First, she emphasizes its disinterest in social differences – such as ones of race, gender, sexual orientation or religion – which are perceived to be irrelevant to political life. Second, and relatedly, she suggests that, because it ignores social differences, the conventional liberal model cannot appreciate the relevance of power imbalances, and especially those dividing majorities and minorities, which are crucially significant in contemporary politics. Third, because the conventional liberal model is based on freedom of conscience, it is narrowly individualistic, and as a result neglects the collective dimension of toleration. This is a significant shortcoming, according to Galeotti (2002, 85), since it prevents liberals from grasping what is at stake when the 'members of a new minority exhibit their differences in some public–political space' and when their representatives seek the 'symbolic recognition' and the 'public acceptance' of their identities.

Putting all of this together, the basic objection she registers against the conventional liberal model is that it does not, and cannot, address the pervasive inequalities of status found amongst different social groups, including religious ones. The idea that minorities might be tolerated without being recognized as full equals is a familiar one in the history of toleration, since from its inception toleration was primarily about protecting vulnerable minorities from persecution, and this was understood to be compatible with inequality of status. So, in seventeenth- and eighteenth-century Europe, for example, religious toleration variously meant putting up with minorities of Catholics, Jews or Protestants, but it did not require treating them as political or social equals. Liberal political theory, however, was supposed to move beyond this, promising as it did equal freedom of conscience for everyone. Unfortunately, however, the conventional liberal model cannot redeem this promise, according to Galeotti, since it is compatible with the social exclusion and stigmatization of minorities, and because it counsels against the only policies that could rectify this – namely, ones to ensure the public visibility and symbolic recognition of minority identities.

The most famous example Galeotti (1993; 2002, 115–36) invokes to illustrate her thesis that the conventional liberal model cannot secure the full and equal inclusion of minorities is the Islamic headscarf. Here, she focuses on a controversy that erupted in France in 1989, after three female Muslim school pupils were expelled for refusing an instruction to remove their headscarves. It was not that the young women had breached a uniform code, since French public schools do not have these. Rather, they had made their religious identities and differences visible, bringing a 'private' matter into a public setting, the classroom, thereby contravening a longstanding norm of French secularism, or *laïcité*, which says that religion ought not to intrude into the public realm. The subsequent and fractious debate was inflamed in 1994, when the Minister of Education, François Bayrou, issued a directive permitting discreet and modest religious symbols but forbidding ostentatious and provocative ones, on the grounds that the latter could be experienced as proselytizing. Although the directive mentioned neither Islam nor headscarves, the distinction it drew between discreet and ostentatious religious symbols seemed unfair to many Muslims, since it could potentially permit Christian crucifixes worn as jewellery whilst forbidding Islamic headscarves. A decade later, this distinction was formalized in a law that banned conspicuous religious symbols in schools, passed on the recommendation of a 2003 official report, written by the ombudsman, Bernard Stasi (for a philosophically rigorous reconstruction of the 'official republican' case in support of this law, see Laborde 2005; for a 'critical republican' critique, see Laborde 2008).

Galeotti refers to this case as 'l'affaire du foulard' (2002, 117). What made it significant, for her, was that liberal theories of toleration seemed incapable of fully grasping what was at stake, and thus could not understand why drawing a distinction between discreet and ostentatious religious symbols was so provocative. Amongst liberals, discussions of the case centred on two issues. First, was the practice autonomously chosen, or had the young Muslim women been brainwashed or coerced into wearing headscarves? Second, was the practice harmful, for instance because the presence of religious clothing in schools exposed other children to unwelcome religious influences, or because it reinforced traditional patriarchal norms? Provided that the practice was freely chosen and did not harm third parties, then liberals concluded that it ought to be tolerated. Meanwhile, Galeotti (2002, 118–19) describes this conclusion as 'simplistic' and 'naïve', and insists that, in treating the decision to wear a headscarf as a basically private matter, liberal analyses miss 'the symbolic meaning of public recognition of differences'. To illustrate this, she memorably observed that, from the conventional liberal perspective, nothing seemed to distinguish the demand made by the three young women from a request to wear a funny hat.

In response, Galeotti proposes an alternative and strongly political reading of the case. According to her, what the young women effectively demanded, in attending school wearing an ostentatious religious symbol, was the 'public acceptance of their cultural difference' (Galeotti 2002, 133). Interpreting their demand in this way requires us to attend closely to the same background context that the liberal model abstracts away from. In particular, as Galeotti (2002, 132) emphasizes, the young women, in common with other Muslims, had been denied full inclusion in society, and experienced a subtle form of discrimination, arising from the 'implicit requirement that different collective identities be invisible'. This requirement, according to Galeotti (2002, 132), 'applies only to social groups that do not form part of the majority in society', because '[t]he collective cultural or ethnic identities of the majority are not even seen as different, but as normal; they constitute the norm in society and set its standards'.

So, then, on Galeotti's interpretation, 'l'affaire du foulard' was really about a demand for the recognition and inclusion of a marginalized identity. Accordingly, it may seem as if her view is similar to Charles Taylor's, examined in chapter 3, since both authors draw a connection between individual dignity and collective recognition. However, there is a subtle but significant difference between the pair (Galeotti 2002, 14–15; Jones 2006, 138–9). As discussed earlier, Taylor suggests that everyone needs the value of their authentic identity to be positively affirmed, and he regards recognition as intrinsically valuable, since it responds to a deep human need.

Meanwhile, for Galeotti, practices of recognition are instrumentally justified, as measures to achieve inclusion. This means that her view is less demanding, and instead of arguing that dignity requires the authentic recognition of all, she insists only that people must have their identities, traits and cultures included as legitimate and normal, as opposed to being excluded or stigmatized as deviant. This means, in short, that one's identity, customs and practices be treated as an ordinary part of society, in the same way as those of dominant social groups already and always are. This sense of normalcy, of course, was absent in the furore over 'l'affaire du foulard', in which minority religious symbols were coded as ostentatious, in contrast to those of the majority, which were assumed to be discreet.

Recognition, for Galeotti (2002, 100), is primarily achieved through acts of 'public toleration', whereby differences are made visible in public settings, and no longer hidden away in the private sphere. Accordingly, her theory might seem to be incompatible with liberal neutrality, since it recommends actively recognizing particular identities. Against this, Galeotti (2002, 103–5) argues that recognition can be justified neutrally, as a means of transforming the symbolic and social orders, making what once seemed deviant appear normal, thereby redeeming the promises of liberal equality and inclusion. In this respect, her argument shares something in common with the pro-accommodation liberals we examined earlier, who likewise believe that special treatment can be justified neutrally, on the basis of the interests everyone shares in common. Thus, full and equal citizenship plays the same role for Galeotti that conscience does for Maclure and Taylor, and which integrity does for Laborde. When it comes to religious accommodations, however, there is a clear difference between her theory and the ones we considered earlier. Crudely put, those thinkers connect the case for accommodations to the distinctive intensity of (some) religious preferences. By contrast, Galeotti connects the case for religious accommodations, and recognition more generally, to the background structure of social relations, and especially inequalities of power and status.

In addition to the objection that her theory is incompatible with liberal neutrality, Galeotti's theory has been criticized for two further reasons. First, for being too narrow, since it concerns only the practices and identities of minorities. Consequently, it cannot provide guidance about whether to tolerate controversial majority practices, or about the identities and practices of groups that are not discriminated against. For instance, her case for permitting Islamic headscarves in schools would cease to apply if Muslims and their practices were no longer symbolically excluded from mainstream society. Second,

Galeotti's theory has also been questioned for whether it qualifies as a theory of toleration, since toleration is usually thought to involve disapproval (Jones 2006). In one sense, this objection is perhaps unfair, since Galeotti's theory does not require the state to evaluate minority identities and practices positively, something often implied by the term 'recognition', and which would clearly be incompatible with toleration. Nevertheless, since recognition for Galeotti (2002, 14–15) involves including minority practices as 'legitimate' or 'normal' options, it implies an attitude quite unlike disapproval. For example, suppose that her theory was fully implemented, and that once-stigmatized minority practices were now regarded as legitimate and normal. Would it be accurate to label this society a tolerant one?

Rethinking secularism

Until recently, most liberal writings on multiculturalism uncritically adopted the model that Galeotti criticized, taking it for granted that liberalism recommends a 'hands-off' approach to religion, and assuming that liberal states ought to be based on the free exercise and non-establishment principles which informed the American constitutional tradition. For example, as indicated in the introduction to this chapter, Kymlicka (in Jewkes and Grégoire 2016, 396) has recently come to see that his own *Multicultural Citizenship*, a landmark text in the emergence of multicultural political theory, contained an 'unreflective commitment to a kind of American-style secularism', reinforced by his assumption – which turned out to be mistaken – that questions about the relationship between religion and the state had been 'more or less settled, both philosophically and politically'. As a result, Kymlicka's (1989a, 1995) initial statements of his own theory assumed that a strict principle of separation was the only way to realize the liberal ideal of neutrality in the religious sphere, arguing that the liberal state should treat different religions with 'benign neglect', meaning that neither majority nor minority faiths should be recognized, much less supported or officially established.

Instead of closely scrutinizing the shortcomings of 'American-style secularism', Kymlicka instead concentrated on trying to persuade his readers that, whilst being appropriate for religion, this model must not be extended to cultural differences more generally. In support of this, he suggested that the 'analogy between religion and culture is mistaken' (Kymlicka 1995, 111) and argued that the separation principle 'is altogether misleading as an account of the relationship between the liberal-democratic state and ethnocultural groups' (Kymlicka 2001a, 25). Later, however, Kymlicka (2009,

324) revised his position, calling the idea that secularism entails a 'rigid separation of church and state' a 'myth', and even arguing for the recognition of minority religions as a way 'to strengthen norms of religious freedom and to deepen democracy'. In other words, he came to see that there were some analogies between culture and religion after all, and that the multicultural case for cultural recognition sometimes carried over in support of the recognition of minority religions too.

Today, an appreciation that 'American-style secularism' is only one alternative amongst others, and perhaps inappropriate for some multifaith societies, is widespread amongst pro-accommodation liberals (one exception to this is Nussbaum 2008). For example, Maclure and Taylor (2011, 26–35) are careful to avoid reducing secularism to the separation of church and state, arguing instead that it can be manifested in a variety of 'regimes', ranging from (strict) republican models to (looser) liberal pluralist ones. According to them, 'secularism rests on two major principles, namely, equality of respect and freedom of conscience, and two operative modes that make the realization of these principles possible: to wit, the separation of church and state and the neutrality of the state towards religions' (Maclure and Taylor 2011, 20). The distinction between 'operative modes' and 'principles' is significant, and they go on to explain that separation and neutrality are not desirable ends in themselves, as equality and freedom are, but instead are merely the institutional 'means' for achieving these ends. This enables them to identify and criticize a troubling tendency in public debates about secularism, such as those prompted by 'l'affaire du foulard', whereby 'the separation between church and state ... assumes greater importance than respect for individuals' freedom of conscience', a pathology they refer to as the 'fetishism of means' (Maclure and Taylor 2011, 28–9; for a provocative discussion of this criticism, see Rudas 2019).

Significantly, Maclure and Taylor (2011, 26) also tentatively suggest that secularism could be compatible with some forms of religious establishment, in which the state confers symbolic and other privileges on an official religion, citing the examples of the United Kingdom and Denmark, where they think that establishment is 'mitigated' and respects the principles of equal respect and freedom of conscience. A number of other authors (e.g. Brudney 2005; Bonotti 2012; Laborde 2017; Miller 2021) have similarly argued that mild or soft forms of establishment can sometimes be compatible with liberalism, including both states with an official church (e.g. Norway, Denmark) and those which recognize or support multiple religions (e.g. Belgium, Germany). Although controversial, these arguments have drawn attention to the various ways in which contemporary liberal democracies already recognize and support religious practices, and especially those of the majority. It is in light of this that a more radical multicultural proposal has begun to take shape, outside the liberal tradition, and in particular in recent writings by Tariq Modood (2007, 2019a), who argues that the connections between religion and the state should be deepened and pluralized.

Modood's is a bottom-up theory, which starts from the observation that, in many states, secularism is 'moderate' rather than 'strict', featuring official recognition of, or support for, at least one religion (Modood and Kastoryano 2006). Rather than attempting to bring these states into line with an ideal based on the American First Amendment or French *laïcité*, Modood (2017b) thinks it would be better to 'multiculturalise' actually existing moderate secularism, especially by using the forms of accommodation and recognition already extended to Christian majorities, and other long-established minorities, as a model for 'new minorities', particularly Muslims. A state might treat these different groups in an 'even-handed' way by, for instance, including non-Christian religions in official ceremonies, collaborating with a variety of religions in the provision of public services, extending the protections Christians receive from blasphemy laws to other religions – for example, by making incitement to religious hatred a crime – or funding non-Christian religious schools on terms similar to those already extended to the major Christian denominations (Modood 2009).

As these examples indicate, the policies Modood favours will generally have the effect of supplying minorities with benefits already enjoyed by the majority. Meanwhile, one frequent objection to his view is that even-handedness could be just as well served by eliminating the privileges currently (and unfairly) enjoyed by historically dominant religious groups. Whether one prefers one option or the other might seem to depend on what one thinks more generally about the public and institutional recognition of religion – something Modood sympathizes with, but that strict secularists oppose. However, Modood (2016, 189) suggests that this is the wrong way to look at things, insisting that the 'most basic argument' for multifaith establishment 'is not by a comparative reference to Christians' but, rather, by comparison 'to the egalitarian accommodation of women, black people, gays etc.'. He thus connects the case for multifaith establishment to the wider argument for multiculturalism, arguing that it would be unfair to exclude specifically *religious* identities from public spaces whilst actively including ones based on gender, race and sexuality.

Although the political theory of multifaith establishment remains provisional and controversial, the phenomenon has proceeded apace in some European countries. For instance, sociologist Christian Joppke (2017, 107) observes that Islam has been supported to an 'astonishing degree' in the Netherlands, noting that mosques have received indirect state financing; that Dutch universities provide training for Imams; that publicly funded Muslim chaplains are provided in the army, prisons and hospitals; that the call for prayer is allowed; and that Muslim television programmes are broadcast on public stations, including in 2010 a musical programme marking Eid al-Fitr. These practices are noteworthy because many of them entail active support for religious activities, and not mere passive tolerance, thereby embroiling the state in religious affairs to a greater degree than some liberal political theorists are comfortable with. Furthermore, many of them follow Modood's recommendations, providing benefits for Muslims that were already extended to more established religious groups.

There is, then, a broadly egalitarian case for multifaith establishment – and, moreover, this kind of arrangement might address some of the issues discussed in chapter 5, if it were to encourage a genuinely multicultural sense of belonging and strengthen the sense of attachment felt by new religious minorities to the national community. However, multifaith establishment might not be able to replicate all of the benefits of traditional, singular, models of establishment. Under that model, whereby one faith is privileged above others and treated as the national faith, the established church is empowered to be a voice for religion in the public sphere and especially in matters of political morality. Of course, it might do so in an exclusionary fashion, in which case minorities might be better off if it were to be disestablished. However, in societies with a broadly multifaith ethos, one might expect an established church to speak for religion in general, and in a broadly inclusive manner. David Miller (2021, 83) suggests that this has already been the case in England, at least in recent years, and he claims that members of religions other than the (established) Church of England 'see the benefit to religion in general of having an institution responsible for speaking on its behalf in public debate'. According to him, this benefit would be lost if the UK were to shift to a model of multifaith establishment, since then there would be no comparable institution able to exercise its voice. In short, he recommends singular establishment with a multifaith ethos, as opposed to multifaith establishment itself.

Conclusion

Multicultural political theorists have become increasingly relaxed about weak varieties of religious establishment, and many have called for the accommodation and even recognition of minority religions, including by making minority religious identities more visible in public life. Amongst liberals, these proposals have mostly been modest, often hesitantly proposed, and rather piecemeal in character, typically presented as occasional and justified departures from a general norm of benign neglect. For them, probably the central issue has been to identify grounds in support of accommodations that do not violate liberal neutrality by unduly favouring religious beliefs and practices over non-religious ones. One possibility, suggested by Maclure and Taylor (2011), is to grant accommodations to protect meaning-giving beliefs and commitments, so as to enable people to uphold their duties of conscience. However, as critics have observed, this formulation is perhaps already biased in favour of religion, and towards one particular branch of religion at that – namely, Protestantism. Another option, which has become increasingly popular in recent writings, is to argue instead that accommodations are justified to protect integrity, such as by enabling people to fulfil their obligations or by protecting their identities from the effects of majority bias.

Meanwhile, other political theorists have criticized mainstream liberal responses to religious diversity for ignoring important social inequalities, including inequalities of power and status. Galeotti, for example, argues for a form of recognition as public toleration, in which social differences – including but not limited to, religious ones – are normalized through public visibility. Galeotti's favoured form of recognition differs from Taylor's, examined in chapter 3, since her theory does not focus on the psychological harms associated with mis- or non-recognition, but instead aims to promote the full inclusion of minorities as equal citizens. Furthermore, it is arguably less demanding, since it does not require the worth or value of religious and cultural differences to be presumed or publicly affirmed. Thus, Galeotti's theory can easily be reconciled with a commitment to liberal neutrality, and in this respect is similar to pro-accommodation liberalism. The same perhaps cannot be said of Modood's attempt to multiculturalize secularism, which stresses the benefits of multi-faith establishment. In common with thinkers like Parekh, examined in chapter 3, Modood puts inclusion, equality and belonging at the centre of his theory of multiculturalism. Often, it will be more effective to achieve these, he argues, by sharing the benefits of religious establishment with multiple religious communities, and not by getting rid of them altogether. Thus, instead of separating church and state, he recommends deepening and pluralizing state–religion connections.

7

Ruling Ourselves: Self-Government Rights for National Minorities and Religious Associations

This chapter considers the right to collective autonomy, whereby a group is empowered to govern some or all of its own affairs with little or no oversight or interference. Though not often considered alongside one another, calls for collective autonomy have come from both national and religious groups. For national minorities, collective autonomy is typically understood as requiring territorial self-government rights, whereby the group controls its traditional homeland, as for Catalonia in Spain, Scotland in the UK, Quebec in Canada, the Åland Islands in Finland, Zanzibar in Tanzania, or Acah in Indonesia. It might be achieved by secession, in which a group exits an existing state and creates a new country (or, less frequently, joins another one). Alternatively, it might take a less dramatic form, such as by devolving significant powers to national parliaments and governments, as in Scotland and Wales in the UK, or by establishing a multinational federation, as happened in Belgium and Canada. Meanwhile, religious groups have sought to control particular and significant institutions, such as churches, schools, hospitals, charities and even the family. For them, collective autonomy might be realized by allowing institutions such as church-run schools or charities to regulate themselves according to their own norms and values, even when these conflict with the norms and values of wider society in areas such as gender discrimination. Or, alternatively, it might involve allowing religious authorities jurisdiction over matters of family – and especially divorce – law, as in contentious debates about the recognition of Islamic, or Sharia, law.

So, whilst some national minorities have sought territorial autonomy, some religious associations have sought institutional autonomy, perhaps manifested in a regime of legal pluralism. These may seem to raise very different issues, especially if territorial autonomy is taken to mean something that approximates full-blown statehood. However, this chapter will attempt to show that, although they are very different in both their substance and justification, the two different kinds of collective autonomy raise surprisingly similar issues, and so are worth considering alongside one another. Both conceivably involve a claim about jurisdictional authority, a claim which might be satisfied through a variety of institutional arrangements, including forms of power-sharing; and both have been criticized for setting back the interests of individuals, including those who are members of, as well as outsiders to, the groups in question.

The first part of the chapter discusses the rights of minority nations, focusing initially on arguments concerning the principle of national self-determination. Multicultural political theorists such as Will Kymlicka (1995, 2001a) and Wayne Norman (2006) have argued that at least some national minorities are entitled to self-government rights, primarily to enable them to protect their culture and traditions in the face of state institutions that would otherwise promote the majority national culture, whether intentionally or not. Typically, these philosophers recommend some form of multinational federalism, which is a particular kind of state made up of (at least) two levels of government: common federal institutions shared by everyone, and self-governing national provinces or subunits (Elazar 1987, 12; Watts 1996, 7). Under these arrangements, although national groups are not fully autonomous, they are meaningfully self-governing and have the final say over some substantive set of policy domains, such as education, language policy or healthcare. Dividing jurisdictional authority in this way means that, although the federal government retains significant influence, perhaps because it has the ultimate say over foreign policy and immigration, it cannot overrule national groups over matters that are especially important for them.

Many of the most difficult normative issues raised by national self-government rights are connected to the assumption that powers of self-government must be exercised over particular territories or homelands. Not only does this often create new minorities (within minorities), but also it has been criticized for reproducing the logic of the nation-state. However, self-government powers do not necessarily have to be exercised territorially, and the second part of the chapter considers claims for similar powers made by religious groups, whose members are nearly always geographically dispersed. Interestingly, these claims have been advanced on grounds similar to those invoked by national minorities – namely, to insulate their beneficiaries from the assimilatory pressures of wider society. In the case of religious associations, however, these pressures have less to do with the culture and identity of the majority, and more to do with its norms and values. In particular, religious groups have sought to protect themselves and their institutions against the spread of civil rights and anti-discrimination laws, especially – but not only – in matters related to sexual orientation and gender identity. Consequently, religious collective autonomy has often been criticized for jeopardizing the interests of vulnerable group members, such as women and girls, LGBTQ+ people and religious dissenters.

Religious collective autonomy has only recently attracted the attentions of legal and political theorists, and two opposing models have emerged as scholars attempt both to explain and to justify it. One treats religious associations as quasi-sovereign entities and denies that civil laws have legitimate jurisdiction over them. This view is arguably incompatible with liberal principles, as well as the democratic constitutional project more generally. The other does not insist that religious associations have state-like rights of jurisdictional authority, but nevertheless allows that they are sometimes entitled to collective exemptions, similar to the individual accommodations considered in chapter 6. Although perhaps preferable, this view struggles to explain whether religious self-governance may permissibly set back the interests of non-members.

Nations and Territories

The principle of national self-determination says that each national community should not be governed from the outside but must instead be trusted to govern its own affairs. In international politics, the principle came of age in early twentieth-century Europe, was later enshrined in the United Nations Charter, and eventually become a cornerstone of decolonization policy. Within the specific context of multicultural political theory, it is usually invoked on behalf of minority nations, either to defend whatever powers they already possess, or to argue in support of additional ones, up to and including those of full statehood. Interestingly, many multiculturalists have suggested that self-government rights within a multinational state are often preferable to full political independence, arguing that devolved or federal political institutions can adequately protect minorities against the identity-shaping effects of majoritarianism. After discussing how these protections could be institutionalized, some notes of scepticism will be registered about the solution favoured by most multiculturalists – territorial autonomy within a multinational federation.

National self-determination

Multicultural discussions about the rights of minority nations have been shaped by two different families of arguments, both supporting the thesis that national communities ought to be self-governing, but for different reasons and, as a result, in different ways. One says that it is better for political communities to be based on shared nationality, and the other emphasizes the value of national identities for individuals.

The first view was encountered already in chapter 5. In its classic form, it says that it is best for states to be nation-states, because citizens who are bound together by national ties will find it easier to achieve a variety of important and valuable outcomes. For instance, David Miller (1995, 90–3) argues that co-nationals will be more likely to co-operate with and trust one another, a claim seemingly vindicated by subsequent empirical research (for a review, see Lenard and Miller 2018). More controversially, Miller (1995, 84–5) also thinks that co-nationals will be more willing to make sacrifices for one another – for instance, by accepting a high taxation burden – and so will be more likely to implement progressive or redistributive economic policies. So, in short, his view is that if we want social co-operation and social justice, then we have good reasons to try and make the boundaries of nations and states coincide.

Another twist on this line of argument appeals to the idea that common bonds of nationality support democracy, either because citizens who share the same language will be better able to deliberate confidently and effectively about politics (Kymlicka 2001a, 213), or because politics will become 'poisoned by division and mutual suspicion' if citizens are not bound together by bonds of unity and affection (Taylor 1993, 197). Supporters of this view fear that a democracy made up of different groups, who do not feel themselves to share a fate in common, will inevitably descend into self-interested and competitive bargaining (Miller 2000, 77). Perhaps, for example, citizens with different national identities will refuse to compromise or to moderate their demands, or maybe they will struggle to entertain seriously opposing views about political matters. If so, then the quality of democratic deliberation will suffer.

Criticisms of the first view come from both directions. Some political theorists object that these arguments overstate the importance of trust and mutual sympathies amongst citizens, suggesting instead that what really matters is that people can trust the major institutions of their society (Mason 1999, 278–9). Meanwhile, others agree about the importance of trust and mutual sympathies, but argue that common nationality is not essential for these, since alternative bases for social solidarity are possible (Caney 2005, 174). Moreover, if social solidarity is what is required, then perhaps shared nationality is not the best place to start from, since, as Parekh (1999, 313–16) has observed, people who are nationalists in the everyday sense, and who express a strong sense of attachment to their nation, do not always exhibit the same warm feelings towards all of their fellow nationals.

Whatever one makes of these objections, the first view about national self-determination clearly poses a challenge to multicultural political theories. As noted already, many multiculturalists believe that the interests of minority nations are often best served by granting them some form of political autonomy, for instance as sub-units within a multinational federation. In such states, the benefits of shared nationality are likely to be experienced, if at all, only within the different national sub-units. Meanwhile, the federation itself, if it is made up of different nationalities, will encounter the various problems these arguments associate with diversity, including its negative effects on trust, co-operation, social justice and democracy. Another challenge these arguments pose for multicultural political theorists concerns small cultural minorities and geographically dispersed groups, such as immigrants. Because these groups are unable to benefit from territorially based self-government rights, the first view is likely to recommend robust civic integration policies for them, which, as discussed in chapter 5, have sometimes been criticized by multiculturalists for being assimilatory.

The other relevant view about national self-determination also claims that it is instrumentally valuable, but in this case the value is experienced directly by members themselves. An influential version of this argument was proposed by Avishai Margalit and Joseph Raz (1990, 448–9), who argued both that a person's national identity provides them with a secure anchor for self-identification and belonging, and that their national culture supplies them with options and conceptions of the good from which they can build life plans:

> Individual well-being depends on the successful pursuit of worthwhile goals and relationships. Goals and relationships are culturally

> determined ... They all depend for their existence on the sharing of
> patterns of expectations, on traditions preserving implicit knowledge
> of how to do what, of tacit conventions regarding what is part of this
> or that enterprise and what is not, what is appropriate and what is not,
> what is valuable and what is not. Familiarity with a culture determines
> the boundaries of the imaginable. Sharing in a culture, being part of it,
> determines the limits of the feasible.

Margalit and Raz conclude that a person's well-being will be compromised if their national culture withers away, if it is diminished or
officially disfavoured, or if it is held in low esteem by one's fellow
citizens. Thus, they propose an instrumental justification for national
self-determination, as an institutional mechanism to secure people's
well-being by protecting them against these fates. In some contexts,
national self-rule may be necessary to restore pride and self-respect to
members, whilst in others it may simply be better for a national group
to govern itself if members are better at protecting and promoting the
things they care about, including their shared culture and heritage.

As Margalit and Raz emphasize, these interests only justify a
conditional right for national self-determination, since they must
be balanced against other people's morally salient interests. For
example, repressive and intolerant nationalist movements should not
be rewarded with states if they will use their powers to undermine
the interests of minorities. Furthermore, if the value of national self-
determination has to do with promoting the culture and self-respect
of members, then it might sometimes be better for it to be realized
in a limited fashion, within the confines of a multinational state. For
instance, it is at least possible that Welsh culture and its language
could be more effectively protected within a larger United Kingdom,
as opposed to an independent Welsh state, and that such arrangements are compatible with the dignity and self-respect of all.

As discussed in chapter 2, Will Kymlicka has proposed an explicitly
multicultural argument for self-government rights along similar lines
to Margalit and Raz's case for national self-determination. Since
this theory has been discussed already, its key features will only be
briefly rehearsed here. Kymlicka's (1995, 37–8) basic justification
for allocating self-government rights has to do with trying to ensure
that the members of a minority 'cannot be outbid or outvoted
by the majority on decisions that are of particular importance to
their culture, such as issues of education, immigration, resource
development, language and family law'. To explain why national
minorities *in particular* are entitled to be protected in this way, he
draws on his novel concept of a societal culture. A societal culture,

recall, supports individual freedom by providing its members with a context of choice. Because societal cultures must be institutionally embedded if they are to survive in the modern world, Kymlicka (1995, 80) suggests that they will 'tend to be national cultures'. Consequently, Kymlicka (1995, 113) concludes that liberals who are concerned to protect individual freedom should 'aim at ensuring that all national groups have the opportunity to maintain themselves as a distinct culture, if they so choose'.

So, on both of these accounts, the purpose of national self-determination, or self-government rights within a multinational federation, is to help national groups to protect their distinctive cultures, and cultures matter because of the role they play in securing the freedom (Kymlicka) or well-being (Margalit and Raz) of their members. As discussed in chapter 4, however, many critics are unconvinced by Kymlicka's context-of-choice argument about the relationship between freedom and culture, and these objections would also seem to apply to Margalit and Raz's view about the relationship between well-being and culture. In particular, if either the essentialist or cosmopolitan critique succeeds, then both of these arguments are in serious difficulty. Conscious of these problems, Wayne Norman (2006) has proposed an alternative and innovative self-defence argument for self-government rights, which also proceeds from the idea that individuals have powerful interests in their national identities and cultures, but which does not depend upon the same controversial philosophical foundations as the theories of Kymlicka or Margalit and Raz.

Norman's (2006, 26) argument starts from the assumption that different national groups will inevitably, and legitimately, seek to engage in what he calls 'nation-building projects', a term he uses to refer to practices orientated towards 'creating, spreading, or shaping a national identity'. These projects sometimes precede claims for national self-determination, as when nationalist entrepreneurs try to build a sense of national consciousness to support a future bid for political independence. Although less often recognized, nation-building projects also continue after a national community has a state of its own, for instance in how literature, language and history are taught in schools, in the content of public broadcasting and the funding of the arts, in language policies, and in decisions about culturally laden issues such as public holidays, flags, anthems and the names of streets and towns. Because political institutions tend to support the nation-building projects of the majority, members of minority nations – with legitimate nation-building and identity-shaping aspirations of their own – will often experience them as unwelcome and assimilatory. In particular, groups with legitimate nation-building and identity-shaping aspirations of their own are likely to regard majoritarian nation-building as exerting an unwelcome assimilatory pressure. In response, Norman (2006, 24) argues that these minorities 'have a right to resist intended and unintended nation-building by the majority', and so should sometimes 'be given the means, through self-government in a federal subunit, to conduct their own nation-building projects'.

So, then, the self-defence justification for self-government rights is that, because majority nation-building is inevitable, political institutions ought to be designed so as to enable national minorities to pursue their own, rival, nation-building projects. For the most part, this will amount to the same kind of multinational federalism that Kymlicka recommends. Furthermore, Norman's argument is broadly consistent with Kymlicka's basic rationale for self-government rights, which had to do with enabling minorities to maintain their cultural distinctiveness and protecting them against majoritarian decision-making. However, Norman does not insist that people's freedom or well-being depends on their national culture, instead basing his argument on the more modest premises that different national groups are entitled to engage in nation-building projects, and that fairness dictates that the state ought not to privilege one of these at the expense of all of the others.

Self-government rights and territorial autonomy

Kymlicka and Norman agree that the two different strands of thinking about national self-determination can be reconciled without giving each nation a state, but instead by equipping different national communities with significant powers of self-government. Their view, in short, is that, instead of making the political community equally accommodating of different national identities, we should make each national community into its own political community, within a broader federation. This solution is attractive because it both respects the interests people have in their national identities, and empowers national communities to protect and promote their own cultures. Consequently, it can potentially help to solve 'a central design challenge for any given federation' – namely, that of 'obviating even the desire by national minorities to want to secede' (Norman 2006, 170; see also Kymlicka 2001a, 91–119).

However, an influential criticism of this approach is that it ends up reproducing the monocultural logic of the nation-state (Carens 2000, 65–9; De Schutter 2005, 2011). This may seem surprising, since Kymlicka and Norman both reject the idea that each state must be united by a single and homogeneous national identity, an idea discredited amongst multiculturalists because of its assimilatory undertones. Nevertheless, they do accept the remarkably similar idea that each national community needs its own territory if it is to preserve its distinctiveness. So, although the self-government rights Kymlicka and Norman favour fall short of full state sovereignty, they are modelled on the very same ideal that lies behind the nation-state – namely, that each nation is entitled to govern itself by controlling its own territory. For example, Kymlicka (1995, 182) refers approvingly to the way in which self-government rights divide society 'into separate "peoples", each with its own historic rights, territories and powers of self-government; and each, therefore, with its own political community'. Again, in a later essay, Kymlicka (2001b, 256) characterizes moving from one region of a multinational state to another as being, 'in important respects, like entering another country'. Similarly, Norman (2006, 165) argues that the best way to protect national minorities from majoritarian nation-building projects is to give them 'territorial autonomy in the form of a federal province exercising powers that will promote the continued existence and flourishing of their group'.

The idea that the interests of national minorities are best served by redrawing internal boundaries and creating territorially defined self-governing communities is, however, only one institutional possibility amongst others. Recall that Kymlicka's basic concern is to ensure that national minorities 'cannot be outbid or outvoted by the majority on decisions that are of particular importance to their culture'. Likewise, Norman starts from the similar idea that national minorities should be supported in protecting their identities against the nation-building projects of the majority. Now it is true, of course, that territorially defined self-government rights are one way to achieve these things. However, other multiculturalists have proposed different solutions, including adjusting public institutions and spaces so that they can be shared by different nationalities on fair terms (De Schutter 2011), extending equal recognition to different nationalities by providing equivalent per capita levels of support (Patten 2014), or creatively remaking state-level national identities to make them more inclusive for citizens with different religious, ethnic and national backgrounds (Uberoi 2018; Modood 2019b). Furthermore, there are at least four reasons to be reluctant about Kymlicka's and Norman's preferred territorial solution.

First is the 'minorities within minorities' problem, which arises when a self-governing territory is also home to the members of another group. This scenario is arguably ubiquitous in multinational federations, since, as Norman (2006, 145) observes, '[t]he mapping out of federal subunits will almost always trap new minorities within minority-controlled subunits (these new minorities may well be members of the national majority) or strand minorities outside of the subunits their members control'. As such, at least some people in a multinational federation will find themselves governed by a national group whose identity they do not share, and whose nation-building efforts they regard as unwelcome.

As an objection to multinational federalism, it is important not to make too much of this worry, since minorities are also created by the boundaries between nation-states, such as the Hungarian-speaking communities living in Romania. Furthermore, finding oneself on the wrong side of a border may be worse in a nation-state than in a multinational federation, since at least the latter is committed to the principle of recognizing different national identities. Nevertheless, there might be distinctive reasons to be concerned about the situation of minorities within the subunits of a multinational federation, especially if the purpose of these subunits is to defend the culture of a minority nation against a majority one, and when that majority culture is also the culture of the internal minority – as is the case for Anglophones in Quebec, say. In these cases, the purpose of self-government rights, for multiculturalists, is to protect the minority nation against the culture and language of the internal minority.

Second is an unfairness objection, which arises because of the restrictions these theories place on the kinds of groups that are entitled to self-government rights. Kymlicka (1995, 18) expressly restricts self-government rights to territorially concentrated intergenerational communities who share a distinct language and history, and which are 'more or less institutionally complete'. Amongst other things, this means that a legitimate beneficiary of self-government rights must already have, at least 'more or less', its own education and legal system, its own economy and employment market, and its own broadcasters and newspapers. However, this requirement will be far too demanding for some groups, including those whose institutional framework has been hollowed out as a result of oppression. This objection bites especially hard for Indigenous communities, whose legal structures and value systems, as well as the territories to which their ways of life are attached, have been profoundly disrupted by colonialism. From Kymlicka's perspective, the culture of these groups, as well as those of many national minorities, is already too fragile to benefit from self-government rights.

Third is the objection that these theories are perhaps 'better suited to a *monocultural* conception of citizenship than a multicultural one', as Joseph Carens (2000, 65) has suggested of Kymlicka's theory. This objection starts from the observation that the sociology underpinning Kymlicka's theory draws heavily on the work of Ernest Gellner (1983), who had argued that modern bureaucratic states and indus- trialized economies depended upon cultural homogeneity to function smoothly. National cultures and identities provide the substance of this homogeneity, which is actively promoted by modern states through standardized education systems and the dispersal of a common language. Although Kymlicka, like Norman, is extremely sensitive to the potentially unwelcome effects of majoritarian nation- building activities on minorities, he retains the Gellnerian assumption that political communities require a high degree of cultural homo- geneity in the first place. Thus, he recommends that minority nations engage in nation-building activities of their own, constructing their own, smaller and territorially demarcated, political communities within the context of a multinational state. However, the ideal to which his theory points – of self-governing and institutionally complete nations living alongside one another – is not so much one of a multinational state as a series of separate 'not quite' nation-states. As a result, it loses sight of the sheer extent to which economic, social and political institutions are shared by all members of multinational states (Carens 2000, 66). For instance, even a multinational feder- ation with a high degree of institutional separation like Belgium – in which the different national groups have their own political parties, newspapers and television stations – still has plenty of shared institu- tions, such as a travel network and national sports teams, as well as much of its economic life.

Fourth, the final objection concerns whether multinational federa- tions of the kind that Kymlicka and Norman recommend can accommodate complex, fluid and hybrid national identities, such as people inhabiting multiple societal cultures or traversing different national identities, or who do not fit easily into a single national group, including children of mixed families and inhabitants of large culturally diverse cities. Certainly, Kymlicka (2001b, 256) sometimes assumes that the members of minority nations have a single and unproblematic national identity, suggesting that most people in Flanders have Belgian citizenship but a Flemish national identity, and that most people in Quebec have Canadian citizenship but a Québécois national identity. Not only is this reductive, since many residents of those places have more complex identities, but it is also false. As De Schutter (2005, 31–2) has observed, people in Flanders are most likely to report themselves as having a double national identity (Belgian and Flemish) and only a very small minority think of their national identity as being 'only Flemish'. Moreover, the same issue also confronts Norman's theory, even though he is keenly aware that national identities are flexible and complex, often shaped by rival nation-building projects (Norman 2006, 29). For example, when he discusses how a federation is to settle on its own ground rules, deciding on matters such as how powers are to be divided between the different levels of government, Norman (1994) assumes – albeit ambivalently – that national groups can speak on behalf of all of their members (Norman 2006, 154, makes this claim more tentatively; for further discussion, see De Schutter 2011 and Shorten 2015a).

In summary, the dominant multicultural approach to accommodating national differences is to allocate significant self-government rights to national groups. The general rationale for these, at least for multiculturalists, is to enable minorities to preserve their national cultures, in the face of majoritarian pressures towards assimilation. In addition, it is usually assumed that national self-government rights must be exercised territorially, which reflects the aspiration that many nationalist movements have to control their own territory or homeland. However, I have suggested that multiculturalists ought to be reluctant about taking these demands at face value, since territorial self-government rights can generate minorities within minorities, discourage hybridity, promote division, and undermine the interests of small, institutionally incomplete or territorially dispersed groups. As such, multiculturalists would do well to consider alternative forms of institutional experimentation so as to find new and better ways to support the interests that national groups have in preserving their cultures and traditions.

Religions and Institutions

Like national groups, religious associations have also sought rights to govern their own affairs, mostly to enable them to regulate themselves according to their own norms and values, when these conflict with the norms and values prevalent in wider society. However, instead of rights to control particular territories, they have sought rights to govern their own institutions, with no or minimal interference from the secular state.

The following section discusses some examples in which the practices of religious associations and institutions come into conflict with laws and policies that apply to non-religious associations and institutions. Unlike the similar cases examined in chapter 6, these all have a collective dimension, since they concern the governance of religious associations and institutions, as opposed to the practices and beliefs of individual religious believers. Then, a difficult puzzle raised by these examples will be examined, concerning how they ought to be characterized, and for which two alternative theoretical models have been proposed. The first of these builds on the separation principle to argue that the secular state has no business interfering in the affairs of religious institutions, who are entitled to govern themselves according to their own values, rules and principles. On this view, religious associations are, or ought to be regarded as, sovereign in their own spheres, with state-like rights of jurisdictional autonomy. The second instead accepts that the secular state does have legitimate jurisdiction over all associations, including religious ones, but argues that religious associations should sometimes be granted special accommodations.

Regulating religious associations

Many religious associations wish to govern themselves according to their own norms and values, even when they conflict with the law. Accommodating this preference is often relatively uncontroversial, as when churches insist that only men be ordained as priests, for example. For cases like this, as liberal William Galston (2002, 111) has remarked, it is widely believed that 'religious associations (and perhaps others as well) enjoy considerable authority within their own sphere to determine their own affairs and in so doing to express their understanding of spiritual matters'. Meanwhile, there are limits to this authority, and religious self-governance has sometimes proven more controversial. For example, there have been protracted debates over the 'ministerial exception', a principle created by the US Supreme Court to disallow judicial interference in the selection of clergy. This has been interpreted to mean that various employment laws have no bearing on the relationships between churches and their ministers, so that, for instance, minimum wage laws do not apply to Catholic seminarians (*Rosas* v. *Corporation of the Catholic Archbishop of Seattle*, 2010). Furthermore, it has also been extended to cover employees who would not usually be regarded as ministers. This meant, for example, that a teacher of non-religious subjects with narcolepsy, working in a Lutheran school, was denied the protection of disability discrimination laws, since she led her class in daily prayers and for that reason was regarded as a minister (*Hosanna-Tabor Evangelical Lutheran Church and School* v. *Equal*

Employment Opportunity Commission et al., 2012), and, in a similar case, a church pianist was denied legal protections against discrimination on grounds of age or disability, since he too was regarded as a minister, and not as an ordinary employee (*Cannata* v. *Catholic Diocese of Austin*, 2012). In these cases, religious employers obtained permission to regulate themselves in ways that would otherwise be unlawful, by arguing that the discretion they enjoy with respect to selecting and employing ministers should be extended to cover a wide range of staff and their activities.

It is not only churches themselves that have sought powers of religious self-governance. For example, a number of businesses with religious owners have refused to provide particular services on grounds of conscience, when otherwise they would be required to do so. Often these are family-run firms, such as the Christian-owned Ashers Baking Company in Northern Ireland, who refused to make a cake bearing a message to promote same-sex marriage, which the owners regarded as contrary to their faith (*Lee* v. *Ashers Baking Company*, 2018). At least one similar case, however, involved a very large firm, Hobby Lobby, which is an American arts and crafts store employing more than 13,000 people and run by a single family, the members of which objected to providing health plans including emergency contraception to their employees, as had been required of them by the Affordable Care Act (*Burwell* v. *Hobby Lobby Stores, Inc.*, 2014).

Publicly funded religious schools, as well as charities and hospitals with a religious ethos, have also sought forms of special legal treatment to enable them to maintain their distinctive character. For instance, state-funded faith schools in the UK have been granted special permissions to use religious criteria when selecting pupils, despite a general prohibition against discriminating on grounds of religion or belief in the provision of goods or services (Clayton et al. 2021). These powers have sometimes been controversial. For instance, the Jewish Free School in London was permitted to give preference to Jewish applicants, since, like other British faith schools, it is permitted to favour applications from co-religionists. However, the school was not allowed to use its preferred definition of Judaism, in which membership is conferred by matrilineal descent, since the courts concluded that this would breach laws prohibiting racial discrimination (*R(E)* v. *Governing Body of JFS*, 2009). Some institutions of higher education have also sought exceptional permission to apply discriminatory admissions policies to sustain a religious ethos. For instance, the Canadian Supreme Court effectively allowed a religious teacher training college to exclude non-celibate homosexuals (*Trinity Western University* v. *British Columbia College of Teachers*, 2001), though it more recently reached the opposite conclusion regarding a proposed law school at the same university (*Trinity Western University* v. *Law Society of Upper Canada*, 2018).

The discretionary powers extended to churches, to firms with religious owners, as well as to schools, hospitals and charities run by religious orders, are a form of religious accommodation. However, unlike the examples discussed in chapter 6, they are exercised not by individuals, but by associations, firms or other institutions. Moreover, whilst the typical accommodation for an individual religious believer takes the form of an exemption, in which the beneficiary is permitted to perform an action that would generally be disallowed, such as riding a motorcycle without a helmet, ones for associations equip beneficiaries with significant powers and immunities (these terms come from Hohfeld 1919; for a detailed explanation, see Shorten 2016, 278–81). So, for example, permitting faith schools to discriminate on otherwise unlawful grounds both equips the school with a power to select and enforce a particular policy, and it disables the state from enforcing its preferred (anti-discrimination) policy within the school (Lægaard 2015, 224; Shorten 2015b, 250). As such, institutional accommodations can have significant effects on the rights and freedoms of individuals, including people who do not belong to the religious association in question (Shorten 2021).

The general rationale for these accommodations has to do with enabling religious associations and their institutions to preserve a particular character or ethos (Shorten 2015b, 244–9). Frequently, though not always, special legal treatment helps to facilitate this goal by ensuring that the religious character of an institution is not undermined by its internal structure (i.e., the formal and informal rules that regulate its internal affairs). For instance, employment and other laws shape and constrain how institutions can govern themselves internally. Unless religious institutions are permitted to opt out of some of these, their distinctive character could be jeopardized – say, if faith schools had to consider hiring atheist teachers, or if the Catholic Church had to consider appointing female priests.

Religious schools are amongst the most frequent beneficiaries of this kind of special legal treatment, having requested accommodations to allow them to give preference to potential pupils and teachers from within their religious communities, and also to ensure that employees uphold the dictates of their faith. For instance, in the United States, a teacher of non-religious subjects was lawfully removed from her post in a Catholic elementary school after entering a second marriage because, although being legally valid, her marriage did not satisfy the requirements of Canon Law (*Little v. Wuerl*, 1991). Had the teacher been employed by a non-religious school, then her employment could not have been terminated for the same reason. More recently, the European Court of Human Rights supported the decision to terminate the employment of a priest who taught religion and ethics in a public school and whose salary was paid by the Spanish state, after it became public knowledge that he was married with three children (*Martinez v. Spain*, 2014). In both cases, teachers were sanctioned for reasons related to their private lives, and in ways that would otherwise have fallen afoul of anti-discrimination laws.

The other main way in which special legal treatment might enable a religious association or institution to preserve its ethos concerns its purposes (i.e., the activities it engages in or the services it provides). For instance, if the law requires services to be provided on a non-discriminatory basis, then religious charities and hospitals might be compelled either to close down or to engage in activities that conflict with their religious doctrines. It is for this reason that some US states permit religious hospitals to refuse to provide abortions, and religious adoption agencies to refuse to place children with LGBTQ+ parents (see, e.g., Corvino, Anderson and Girgis 2017, 113–14; Tebbe 2017, 193–4). Further, it is not only public service providers that have sought permission to discriminate in the provision of services. For example, the US courts have recently confronted cases in which a bakery and a florist refused to provide services for gay weddings on religious grounds (*Masterpiece Cakeshop v. Colorado Civil Rights Commission*, 2018; *State of Washington v. Arlene's Flowers*, 2019).

Locating jurisdictional authority

Until recently, legal and political theorists had not discussed these phenomena systematically, and as a result they remain under-theorized. Nevertheless, two contrasting frameworks have begun to take shape, each of which attempts to identify the justificatory basis for these forms of religious self-governance. After describing and assessing these, I will suggest that both of them fail to account properly for the effects of religious self-governance on outsiders, and recommend a dialogical approach to address this deficiency.

The first view is the most radical and it goes under a number of different titles, including 'church autonomy' (Laycock 2009), 'sphere sovereignty' (Horwitz 2009), 'religious institutionalism' (Schragger and Schwartzman 2013) and 'jurisdictional pluralism' (Cohen 2015, 2017). Whatever term is used, its key thesis is that churches and other religious institutions have rights akin to those of sovereign states. This idea is captured by Paul Horwitz's (2009, 83) description of religious bodies as 'sovereign within their own spheres', and by Richard Garnett's (2016, 50) recommendation for the state to respect the autonomy of the church as an 'organized society with its own laws and jurisdiction'. Distinctively, this approach invokes a 'pluralist' reading of sovereignty, which rejects the assumption – widespread in modern political thought – that the state alone is sovereign, without rivals and with full authority over all of its citizens as well as all of the intermediate bodies that compose civil society, such as churches, mosques, guilds, trades unions and universities (Cohen 2017, 86–93; see also Muñiz-Fraticelli 2014; Levy 2015). Instead, it insists that religious bodies are authoritative sources of binding norms, whose legitimacy does not depend 'on the state's acquiescence or permission' (Muñiz-Fraticelli 2014, 32). Strikingly, this implies that when it comes to cases like those described in the previous section, the proper question to ask is not whether a religious association should be given exceptional permission to opt out of a particular law, but whether the state has the authority in the first place to direct religious associations about their own affairs.

Like the kind of multinational federalism examined earlier, this view challenges the traditional model of a unitary sovereign state underlying much political thought, though arguably at an even deeper level. As we have seen, multinational federations disperse decision-making authority to two or more levels of government – the federation itself and its national subunits. Both of these, however, derive their legitimacy democratically. Meanwhile, this view also disperses decision-making authority to two different kinds of bodies, but only one of them has democratic legitimacy, whilst the other derives its authority from elsewhere. In doing so, as Jean Cohen (2015) has suggested, it seemingly resurrects an old 'two worlds' theory of separate jurisdictional domains, dividing authority between two autonomous sovereigns – Church (God) and State (King).

Despite its controversial foundations, a number of broadly secular grounds can be marshalled in support of this view. For instance, it can be defended on political grounds, as a mechanism for limiting government, protecting vibrant public discourse, and providing a check against potentially overweening states (Garvey 1996, 153; Horwitz 2009, 83). Furthermore, it conceivably protects a distinctive and valuable manifestation of freedom of conscience, recognizing that what matters is not so much the individual and self-regarding freedom emphasized by orthodox liberals, but rather the ability to worship collectively, alongside and in communion with others, with whom one can jointly explore religious life and share religious experiences (Baumeister 2019, 100–6).

Arguably, however, the most fundamental reason in its support is a controversial interpretation of state neutrality (Cohen 2015, 188). According to this, a neutral state cannot consistently affirm its own supremacy because it cannot authoritatively deny the claims of religious believers to be subject to a higher authority (McConnell 1985, 15). Given this, secular authorities cannot simply presume themselves to have a right to govern the affairs of religious associations, and it is the latter who are entitled to decide where the limits of their own authority rest. Accordingly, the fact that collective accommodations happen almost always to be exemptions from anti-discrimination laws is coincidental, and the liberal democratic state lacks the authority to trespass on the sovereignty of religious associations in other areas of the law too.

Criticisms of this view tend to emphasize its incompatibility with liberal principles, as well as with the modern democratic constitutional tradition (Cohen 2015; Laborde 2017, 167–71). Most obviously, it disempowers citizens, removing significant and influential social institutions from the purview of democratic accountability and control, locating them instead under the remit of divine law and authority. As a result, it implies that citizens lack the standing, at least in their capacity as citizens, to challenge the internal regulation of religious associations, or the ways in which they act in the world, something that would surely be regarded as unacceptable for other collective bodies, such as commercial firms. Furthermore, this approach also threatens individual rights and freedoms, especially by weakening important civic entitlements and protections. For instance, consider the way in which the Hobby Lobby decision, allowing the firm to remove emergency contraception from its health insurance coverage, had the effect of denying important social benefits to its employees, many of whom belonged to different churches than the owners of the firm, or to none at all.

Another objection to this view is that it trades on an ambivalence, meaning that, in the end, talk of jurisdictional autonomy amounts to little more than a 'rhetorical device' (Laborde 2017, 169). Few people think that the state has no grounds whatsoever for interfering in the internal affairs of religious organizations, and even if religious associations are sovereign bodies, they still have duties to respect individual rights, including those of members and outsiders. But once one accepts that religious associations do not have a completely free hand, then it seemingly follows that someone must be entitled to oversee, and if necessary interfere in, their affairs, and the most viable candidate for doing so is the democratic state, since the members of religious associations are also citizens.

The second view makes no such radical claims about sovereignty, and instead holds that liberal democratic states have reasons of justice to support religious associations in their efforts to preserve a distinctive ethos. One argument for this conclusion starts from a complaint about 'secular bias' in government programmes and public institutions, such as schools, hospitals, universities and care homes (Tomasi 2004, 339). To counteract this, and on grounds similar to the self-defence argument considered in the previous section, scholars such as John Tomasi (2004), Mitch McConnell (2000) and Veit Bader (2007) recommend subsidizing separate religious institutions, to give religious citizens an adequate range of options. However, as a case for religious self-governance, this argument is incomplete in two respects. First, even if public institutions happen to be biased against religious worldviews, this is not inevitable, and other scholars have argued that religious citizens can be fairly accommodated within inclusive public institutions (Maclure and Taylor 2011; Laborde 2017). Second, counteracting secular bias does not explain the necessity of institutional autonomy, since the state could subsidize and support religious service providers without permitting their institutions to discriminate in otherwise unlawful ways.

Another, stronger, argument for the same conclusion appeals to the interests people have in freely associating with one another on their own terms, including by creating institutions to pursue collective purposes and regulating those institutions with their own procedures and norms. Respect for freedom of association does not block the state from ever interfering in these institutions, but that interference must be justified by good reasons. Generally speaking, most liberals – Kukathas excepted – think that protecting people against discrimination is a good reason (White 1997). Notwithstanding this, some political theorists have also argued that the members of particular associations can have morally weighty interests in being granted extra latitude, to allow their institutions to apply discriminatory rules that would otherwise be unlawful (Schragger and Schwartzman 2013; Shorten 2015b; Sager 2016).

Cécile Laborde (2017) has proposed the most thorough argument to this effect. Her account emphasizes two interests that group members sometimes have in maintaining their 'collective integrity'. The first has to do with associational 'coherence' and is satisfied when the activities an association engages in, as well as the rules governing its internal affairs, remain consistent with its underlying ethos or character. Anti-discrimination laws potentially

jeopardize this interest by blunting the ability of religious associations 'to prohibit apostasy and blasphemy from their members,
to excommunicate heretics and dissidents, and to refuse entry to
nonbelievers' (Laborde 2017, 179). To avoid this, Laborde recommends extending 'collective exemptions', so that associations are
not compelled to adopt structures or purposes contrary to their
ethos. Meanwhile, the second interest she highlights has to do with
the special expertise associations possess to interpret their own
standards, purposes and commitments. Laborde calls these 'competence' interests, arguing that they justify deferring to the judgements
of religious associations themselves, or their traditional authorities,
over matters such as whether a priest has 'the requisite spiritual
qualities' or 'preached an inaccurate interpretation of the Gospels'
(Laborde 2017, 192).

Some of the collective exemptions Laborde (2017, 180) endorses
are controversial, including permitting white supremacist churches
to refuse entry to non-whites. However, she places strict limits on
the kinds of associations who can benefit from them, recommending
special privileges only for identificatory groups that are formally
constituted as voluntary associations. Consequently, Hobby Lobby
was not entitled to special treatment on her view, because, with over
13,000 employees and 500 stores, it was too large an organization
to infer that its members share the religious ethos of its owners. In
other words, it was not an identificatory association in Laborde's
sense. Likewise, groups like 'the Hindu community' or 'the Muslim
community' do not qualify for collective exemptions on Laborde's
(2017, 181) account, because they are too 'diffuse' and lack formal
structures of authority.

Interestingly, Laborde (2017, 185) entirely rules out granting
accommodations to schools, hospitals, firms and other organizations
providing services to the general public, arguing that 'as soon as an
organisation claims to serve the public, it is not "religious" in the
sense that matters'. However, this is arguably too strict, since, by
the lights of her own argument, the people operating and supporting
these institutions might well have weighty coherence interests. For
example, consider a school with a religious ethos, which initially
admits pupils only from one faith community, and so at this time
does not serve the general public, but which later decides to offer
places to all children. It seems at least possible that, after widening its
admissions criteria, the members of the school could retain coherence
interests in preferring to appoint co-religionists onto its teaching staff
(Shorten 2019). Why should those interests now be discounted, when
they mattered before?

Another potential problem concerns the role of consent in justifying collective exemptions. According to Laborde (2017, 174), only voluntary and formally constituted associations should be granted special privileges to discriminate, since we can 'presume' that members 'consent' to the 'formal authority structures' of their associations. However, as discussed in chapters 3 and 5, some political theorists are wary about presuming that membership entails meaningful consent, especially for patriarchal groups. Moreover, collective exemptions for religious associations often affect the dignity and standing of outsiders as well as members, who have no credible opportunity to consent. For example, recall the parents whose children were denied places at the Jewish Free School, the church pianist denied the protection of discrimination laws, and the teachers sacked for reasons related to their private conduct.

So, then, like the first view, Laborde's argument seems to neglect the effects of religious self-governance on non-members. The significance of this shortcoming can be illustrated by considering whether religious adoption agencies should ever be permitted to refuse to offer services to same-sex couples, as was temporarily the case in the UK after the 2007 Equality Act (Sexual Orientation) Regulations became law. For Laborde, the crucial question is whether the adoption agencies in question serve the general public. If they do, then no exemption should be granted. But, if they restrict their services to co-religionists, then Laborde should presumably concur with Annabelle Lever (2017, 236–7), who argues that '[t]he state cannot reasonably object to adoption agencies that refuse to place children with homosexual couples, so long as the adoption agency serves *only* those who accept Church teaching on these matters, and there are suitable alternatives for everyone else'. However, this conclusion neglects the broader social effects of allowing discrimination on grounds of sexuality. This point was not lost on a British tribunal, tasked with considering a request from Catholic Care Leeds, a religious adoption agency who wanted to restrict their services to heterosexual parents. The tribunal concluded that being able to access adoption services elsewhere 'did not remove the harm that would be caused to [same-sex couples] through feeling that discrimination on grounds of sexual orientation was practised at some point in the adoption system nor would it remove the harm to the general social value of promotion of equality of treatment for heterosexuals and homosexuals' (*Catholic Care (Diocese of Leeds)* v. *Charity Commission*, 2012; see Baumeister 2019 for a discussion of this example). So, what the tribunal appreciated, and Laborde's view does not, is that discrimination by and within voluntary religious associations can have profound effects on the social standing of outsiders, and the recognition accorded to them.

Conclusion

Arguments for religious self-governance have been framed in terms of both sovereignty and justice, and each approach faces serious objections. Whilst arguments from sovereignty unacceptably disempower citizens, those appealing to justice neglect the legitimate interests of outsiders in how religious institutions conduct their affairs. Perhaps, however, the case for religious self-governance can be rescued, by framing it instead within something like Parekh's dialogical approach, examined in chapter 3. Furthermore, something like this solution might also help to address some of the challenges faced by multinational societies for whom territorial autonomy within a multinational federation is inappropriate.

In the case of religious self-governance, exemptions from anti-discrimination laws for religious institutions could be conditional on the approval of both members and outsiders, after a dialogue involving those responsible for the institutions themselves, the members of the related religious associations, and the general public. Such a dialogue, of course, may prompt a religious institution to redefine its structures or purposes, so that its ethos becomes consistent with anti-discrimination norms, as when some Protestant denominations accepted female clergy, or when religious schools ceased giving preference to co-religionists in admissions. Alternatively, it might encourage outsiders to appreciate that the costs of accommodating a religious association are worth paying. Or, instead, after listening to the group and its members, wider society might decide to permit an exemption but also insist on legal mechanisms to protect the vulnerable.

This proposal is consistent with the model of 'joint governance', suggested in a different but related context by Ayelet Shachar (2001). Joint governance gives a group substantial (but incomplete) jurisdictional autonomy over a particular legal or social domain, without rigidly 'fixing' the balance of power between it and the state, and instead allowing for the competences of different authorities to be a matter of ongoing negotiation. Although joint governance falls well short of allocating unfettered dominion to religious institutions over their own affairs, it does not entirely suppress the freedoms of association and religion, and it still allows for considerable institutional autonomy (Shorten 2017).

With respect to national differences, a dialogical and joint governance approach would treat the powers held by the different levels of government as unfixed, subject to ongoing contestation and potentially revisable. This might have the welcome effect of empowering minorities to register grievances, thereby encouraging majority and minority national identities to be reimagined in more inclusive ways. Furthermore, it could help to weaken the links between particular nations and particular territories without altogether eliminating them. Thus, national groups could still think of particular territories as 'theirs', even if they lack exclusive powers of jurisdiction over them. In addition to underlining the idea that territories must always be shared, and on fair terms, this might also better accommodate hybridity and complexity, allowing for the emergence of new national identities. Finally, and as we saw in chapter 3, dialogue should also be welcomed for having a kind of intrinsic value, enabling its participants to better understand themselves, their society and one another.

8

Speaking with Dignity: Linguistic Justice for National Minorities and Immigrants

It is estimated that more than 7,000 languages are spoken in the world today (Eberhard, Simons and Fennig 2020). Since there are fewer than 200 different countries – the UN currently has 193 members – it should come as no surprise that each state contains some degree of linguistic diversity. Amongst multicultural political theorists, two different forms of multilingualism have attracted the most attention. First are societies containing multiple long-settled language groups, such as Canada (English and French), Belgium (Dutch, French and German), Sri Lanka (Sinhala and Tamil) and Switzerland (French, German, Italian and Romansh). This variety of linguistic diversity is sometimes truly impressive – for instance, over 400 languages are spoken in India, which recognizes 2 of them as official (Hindi and English) and lists 22 as 'scheduled languages' (including Hindi, but not English). The second variety of multilingualism, meanwhile, results from migration, including the languages spoken by newly arrived immigrants as well as those in the second or third generation, some of whom wish to preserve a connection to the culture of their parents and grandparents. Immigrants have introduced significant linguistic diversity even into societies with a single dominant language. For example, the US Census Bureau recently estimated that approximately 22 per cent of residents speak languages other than English at home (US Census Bureau 2019).

This chapter examines both kinds of diversity. It begins by discussing the claims of long-settled linguistic minorities, including large groups – such as French speakers in Canada, and Catalan speakers in Spain – as well as smaller ones – such as speakers of

Scottish Gaelic in the United Kingdom, and German in the South Tyrol region of Italy and the eastern parts of Belgium. As demonstrated in chapters 2 and 3, the claims of some of these groups, most notably Canadian francophones, had a tremendous influence on the first wave of multicultural political theory, especially the writings of Taylor and Kymlicka. Here the work of another Canadian political theorist, Alan Patten, will be examined. His *Equal Recognition* (2014) extends and updates Kymlicka's theory of liberal multiculturalism, arguing that speakers of minority languages often have a moral right for their language to be used by public institutions, such as courts, bureaucracies, hospitals, schools and universities. Furthermore, he suggests that the official recognition of languages should be distributed equally, not reserved solely for the majority or dominant language.

Patten describes the kind of language rights that he and his critics are interested in as promotion rights, since they aim to promote particular patterns of language use, status and competence within society (sociolinguists refer to this as 'language planning'). There are a number of ways in which a state might promote a majority or a minority language, such as by teaching it in schools or by using it in public institutions and administration. The promotion of majority languages often goes unnoticed, at least by its speakers, since it is the consequence of their language serving as the norm for political, educational and administrative purposes. Meanwhile, minority language promotion is usually an intentional – and controversial – public policy, perhaps aiming to maintain the cultural distinctiveness of a specific region, as in Catalonia and Quebec, or perhaps instead to help preserve and encourage a vulnerable language, as for Welsh in the United Kingdom and Irish in Ireland. Promoting a minority language typically requires more than ensuring that people be able to speak and understand it – in order to prevent it from becoming marginalized, people must be encouraged to use it, and especially in high-status settings and institutions, such as businesses, universities and parliaments, or on tax forms, in courts and when casting votes.

Advocates disagree about how language promotion policies should be implemented. One view, known as the territoriality principle, says that language rights and policies ought to vary according to geography. For example, the Swiss confederation is composed of twenty-six cantons, twenty-two of which are officially monolingual, and, in each of these, public services are available only in a single language. So, although Switzerland itself recognizes four official languages, most of its population live in regions using only one of these. Citizens are free to move from one place to another, but if they do so they must adapt themselves to their new linguistic circumstances. A powerful reason in support of the territoriality principle is that it better supports vulnerable languages. For instance, Philippe Van Parijs (2011, 146–9) has argued that making one language 'queen' in a given territory will strongly incentivize people living there to learn and use it. Meanwhile, the other view is known as the personality principle, and it says that language rights should follow citizens, meaning that speakers of official languages should be able to access public institutions in their own language wherever they happen to be. So, for example, the city of Brussels is bilingual, and speakers of both French and Flemish can access services in their preferred language. According to its defenders, this principle is particularly suitable where language groups are messily dispersed, without clear geographical boundaries, or when one is especially concerned about the fate of minorities within minorities (De Schutter 2008; Patten 2014, 227–31).

As well as promotion rights, other rights also have a linguistic dimension. Most fundamental is the right for one's private language choices to be tolerated, so that people are able to use their preferred language in private settings, including in the home or on the streets as well as in newspapers and on television (following Heinz Kloss 1977, contemporary theorists of linguistic justice such as May 2012 and Patten 2014 distinguish between 'promotion-oriented' and 'tolerance-oriented' language rights). Examples of linguistic intolerance from colonial societies remain shocking, despite their notoriety. For instance, in their ground-breaking collection *Linguistic Human Rights*, Tove Skutnabb-Kangas and Robert Phillipson (1994, 19) highlight the British colonial practice of punishing school-children in Kenya for using their own language rather than English, an offence that could attract violent and humiliating penalties, including caning and being made to wear a sign describing the bearer as 'stupid' or as a 'donkey'.

Beyond mere toleration, some speakers of minority languages, especially immigrants, have sought additional supports to enable them to communicate with public institutions when they are not proficient users of the majority or official language. Falling loosely within Kymlicka's category of polyethnic rights, these include things like translation and interpretation services in hospitals and courts, employing bilingual staff to provide some public services, and printing administrative forms and public information materials in multiple languages (Shorten forthcoming). In practice, the extent and quality of such provisions varies considerably, even within countries (Dunbar and McKelvey 2018, 94). Like tolerance-oriented rights, these supports are arguably not language rights proper, at least not in the 'strict sense', because they do not entail supporting, promoting or extending official recognition to any particular languages (Rubio-Marín 2003, 67). Rather, they are typically understood as temporary or bridging measures, appropriate for people whose linguistic integration is a work in progress, or for whom majority language learning is an unrealistic aspiration, such as the elderly.

As Patten (2014, 188–91) has noted, from the perspective of political theory, many of these measures are 'not especially controversial', since they are necessary 'instruments' to secure people's enjoyment of their basic 'rights and entitlements', such as the right to a fair trial or the right to literacy. However, in politics itself, the public funding of translation and interpretation services has come under fire, especially in countries experiencing the kind of backlash against multiculturalism discussed in chapter 5. In particular, it is often claimed that providing such services discourages migrants from learning the majority language, thereby setting back their interests in the longer term (see, e.g., Schäffner 2009; Schuck 2009). For instance, this was suggested in 2013 by the UK's Secretary of State for Communities and Local Government, who then stated that 'translation services have an unintentional, adverse impact on integration by reducing the incentive for some migrant communities to learn English' (Eric Pickles, quoted in Pokorn and Čibej 2018, 113). Interestingly, this hypothesis is not supported by empirical evidence (Gonzáles Núñez, 2016, 239), and at least one recent study casts doubt on it, albeit in the specific case of asylum seekers (Pokorn and Čibej 2018). Nevertheless, the underlying assumption remains widespread in political discourse.

Regardless of whether states are obliged to provide extensive translation and interpretation services, there is little public support for actively promoting the languages of immigrants. Many political theorists share this view (e.g., Kymlicka 1995, 95–100; Van Parijs 2011, 149–51; Patten 2014, 269–97), and the second half of the chapter will examine some of the arguments multiculturalists have given in support of discriminating between the languages of long-settled groups and those spoken by minorities. Importantly, these arguments typically apply to a wide range of cultural rights, and not only to language policies. For example, Kymlicka (1995, 96) argues that immigrants waive their cultural rights because, as he puts it, '[i]n deciding to uproot themselves, immigrants voluntarily relinquish some of the rights that go along with their original national membership'. Similarly, Patten (2014, 291) has claimed that host societies are morally permitted to make relinquishing one's language rights a condition for entry, both because existing citizens have legitimate expectations that their linguistic environment not be dramatically altered, and because existing citizens are entitled 'to show some level of partiality to their own languages'. As we shall see, these arguments are philosophically contentious, even if they reflect the practices of nearly all existing states.

Language Promotion and Equal Recognition

According to Patten (2014), speakers of minority languages sometimes have a moral right for their language to be used by public institutions. The public recognition of multiple languages can be central to a country's self-understanding, as in Belgium, Switzerland and Canada. Elsewhere, it can be controversial. For example, consider the UK, where the recognition of Welsh in Wales and Scottish Gaelic in Scotland have been broadly welcomed, but where proposals to recognize Irish, and perhaps Ulster Scots, in Northern Ireland have attracted acrimony. Or consider France, whose constitution identifies French (and only French) as its official language, and where recognition has been denied to regional languages such as Alsatian, Basque and Breton.

Patten's case for language recognition combines two key features. First, he defends a proceduralist approach to language rights, arguing against the intuitively plausible view that language policies should aim at particular outcomes, such as preserving vulnerable languages or promoting a common national language. Second, he defends a particular principle of linguistic justice, which says that recognition ought to be distributed equally to the speakers of different languages, and that this means the state ought to provide supports to different languages broadly in proportion to the number of speakers they have. After setting out these two parts of Patten's theory, some friendly criticisms that have been registered against each of them will be considered. Taken together, these suggest that Patten's principle of equal recognition may be too frugal and that a proceduralist approach to language rights will sometimes need to be corrected.

Outcomes and procedures

An intuitive way to think about language promotion rights is in terms of the outcomes a society wants to bring about, such as preserving a vulnerable minority language or achieving convergence on a single national language. Once the desired goals are agreed upon, then a system of language rights and policies can be designed around them. However, an oft-made complaint about these approaches is that they risk treating speakers of different languages unequally, perhaps even alienating some of them from their own political community and its institutions, if the outcome society aims at is one they personally oppose. For example, some anglophone residents object that Quebec's language policy is disrespectful, believing it to favour their francophone neighbours unfairly. Similarly, other minorities have complained about policies to promote convergence on a single national or common language, on the grounds that doing so neglects their interests in having their own languages publicly affirmed and supported too.

Instead of selecting a set of linguistic outcomes for society to aim at, Patten recommends thinking about the justification of language rights and policies in procedural terms. To get a sense of what he means by this, consider the widely shared intuition that when the rules of the game are fair, then the outcomes arising from them will be too. So, for example, we generally do not think it unfair to lose a game because the other side played better, or got lucky, but we would do if the rules were rigged in their favour, or if the umpire was biased towards them. When it comes to how society treats languages, Patten suggests that something similar might apply, since, even though the speakers of different languages may not think of themselves as competing against one another, each language group is nevertheless striving for survival and success. The challenge, then, is to find the ideal set of language rights and policies, or rules of the game, so that no one has a legitimate complaint about whether a particular language flourishes or declines over time.

What kinds of language rights and policies could confer legitimacy on the linguistic outcomes that happen to arise? One obvious possibility is to treat linguistic differences in much the same way as traditional theories of liberalism treat religious differences, with the state neither encouraging nor discouraging any particular language, since then no one could complain that someone else's language was unfairly supported. Unfortunately, whether or not such an approach is desirable, a policy of 'linguistic disestablishment' does not seem feasible, because even countries without an official language, like the US, still have to choose which language(s) to use in the public education system, the courts and for administrative purposes, for example (Pool 1991, 496; Kymlicka 1995, 111; Carens 2000, 77–8; Patten 2014, 7–8).

Another option that suggests itself is to select language policies via democratic competition, an approach that also treats people as equals, since – in principle at least – everyone has the same influence over the final decision. An important attraction of this solution is its acknowledgement that disagreements about linguistic matters are reasonable, including those within language communities, reflecting the fact that people have different preferences and beliefs about the significance of their linguistic identities. Democratic procedures may therefore yield language policies that are perceived to be legitimate, if citizens themselves have been empowered to mobilize support for their preferred policies – for instance, by forming interest groups, campaigning or building coalitions. Of course, one might want to modify this procedure by imposing limits on the scope of democratic decision-making, perhaps constraining it with a scheme of liberal rights (see Laitin and Reich 2003 for a worked-out version of this proposal). So, for example, one might decide by majority vote which languages to use in major social institutions, but not the languages people can speak in their own homes.

Unlike the first proposal, a democratic procedure for settling on a scheme of language rights is certainly feasible. However, it is vulnerable to a different objection. This is that there is no certainty that majoritarian decision-making, even when constrained by a scheme of liberal rights, will respect the interests minority language speakers have in their own languages. For instance, in a society where two languages are spoken, one by a far larger proportion of the population, the minority may find itself consistently on the losing side in democratic competition. Although simply losing out in a democratic decision is not itself unjust, it would be if it jeopardized some of the basic interests that people have in the languages they speak. These interests are weighty enough for Patten to conclude that the members of linguistic minorities have a genuine moral claim for their languages to be publicly recognized and supported, regardless of the preferences of the majority. Since the democratic approach cannot guarantee this, it is unacceptable.

Linguistic interests

Some of the interests we have regarding languages are essentially communicative, such as being able to converse with potential employers or fellow citizens, or being able to engage with public institutions. Although significant, these cannot ground a moral claim for one's own language to be publicly recognized and supported, since communication is possible in any language, or through translation and interpretation. Meanwhile, Patten (2014, 202–3) thinks that people have two additional linguistic interests, both of which can ground such a claim. The first has to do with being able to access options one values, something that depends on the viability of one's language community. Drawing on Kymlicka, Patten argues that people who share the same language will often share preferences about art, food, work, social practices and the like. Since people have an interest in being able to access the options they value, and living a life according to their own plan, this means that they also have strong interests in the flourishing of their language group, because this will give them better access to the opportunities that matter to them. The second interest, meanwhile, has to do with identity, and satisfying it requires that one's language be afforded appropriate respect. Patten points out that many people are proud of their language, take pleasure in using it and enjoy its subtleties and intricacies, and feel denigrated when others do not afford it adequate respect or refuse to use it. As such, because people have an interest in their own identity, Patten concludes that they also have an interest in the social status and official recognition of their language, since these are clear indicators of public esteem and respect.

Taken together, these two interests suggest that each of us has a morally salient interest in having our own language recognized, and in having services and opportunities made available in it. Of course, it may not be feasible for a state to do so for every language its citizens speak, and so principled grounds will be required to justify withholding recognition from some of them, such as favouring the languages of long-settled minorities over those spoken by immigrants. In any case, amongst those languages to be recognized, Patten (2014) favours distributing recognition according to a principle of 'equal recognition', which he interprets to count in favour of a policy of 'prorated official multilingualism'.

To see what prorated official multilingualism might entail, first consider what a non-prorated policy would consist in. Under this rule, all official languages are treated in the same way – so if I can pay my taxes in one of them, then I should be able to do so in any of them, and if I can have my child publicly educated in one language, then I should be able to do so in any official language. Importantly, whether someone is allowed to avail of these opportunities has nothing to do with their language skills. Under this policy, someone is entitled to medical care in their own language even if they can speak the majority one, for example. Non-prorated official multilingualism, then, treats languages as equals, so that services and opportunities are offered in each language on similar terms. Meanwhile, Patten's prorated official multilingualism modifies this scheme by considering the number of people seeking services in each official language, so that the extent of support each receives depends on how many speakers it has. As Patten (2014, 200) acknowledges, this means that 'a more restricted set of public services may be offered in less widely spoken languages, or speakers of such languages might be expected to travel farther to find services in their own language, or the eligibility of such people to receive services in their own language may be constrained by a "where numbers warrant" proviso'.

It may seem surprising for Patten to claim that the basic rationale for prorated official multilingualism is that it satisfies the principle of equal recognition, since the policy he recommends seems to discriminate amongst different languages according to how many speakers they have. However, according to Patten (2014, 162), providing the same support for languages, regardless of how many speakers they have, would itself be unfair:

> Suppose that 99 percent of citizens speak and value language P and 1 percent speak and value language Q. Do we really want to say that equal recognition of those who value P and those who value Q requires that the state spend the same amount of money on services in each language, or provide the same facilities (same networks of schools, hospitals, etc.) in both P and Q?

The prorated version of official multilingualism that he supports escapes this objection, since it does not aim to be fair to languages themselves, but rather to 'establish fair conditions for individuals who speak different languages' (Patten 2014, 200). To illustrate his preferred view, Patten (2014, 162) invokes a hypothetical market, imagining that people are given an equal budget of purchasing tokens to spend on supporting their preferred language(s). The result of their decisions, he thinks, must be fair, since each has the same influence over the outcome. Further, assuming that most people would prefer to spend their tokens on their own languages, the hypothetical market would result in something very much like his favoured prorated model.

Debating equal recognition

Patten's (2014, 200–1) view, then, is that 'fairness to individuals requires offering the same per capita level of assistance to the different languages those individuals speak', and that equality is realized 'when people receive services in their own language equivalent in value to their fair claim on public resources rather than when they receive equivalent services'. Recognition, for him, does not mean what either Taylor or Galeotti intended by it – views considered in chapters 3 and 6, respectively. Instead, it has to do with the provision of financial and other supports. So, the more recognition granted to a language, the larger its share of direct and indirect state subsidies. Importantly, although his theory aims to explain when minorities have a moral claim to the public use of their language, he does not believe it to be the state's responsibility to secure the long-term sustainability of any particular language, since principles of linguistic justice concern procedures rather than outcomes. Consequently, his theory can be criticized in at least two different ways. On the one hand, one might accept his proceduralism but reject his prorated official multilingualism. Or, on the other hand, one might reject his proceduralism in favour of an outcome-based approach.

A compelling version of the first criticism has been suggested by Belgian philosopher Helder De Schutter (2017), who rejects Patten's prorated official multilingualism and instead endorses an equal services principle. According to this, public services provided in one language should be provided in all official languages, regardless of how many speakers they have, 'and in principle until the last speaker of each language dies' (De Schutter 2017, 77). By way of illustration, De Schutter (2017, 75) refers to Brussels, a bilingual city with far more French than Dutch speakers, but where, nevertheless, 'Dutch and French enjoy equal status and where state services (such as voting ballots, administrative and police services, public schools, state-subsidized theaters and museums, and so on) are offered in both languages'. An important implication of De Schutter's principle is that minorities will sometimes need to be allocated more than what Patten would regard as their fair share of resources. This might be because, for example, a per capita division of resources would mean that certain services could not be provided at all, such as a minority-language television station or school. Or it might be because economies of scale mean that some minority-language provisions are more expensive, such as school textbooks.

De Schutter (2017, 79) identifies a number of advantages of his preferred principle, such as it being more likely to support the survival of vulnerable languages, whose speakers can be confident that services and opportunities will always be available in their language, thereby countering the incentive for them to shift to the majority language. Further, he also points out that Patten's prorated approach might sometimes be bizarrely counter-intuitive, especially when it comes to things like visual symbols and anthems (De Schutter

2017, 81–2). For instance, the words 'European Parliament' are transcribed in all twenty-four official languages on the building in Brussels where it sits, and it would defeat the purpose of doing so if space were to be distributed according to the size of each language group. Notwithstanding these advantages, however, De Schutter thinks that the main principled grounds in support of his equal services approach is an appeal to fairness. Recall that, according to Patten, it would be unfair to ask the speakers of a large language to subsidize the linguistic preferences of a minority. Against this, De Schutter argues that Patten's hypothetical market is itself unfair, since it deprives minority-language speakers of the opportunity to secure the morally significant interests they have in their own languages (interests that, recall, have to do with options and identity). For instance, if 90 per cent of the population speak one language, and 10 per cent speak another, then members of the minority will know from the outset that they will be unable to get enough support for their language. It is this which is unfair, De Schutter argues, because it is simply a matter of bad luck that they happen to find themselves part of the minority. Since people should not be disadvantaged for reasons for which they are not responsible, De Schutter (2017, 83) concludes that speakers of minority languages ought to be given special and additional supports, including subsidies from speakers of the majority language, as recommended by his own equal services principle (see also De Schutter and Ypi 2012).

De Schutter's approach is an improvement on Patten's. However, it arguably still falls short in two ways. First, because it is narrowly focused on services provided by public institutions, it neglects some significant linguistic inequalities that occur elsewhere, such as in civil society or the marketplace (see Shorten 2018 for a more general discussion of this issue). For instance, speakers of minority languages are often frustrated by the unequal provision of commercial services, as when banks and shops operate only in the majority language, but De Schutter's equal services principle does not directly address these. Similarly, consider the demands made by linguistic minorities for publicly funded broadcasting services or arts festivals. Often, the rationale for these is not that the state already provides equivalent services for the majority, something that would be captured by De Schutter's principle, but rather that they are already available without public subsidies in the majority language, something which De Schutter's principle does not capture. Meanwhile, the second shortcoming of De Schutter's approach is that equal services do not guarantee equal recognition, since the influence of social attitudes and dominant language ideologies may mean that people who are able to speak the majority language are reluctant to request services in their own, minority, language. For instance, assessing the usage and provision of public services in Welsh, Huw Lewis (2017) has demonstrated that people are often unwilling to assert their right to Welsh-language services, instead communicating with public institutions through the medium of English, even when they would prefer not to.

The other way to criticize Patten's approach is to question his proceduralism. This, recall, refers to the idea that public institutions should not be designed with a view to achieving certain linguistic outcomes, such as the preservation of a vulnerable language or the dispersal of a common national language. Rather, they should establish a set of language rights and policies, or rules of the game, that treat the speakers of different languages fairly. However, rather than letting the chips fall where they will, some political theorists have instead argued for outcome-based approaches, including by drawing on values and concepts that closely resemble Patten's principle of equal recognition. One influential example of this is Philippe Van Parijs's (2011, 119) principle of 'parity of esteem', which insists that people not be 'stigmatized, despised, disparaged, or humiliated because of their collective identity'.

Neither Patten's prorated official multilingualism nor De Schutter's equal services approach can guarantee parity of esteem, since both procedures may yield outcomes experienced by speakers of minority languages as humiliating or stigmatizing. For example, consider a society where two languages are spoken, one of which is perceived to have high status, and the other, low status. Even if linguistic resources are distributed according to Patten's per capita formula, or if public services are provided equally, as De Schutter advises, it will still be very likely that the pressure to learn and use a language other than one's own will be distributed unequally. Whilst speakers of the low-status language will feel compelled to learn the other language, speakers of the high-status language will not. Consequently, when speakers of different languages meet and work together, they will systematically favour the high-status language. According to Van Parijs (2011, 141), this implicates speakers of the low-status language in a kind of 'linguistic bowing', an experience 'analogous to situations in which it is always the members of the same caste or gender that need to bow when meeting members of the other, or to get off the pavement where it is too narrow for two people to walk past each other'. Alternatively, consider a society in which a minority language gradually becomes ever more marginalized, despite getting its fair share of linguistic resources, or despite the availability of public services. If it were possible for the state to reverse this course without violating anyone else's rights, and if it instead follows a policy of official indifference, then speakers of that language will justifiably feel as if they and their language have been stigmatized as inferior (Van Parijs 2011, 146).

These examples suggest that we should either abandon proceduralism and instead embrace an outcome-orientated theory of linguistic justice, such as one that prioritizes parity of esteem, or instead accept that proceduralist principles will sometimes need to be supplemented by a concern with outcomes. Patten (2014, 210–31) himself ends up taking the latter course, endorsing a hybrid theory of language rights that allows occasional deviations from the principle of equal recognition. For instance, he argues that children whose parents speak languages spoken by only a small number of people must sometimes be required to learn a majority language, to ensure that as adults they will have an adequate range of opportunities for employment and social mobility. Likewise, he also acknowledges that equal recognition alone is not enough to correct some linguistic injustices, arguing for policies of affirmative action to support speakers of less prestigious languages, or languages whose speakers were discriminated against in the recent past.

Language Rights for Immigrants?

Some of the most prominent political theorists who defend official recognition or language promotion policies for minority languages, including both Patten (2014, 269–97) and Van Parijs (2011, 149–51), argue against the same measures when it comes to the languages spoken by immigrants. In this respect, they are following the lead of Kymlicka (1995, 95–100), who defended the similar and more general thesis that immigrants are not entitled to the same extensive set of cultural rights as national minorities and Indigenous peoples are. Furthermore, this distinction between the claims of settled minorities on the one hand, and immigrants on the other, is also reflected in both domestic and international public policy. For instance, the European Charter of Regional or Minority Languages requires its signatories to support and recognize their historical languages, but expressly excludes immigrant languages from its remit. This section will examine whether there are credible philosophical grounds for treating immigrants differently when it comes to cultural and linguistic rights, focusing on arguments suggested by Kymlicka and Patten.

To begin, it is worth noting that, although rarely, immigrants do indeed sometimes seek official recognition for their languages. For example, Patten (2014, 269) records a demand made by Abou Jahjah, a Belgian citizen originally from Lebanon, who called for Belgium to recognize Arabic alongside Dutch, French and German. Moreover, immigrants also often exhibit the kinds of identity- and autonomy-related interests that Patten and Kymlicka think can justify language promotion rights. Regarding identity, the strong and enduring attachments of many migrants to their first languages is a common literary theme, especially amongst exiles and émigrés. For example, reflecting on his life in exile in Paris, the South African writer and anti-Apartheid activist Breyten Breytenbach (1986, 20) observed that, although he had taken his language, Afrikaans, with him, it was 'rather like carrying the bones of your ancestors with you in a bag: they are white with silence, they do not talk back'. Meanwhile, the fate of Antoni Slonimski illustrates some of the autonomy-related interests that immigrants have in their languages. Slonimski was a Polish poet who took refuge in London during the Second World War, and who decided to return to Poland in 1951, of all moments. Asked why, he said that he had no qualms about living under capitalism, claimed to have nothing against the English and their ways, and denied feeling lonely, materially underprivileged or socially degraded. Rather, what he could no longer stand was that, whenever he tried to tell a joke to an English friend, his wit somehow abandoned him, and that every joke he told amongst the English was a dud, regardless of his tireless preparations. Thus, he resolved to cross the continent once again, this time for good, since at least there, regardless of the hardships and censorship, he could at least sit down at his regular table in his favourite cafe, crack a joke, and hear his admirers laugh (Baranczak 1989).

Given their professions, Breytenbach's and Slominski's connections to their ancestral languages were perhaps unusually strong. However, there is compelling empirical evidence to suggest that immigrants in general, as well as their children and grandchildren, have similar interests, taking a unique pleasure in using their own language and concerned to maintain links with it (see, e.g., Basch, Schiller and Blanc 1994; Ong 1999; Castles 2000). Accordingly, political theorists who wish to maintain a distinction between the claims of immigrants and those of established linguistic minorities cannot argue that only the latter have significant interests in their own languages, since it seems as if both groups can have broadly similar interests. Instead, then, they must find alternative grounds to reject immigrant language rights.

Properties, preferences and consent

Because Kymlicka was the first multiculturalist to argue expressly for a distinction between national minorities and immigrants, it makes sense to begin with his analysis. According to him, although immigrants are entitled to express their cultural identities, as well as to fair terms of integration including accommodations and other supports, three reasons explain why they are not entitled to the same cultural rights as national minorities, including rights to preserve and promote their language and culture.

First, immigrants usually lack some of the essential properties that are needed by groups to exercise their cultural rights, since they tend to be geographically dispersed, with few institutions, and so do not meet the 'territorial and institutional prerequisites for self-government' (Kymlicka 1995, 96). The relevance of this reason depends on the close connection Kymlicka draws between cultural rights and territorial self-governance rights, an issue examined in chapter 7 and so not considered again here. However, it is worth noting that Kymlicka's insistence on these prerequisites would probably disqualify a number of smaller regional or heritage languages, including ones currently recognized or supported by their states, such as Scottish Gaelic in the UK.

Second, immigrants themselves usually do not seek cultural rights, and instead prioritize accessing opportunities in the language(s) of their host society over replicating their culture of origin. A likely explanation for this is that immigrants are often keenly aware that their own future prospects, as well as those of their children, depend on successfully integrating into their new community (Kymlicka 1995, 61–3, 97–8, 176–81). Kymlicka's position here is rather more subtle than he is sometimes given credit for. For instance, when it comes to education, he criticizes a view defended by some anti-multiculturalists (e.g. Barry 2001a; Pogge 2003). This says that schools should try to mould the children of immigrants so they resemble unilingual native speakers, something that Kymlicka (1995, 97) describes as 'a deeply misguided policy'. Instead, according to him, immigrant parents might legitimately prefer for their children to be educated in their first language as well as that of the host society, both because bilingual education can be educationally beneficial, since children learn more effectively in a language they are familiar with, and because it serves their identity interests by retaining a link with their ancestral culture.

Third, and most importantly, Kymlicka suggests that, by voluntarily uprooting themselves, immigrants effectively waive their cultural rights. This is the consent argument, which he illustrates by imagining a group of Americans who choose to move to Sweden. According to Kymlicka, these immigrants would have no plausible claim on the Swedish government for institutions of self-government or public services in English. Even if Swedish society would be enriched by recreating the immigrants' culture – for instance, by endowing the Americans with extensive language and cultural rights – the immigrants themselves would 'have no right to such policies, for in choosing to leave the United States they relinquish the national rights that go with membership in their original culture' (Kymlicka 1995, 96).

Although powerful, the consent argument has only limited application. For one thing, it can only apply to first-generation immigrants, and not their children or grandchildren (Banai 2013, 198). Consequently, it cannot be employed to justify withholding language rights from people who are descendants of immigrants, such as Hispanics in the US or Turkish speakers in Germany. Further, as Kymlicka himself emphasizes, it can only apply to voluntary immigrants, and not, for example, to refugees, who did not consent to anything. Moreover, as Kymlicka (1995, 99) acknowledges, '[t]he line between involuntary refugees and voluntary immigrants is difficult to draw, especially in a world with massive injustice in the international distribution of resources, and with different levels of resources for human rights'. Although we can perhaps be confident that Kymlicka's Americans who moved to Sweden did so voluntarily, thereby waiving their cultural rights, we cannot be so confident about this also being true for many of today's migrants, especially those moving from poor regions to richer ones.

Another problem with the consent argument is that, at least according to some liberal political theorists, the most important individual rights are inalienable, such as rights to legal due process or freedom of religion. This observation puts Kymlicka in a tight spot. On the one hand, he might say that cultural rights can be waived because they are not as fundamental as these other rights. But this would seem to call into question the importance he elsewhere attributes to them (Carens 2000, 81). On the other hand, he might insist that cultural rights are just as significant as these rights, but that they are different in that they can be waived. However, if it is true that access to one's own societal culture really is a necessary precondition for freedom, as Kymlicka himself argues, then it is surely unlikely that anyone, including immigrants, could waive their cultural rights, since in doing so they would also be waiving their right to freedom. In response to this point, Alan Patten (2014, 283–4) has suggested that Kymlicka should have been more careful when presenting his own theory. True, Kymlicka does believe that people need access to a societal culture, and that this interest can justify cultural rights. However, he does not insist that people need access to their own culture, only that this is a reasonable expectation. Given this, the correct position for Kymlicka to have endorsed would have been that people have interests in being able to access their own societal culture, but that someone's freedom would not be 'fatally compromised' for being cut off from that culture (Patten 2014, 284). If this is the case, then one can consent to waiving one's cultural rights.

Conditional admission

Even if some immigrants can relinquish their cultural rights, perhaps this is an unreasonable thing to ask of them. Indeed, given the powerful attachments that bind people to their ancestral cultures and languages, it could be humiliating to demand they surrender their cultural rights in exchange for admission. Although Kymlicka did not consider this issue, Patten's analysis foregrounds it, and he proposes two arguments in support of allowing liberal democracies to prioritize the languages already spoken by members over those spoken by newcomers.

The first argument concerns a message that official recognition conveys to speakers of different languages. According to Patten (2014, 289), official recognition sends a signal that the state is 'throwing its support behind the culture or language in question', indicating to speakers that they should be confident about educating their children in it, and that they can reasonably expect opportunities to be available in it for some time to come. Meanwhile, official recognition could no longer send this signal if it became known that the state might summarily withdraw its recognition. For instance, imagine that a state withdraws recognition from an established language spoken by a small minority because a larger group of immigrants arrive, seeking cultural rights for themselves. Simply being aware of this possibility would leave speakers of all minority languages fearful that they too could find themselves left in the lurch one day. Consequently, Patten concludes that, if a state already extends recognition to its speakers of established languages, as it should do, then their claims ought to have priority over claims made by immigrants, since people plan their goals and projects around a set of expectations informed by the status quo.

The second argument is that it would be unreasonable to expect citizens to be impartial about the question of which languages should be recognized, since each of us is strongly attached to our own language. As such, it would ask too much of current citizens to insist that they give the same consideration to immigrant languages as to their own. Patten (2014, 293) is careful here to avoid saying that citizens, in their capacities as democratic co-legislators, are permitted to favour their own language over minority languages spoken by their fellow citizens, since, as 'public legislators', they 'have fairly strict obligations of impartiality to their fellow citizens'. Rather, he suggests that this does not apply to citizens taken collectively, who Patten thinks may permissibly prioritize their own languages and cultures over those of foreigners.

Both of these arguments depend on the assumption that language recognition is a scarce resource that is important to people, but not essential. If recognition were essential, of course, then it would be unacceptable to ask immigrants to relinquish their claims to it as a condition for entry. Conversely, if it were not important, in the sense of being connected to significant interests, then there would be no objection to making this request. Meanwhile, the scarcity thesis is built into Patten's per capita approach, which measures recognition according to the amount of resources and supports the state provides for each language, and which requires him to conclude that recognition cannot be extended to all languages.

One might doubt, however, that recognizing an immigrant language must consume a depleting pool of resources or indeed set back the interests of speakers of other languages, as Patten assumes. For instance, symbolic forms of recognition for immigrant languages need not undermine the status of established languages, and many citizens will hardly notice the use of one or two additional languages in official ceremonies or documents. Furthermore, even when it seems as if there is a limit to how many languages can be simultaneously recognized, creative ways of lifting that limit can often be found. For instance, some countries require that public servants such as police officers be competent in each official language, and it would surely be too much to expect these officials to learn multiple immigrant languages in addition to those already recognized. However, it certainly is not too much to expect public institutions, including especially police forces, to employ people from a representative range of immigrant backgrounds, meaning that at least some of their employees will speak the languages spoken by immigrants.

So, then, Patten's scarcity assumption is perhaps an exaggeration, since recognizing immigrant languages need not come at the expense of long-established ones. Furthermore, even if one accepts that recognition is sometimes a scarce good, as Patten does, there are still reasons to be sceptical about the specific grounds he gives for prioritizing the languages of national minorities over those of immigrants. The first argument assumes that the expectations citizens have about their language being recognized now and into the future are legitimate, but this is to beg the question, since it is the legitimacy of these expectations which is at stake. For instance, imagine a society in which one group of citizens currently benefits from the exploitation of another group, and that this exploitation is written into their shared constitution. Members of the first group might form life plans on the basis of expectations about maintaining their currently advantageous social position, but surely they would have no justice-based complaint if their exploitation were to be halted. By the same token, speakers of minority languages who already benefit from immigrant languages not being recognized surely cannot justify maintaining the status quo, thereby depriving future immigrants of an important social good, simply because they happen to have made plans on that basis.

Meanwhile, the second argument about permissible partiality trades on a distinction between local languages (amongst which citizens must be rigorously impartial) and immigrant languages (which citizens may permissibly disfavour). However, since what makes a language a local one is that it is spoken by citizens, then in practice nearly all immigrant languages will also be local ones too. Recall that Patten says that citizens 'have fairly strict obligations of impartiality to their fellow citizens', and so cannot favour their own languages ahead of those spoken by their fellow citizens. Even supposing, as Patten does, that citizens do not have the same 'strict obligation of impartiality' to foreigners, they still cannot disfavour the languages foreigners speak, if they are also spoken by their fellow citizens, which will often be the case.

Conclusion

In discussions of language rights and linguistic justice, multicultural political theorists have focused on language policies that aim to protect the rights and interests of people who do not speak the dominant or official language(s). Some of these are policies to provide things like translation and interpretation services for people without proficiency in the official language(s), thereby enabling them to access opportunities available in it. Others involve officially recognizing or promoting minority languages – for instance, by requiring them to be used in public institutions, by teaching them in schools, by funding newspapers or broadcasting, or even by trying to make them locally dominant. Following Kymlicka's framework, outlined in chapter 1, policies of the first kind are usually subsumed under the heading of polyethnic rights, since they aim to secure fair terms of integration for immigrants. Meanwhile, policies included in the second kind of approach are understood to be justified by language rights in the proper or in the strict sense, since they aim to support and encourage particular languages. Official recognition and language promotion rights are usually reserved for languages spoken by national minorities, and not immigrants. The practices of many states also reflect this distinction, and official recognition is currently universally restricted to languages spoken by long-settled minorities.

This chapter examined Kymlicka's and Patten's attempts to justify this distinction, and for denying cultural rights more generally to immigrants. It is surprisingly difficult to explain why language rights in the strict sense can be rightfully withheld from immigrants, and I have suggested that neither Kymlicka nor Patten entirely succeed in doing so. Kymlicka suggests that at least some migrants can be interpreted as having waived their cultural rights by voluntarily choosing to leave their country of origin. However, this clearly is not true of all migrants, and quite possibly is not the case for migrants in general. Meanwhile, Patten points out that, in addition to migrants consenting to waive their cultural rights, it must also be the case that host societies can legitimately ask this of them. However, both of the arguments he proposes to explain why democratic states can permissibly favour their own languages over those spoken by immigrants face difficulties.

When it comes to the content of a scheme of language rights, Patten suggests that instead of thinking about the linguistic outcomes a society wants to achieve, such as establishing a single national language or reviving a vulnerable one, it would be better to focus on getting the rules of the game right. One of the merits of this approach, as Patten emphasizes, is that it better reflects the liberal commitment to neutrality. However, as he also acknowledges, procedural approaches to linguistic justice have their limits, and at some point will need to incorporate a concern with avoiding particular outcomes. More importantly, the particular principle of linguistic justice that Patten defends – equal recognition – is arguably too frugal, not least because Patten's interpretation of recognition remains narrowly focused on the distribution of linguistic resources and says little about inequalities of power and status.

9

Conclusion

Multicultural political theory emerged during the 1990s, and by the turn of the millennium had assumed a prominent place within the wider sub-discipline of political theory. For example, widely used introductions to political theory added or included full chapters on the topic (e.g. Kymlicka 2001c; Farrelly 2004; Heywood 2004; McKinnon 2008), as did handbooks published for more advanced readers (e.g. Gaus and Kukathas 2004; Dryzek, Honig and Phillips 2006), and within a few years specialized textbooks dedicated to it began to appear (e.g. Murphy 2012; Crowder 2013). Since then, it may seem as if its star has been on the wane, as multiculturalism is less often named as the subject of professional colloquia, monographs or edited volumes, for instance. However, much like the supposed retreat of multiculturalism as a public policy orientation, discussed in chapter 5, this appearance is deceptive, and the topics and puzzles addressed by the multiculturalists of the 1990s and 2000s still preoccupy contemporary political theorists, albeit in new guises. The more accurate picture, I have suggested, is that the ambitious and comprehensive theories of multiculturalism developed by the likes of Kymlicka, Kukathas, Taylor and Parekh have been replaced by more fine-grained theories addressing particular issues and problems. However, these recent debates about language, nationality and religion are very much the offspring of those earlier multicultural theories, whose influence remains critical. So, overall, we are seeing not so much the decline or even death of multicultural political theory, but rather its dissipation into a number of different strands.

Today's politics of cultural diversity is sometimes understood as part of a broader category of identity politics. This term is used to describe a range of loosely connected social and political movements, representing groups defined by their members' shared experiences of injustice, marginalization and oppression. Amongst other things, identity politics encompasses political claims and projects associated with differences of race, gender and sexuality, as well as the differences emphasized by multiculturalists. It has a longer pedigree than multiculturalism, and is often traced back to the civil rights, feminist and gay rights movements that emerged during the second half of the twentieth century. Nevertheless, it has been reinvigorated in recent years, as a result of theoretical innovations, such as those drawing on the concepts of intersectionality (Crenshaw 1990; Hill Collins and Bilge 2016) and structural injustice (Young 2011), as well as in response to political developments, including the #MeToo and Black Lives Matter movements, for instance. Indeed, the language of identity politics has become so prevalent that it is now even invoked by populist and radical right-wing political movements, exploiting the decline of class-based politics and responding to disaffection among white men (Fukuyama 2018).

Locating multiculturalism within this wider context of identity politics is certainly not inappropriate, since there are clear parallels between the experiences, interests, struggles and strategies of the groups identified by each term (Appiah 2005, 2018). However, assimilating multiculturalism into identity politics, let alone allowing the label of identity politics to displace that of multiculturalism, risks obscuring the distinctive and original contributions made by multicultural political theory. Vigilant of this possibility, this book has presented multiculturalism as a distinctive body of ideas and arguments, overlapping in important ways with other political movements, and drawing on a variety of intellectual traditions, but also with its own concerns and organizing concepts, which include autonomy, toleration, recognition, dialogue and belonging. Moreover, it has sought to establish the continuing relevance of these concepts and arguments, especially during the last three chapters, each of which illustrated how the various strands of multicultural political theory can fruitfully be brought to bear on a wide variety of political claims advanced by cultural minorities today.

As it has been represented here, multicultural political theory is far from being an internally consistent or systematic body of arguments. This is not to deny that there are individual theories of multiculturalism which exhibit these properties, and indeed some of these were discussed in chapters 2 and 3. Rather, what I have suggested is that multicultural political theory as a whole contains multiple strands, drawn from different traditions, sometimes in tension with one another, but nevertheless making important contributions to how we might understand and address the different challenges of cultural diversity. Though we must not eliminate the possibility of doing so in the future, for the time being it would be prudent to give up on the project of developing a single, cohesive and overarching framework from which to address all of the issues raised by the politics of diversity. Instead, it is better to think of multicultural political theory as a set of overlapping responses to a series of interrelated, but distinctive, problems.

This way of thinking about multicultural political theory carries two implications that are worth emphasizing. First, multiculturalism is not simply an extension of liberalism. True, many liberal multiculturalists have tried to demonstrate that their own preferred version of liberalism already contains a satisfactory response to multiculturalism, and in doing so have revealed how rich and malleable a tradition liberal political theory is. However, too often, liberals treat multiculturalism as continuous, or even synonymous, with liberalism, and this comes at the cost of missing the opportunity to learn from other intellectual and cultural traditions. Second, multiculturalism is not a comprehensive political theory, and nor should it aspire to be one. As I have suggested, its arguments have significant limitations and gaps, especially when it comes to addressing racism, as well as the legacies and ongoing impact of settler colonialism. So, in the end, arguments drawn from multicultural political theory can only provide tentative guidance for real-world politics, and will need to be supported by ideas drawn from other branches of political theory.

Bibliography

Appiah, K. (1994) 'Identity, Authenticity, Survival: Multicultural Societies and Social Reproduction' in A. Gutmann (ed.) *Multiculturalism and the Politics of Recognition* (Princeton University Press)

Appiah, K. (1997) 'The Multiculturalist Misunderstanding', *New York Review of Books*, October 9

Appiah, K. (2005) *The Ethics of Identity* (Princeton University Press)

Appiah, K. (2006) *Cosmopolitanism: Ethics in a World of Strangers* (New York: W. W. Norton)

Appiah, K. (2018) *The Lies That Bind: Rethinking Identity* (London: Profile Books)

Arneson, R. (2003) 'Liberal Neutrality on the Good: An Autopsy' in S. Wall and G. Klosko (eds.) *Perfectionism and Neutrality: Essays in Liberal Theory* (Lanham, MD: Rowman & Littlefield)

Arneson, R. (2010) 'Against Freedom of Conscience', *San Diego Law Review*, 47, 1015–40.

Bader, V. (2007) *Secularism or Democracy? Associational Governance of Religious Diversity* (Amsterdam University Press).

Balint, P. (2017) *Respecting Toleration: Traditional Liberalism and Contemporary Diversity* (Oxford University Press)

Banai, A. (2013) 'Language Recognition and the Fair Terms of Inclusion: Minority Languages in the European Union' in P. Balint and S. G. de Latour (eds.) *Liberal Multiculturalism and the Fair Terms of Integration* (Basingstoke: Palgrave)

Banting, K. (2014) 'Transatlantic Convergence? The Archaeology of Immigrant Integration in Canada and Europe', *International Journal*, 69/1, 66–84

Banting, K., R. Johnston, W. Kymlicka and S. Soroka (2006) 'Do Multiculturalism Policies Erode the Welfare State? An Empirical Analysis' in K. Banting and W. Kymlicka (eds.) *Multiculturalism and the Welfare State: Recognition and Redistribution in Contemporary Democracies* (Oxford University Press)

Banting, K., and W. Kymlicka (eds.) (2006) *Multiculturalism and the Welfare State: Recognition and Redistribution in Contemporary Democracies* (Oxford University Press)

Banting, K., and W. Kymlicka (2013) 'Is There Really a Retreat from Multiculturalism Policies?' *Comparative European Politics*, 11/5, 577–98

Banting, K., and W. Kymlicka (eds.) (2017) *The Strains of Commitment: The Political Sources of Solidarity in Diverse Societies* (Oxford University Press)

Baranczak, S. (1989) 'Tongue Tied Eloquence: Notes on Language, Exile, and Writing', *University of Toronto Quarterly*, 58, 429–38

Bardon, A., and E. Ceva (2018) 'The Ethics of Toleration and Religious Accommodation' in A. Lever and A. Poama (eds.) *The Routledge Handbook of Ethics and Public Policy* (Abingdon: Routledge)

Barry, B. (2001a) *Culture and Equality: An Egalitarian Critique of Multiculturalism* (Cambridge: Polity)

Barry, B. (2001b) 'The Muddles of Multiculturalism', *New Left Review*, 8, 49–71

Barry, B. (2002) 'Second Thoughts, and Some First Thoughts Revived' in P. Kelly (ed.) *Multiculturalism Reconsidered* (Cambridge: Polity)

Basch, L., N. Schiller and C. Blanc (1994) *Nations Unbound: Transnational Projects, Postcolonial Predicaments and Deterritorialised Nation-States* (Abingdon: Routledge)

Baumeister, A. (2019) 'Religion and the Claims of Citizenship: The Dangers of Institutional Accommodation' in J. Seglow and A. Shorten (eds.) *Religion and Political Theory* (London: ECPR / Rowman & Littlefield)

Baumgartner, C. (2019) '(Not) Shaking Hands with People of the Opposite Sex: Civility, National Identity, and Accommodation' in J. Seglow and A. Shorten (eds.) *Religion and Political Theory* (London: ECPR / Rowman & Littlefield)

Baycan, E., and M. Gianni (2019) 'What is Wrong with the Swiss Minaret Ban?' in J. Seglow and A. Shorten (eds.) *Religion and Political Theory* (London: ECPR / Rowman & Littlefield)

Bell, D. (2014) 'What Is Liberalism?' *Political Theory*, 42/6, 682–715

Benhabib, S. (2002) *The Claims of Culture: Equality and Diversity in the Global Era* (Princeton University Press)

Bhargava, R. (2015) 'Is European Secularism Secular Enough?' in J. Cohen and C. Laborde (eds.) *Religion, Secularism, and Constitutional Democracy* (New York: Columbia University Press)

Bonotti, M. (2012) 'Beyond Establishment and Separation: Political Liberalism, Religion and Democracy', *Res Publica*, 18/4, 333–49

Bouchard, G. (2011) 'What is Interculturalism?' *McGill Law Journal*, 56/2, 435–68

Bouchard, G. (2015) *Interculturalism: A View from Quebec*, trans. H. Scott (University of Toronto Press)

Bouchard, G. (2016) 'Quebec Interculturalism and Canadian Multiculturalism' in N. Meer, T. Modood and R. Zapata-Barrero (eds.) *Multiculturalism and Interculturalism: Debating the Dividing Lines* (Edinburgh University Press)

Bouchard, G., and C. Taylor (2008) *Building for the Future: A Time for Reconciliation* (Report on the Consultation Commission on Accommodation Practices Related to Cultural Differences) (Quebec City: Government of Quebec)

Bou-Habib, P. (2006) 'A Theory of Religious Accommodation', *Journal of Applied Philosophy*, 23/1, 109–26

Bowen, J. (2011) *Can Islam Be French? Pluralism and Pragmatism in a Secularist State* (Princeton University Press)

Brennan, T. (1997) *At Home in the World: Cosmopolitanism Now* (Cambridge, MA: Harvard University Press)

Breytenbach, B. (1986) *End Papers: Essays, Letters, Articles of Faith, Workbook Notes* (London: Faber)

Brudney, D. (2005) 'On Noncoercive Establishment', *Political Theory*, 33, 812–39

Buchanan, A. (1991) *Secession: The Morality of Political Divorce from Fort Sumter to Lithuania and Quebec* (Boulder: Westview Press)

Caney, S. (2005) *Justice Beyond Borders: A Global Political Theory* (Oxford University Press)

Caney, S. (2010) 'Cosmopolitanism' in D. Bell (ed.) *Ethics and World Politics* (Oxford University Press)

Cantle, T. (2001) *Community Cohesion: A Report of the Independent Review Team (The 'Cantle Report')* (London: UK Home Office)

Cantle, T. (2008) *Community Cohesion: A New Framework for Race and Diversity* (Basingstoke: Palgrave Macmillan)

Cantle, T. (2012) *Interculturalism: For the Era of Cohesion and Diversity* (Basingstoke: Palgrave Macmillan)

Cantle, T. (2016) 'The Case for Interculturalism, Plural Identities and

Cohesion' in N. Meer, T. Modood and R. Zapata-Barrero (eds.) *Multiculturalism and Interculturalism: Debating the Dividing Lines* (Edinburgh University Press)

Carens, J. (2000) *Culture, Citizenship, and Community: A Contextual Exploration of Justice as Evenhandedness* (Oxford University Press)

Castles, S. (2000) *Ethnicity and Globalization: From Migrant Worker to Transnational Citizen* (London: Sage)

Chin, C. (2019) 'The Concept of Belonging: Critical, Normative and Multicultural', *Ethnicities*, 19/5, 715–39

Chin, R. (2017) *The Crisis of Multiculturalism in Europe: A History* (Princeton University Press)

Clayton, M., A. Mason, A. Swift and R. Wareham (2021) 'The Political Morality of School Composition: The Case of Religious Selection', *British Journal of Political Science*, 51/2, 827–44

CMEB (Commission on the Future of Multi-Ethnic Britain) (2000) *The Future of Multi-Ethnic Britain* (London: Profile Books)

Cohen, J. (2015) 'Freedom of Religion, Inc: Whose Sovereignty?' *Netherlands Journal of Legal Philosophy*, 3, 169–210

Cohen, J. (2017) 'Sovereignty, the Corporate Religious, and Jurisdictional/Political Pluralism' in C. Laborde and A. Bardon (eds.) *Religion in Liberal Political Philosophy* (Oxford University Press)

Corvino, J., R. Anderson and S. Girgis (2017) *Debating Religious Liberty and Discrimination* (New York: Oxford University Press)

Coulthard, G. (2007) 'Subjects of Empire: Indigenous Peoples and the "Politics of Recognition" in Canada', *Contemporary Political Theory*, 6/4, 437–60

Coulthard, G. (2014) *Red Skin, White Masks: Rejecting the Colonial Politics of Recognition* (Minneapolis: University of Minnesota Press)

Council of Europe (2008) *White Paper on Intercultural Dialogue: 'Living Together as Equals in Dignity'* (Strasbourg: Council of Europe)

Crenshaw, K. (1990) 'Mapping the Margins: Intersectionality, Identity Politics, and Violence Against Women of Color', *Stanford Law Review*, 43/6, 1241–99

Crowder, G. (2013) *Theories of Multiculturalism: An Introduction* (Cambridge: Polity)

De Schutter, H. (2005) 'Nations, Boundaries and Justice: On Will Kymlicka's Theory of Multinationalism', *Ethical Perspectives*, 12/1, 17–40

De Schutter, H. (2008) 'The Linguistic Territoriality Principle: A Critique', *Journal of Applied Philosophy*, 25/2, 105–20

De Schutter, H. (2011) 'Federalism as Fairness', *The Journal of Political Philosophy*, 19/2, 167–89

De Schutter, H. (2017) 'Two Principles of Equal Language Recognition', *Critical Review of International Social and Political Philosophy*, 20/1, 75–87

De Schutter, H., and L. Ypi (2012) 'Language and Luck', *Politics, Philosophy & Economics*, 11/4, 357–81

Deveaux, M. (2000) *Cultural Pluralism and Dilemmas of Justice* (Ithaca: Cornell University Press)

Deveaux, M. (2005) 'A Deliberative Approach to Conflicts of Culture' in A. Eisenberg and J. Spinner-Halev (eds.) *Minorities Within Minorities: Equality, Rights and Diversity* (Cambridge University Press)

Deveaux, M. (2006) *Gender and Justice in Multicultural Liberal States* (Oxford University Press)

Dryzek, J., B. Honig and A. Phillips (eds.) (2006) *The Oxford Handbook of Political Theory* (Oxford University Press)

Dunbar, R., and R. McKelvey (2018) 'Must States Provide Services to Migrants in their Own Languages?' in F. Grin, M. Célio Conceição, P. A. Kraus, et al. (eds.) *The MIME Vademecum* (Switzerland: Mobility and Inclusion in Multilingual Europe)

Dworkin, R. (1985) *A Matter of Principle* (Cambridge, MA: Harvard University Press)

Dworkin, R. (2011) *Justice for Hedgehogs* (Cambridge, MA: Harvard University Press)

Dworkin, R. (2013) *Religion without God* (Cambridge, MA: Harvard University Press)

Eberhard, D., G. Simons and C. Fennig (eds.) (2020) *Ethnologue: Languages of the World, Twenty-Third Edition* (Dallas, TX: SIL International). Online version: www.ethnologue.com

Elazar, D. (1987) *Exploring Federalism* (Tuscaloosa: University of Alabama Press)

Farrelly, C. (2004) *Introduction to Contemporary Political Theory* (London: Sage)

Festenstein, M. (2005) *Negotiating Diversity: Culture, Deliberation, Trust* (Cambridge: Polity)

Fraser, N. (2001) 'Recognition Without Ethics', *Theory, Culture & Society*, 18, 21–42

Fraser, N. (2008) *Adding Insult to Injury* (London: Verso)

Fraser, N., and A. Honneth (2003) *Redistribution or Recognition: A Political-Philosophical Exchange* (London: Verso)

Freeden, M. (1996) *Ideologies and Political Theory: A Conceptual Approach* (Oxford University Press)

Freeden, M. (2005) *Liberal Languages: Ideological Imaginations and Twentieth-Century Progressive Thought* (Princeton University Press)

Fukuyama, F. (2018) *Identity: The Demand for Dignity and the Politics of Resentment* (New York: Farrar, Straus, and Giroux)

Gagnon, A.-G., and R. Iacovino (2004) 'Interculturalism: Expanding the Boundaries of Citizenship' in R. Máiz and F. Requejo (eds.) *Democracy, Nationalism and Multiculturalism* (London: Frank Cass)

Galeotti, A. E. (1993) 'Citizenship and Equality: The Place for Toleration', *Political Theory*, 21/4, 585–605

Galeotti, A. E. (2002) *Toleration as Recognition* (Cambridge University Press)

Galston, W. (1995) 'Two Concepts of Liberalism', *Ethics*, 105/3, 516–34

Galston, W. (2002) *Liberal Pluralism: The Implications of Value Pluralism for Political Theory and Practice* (Cambridge University Press)

Garnett, R. (2016) 'The Freedom of the Church: (Toward) An Exposition, Translation and Defence' in M. Schwartzman, C. Flanders and Z. Robinson (eds.) *The Rise of Corporate Religious Liberty* (Oxford University Press)

Garvey, J. H. (1996) *What are Freedoms For?* (Cambridge, MA: Harvard University Press)

Gaus, G. (2011) *The Order of Public Reason: A Theory of Freedom and Morality in a Diverse and Bounded World* (Cambridge University Press)

Gaus, G., and C. Kukathas (eds.) (2004) *Handbook of Political Theory* (London: Sage)

Gellner, E. (1983) *Nations and Nationalism* (Ithaca: Cornell University Press)

Gonzáles Núñez, G. (2016) *Translating in Linguistically Diverse Societies: Translation Policy in the United Kingdom* (Amsterdam: John Benjamins)

Goodin, R. (2006) 'Liberal Multiculturalism: Protective and Polyglot', *Political Theory*, 34, 289–303

Goodman, S. (2014) *Immigration and Membership Politics in Western Europe* (Cambridge University Press)

Gray, J. (1986) *Liberalism* (Milton Keynes: Open University Press)

Green, L. (1994) 'Internal Minorities and their Rights' in J. Baker (ed.) *Group Rights* (Toronto University Press)

Greenawalt, K. (2008) *Religion and the Constitution*, Volume II: *Establishment and Fairness* (Princeton University Press)

Grillo, R. (2007) 'An Excess of Alterity? Debating Difference in a Multicultural Society', *Ethnic and Racial Studies*, 30/6, 979–98

Habermas, J. (1996) *Between Facts and Norms: Contributions to a Discourse Theory of Law and Democracy*, trans. W. Rehg (Cambridge: Polity)

Habermas, J. (1998) *The Inclusion of the Other: Studies in Political Theory* (Cambridge: Polity)

Hall, S. (2000) 'Conclusion: The Multicultural Question' in B. Hesse (ed.) *Un/settled Multiculturalisms: Diasporas, Entanglements, Transruptions* (London: Zed Books)

Haslanger, S. (2000) 'Gender and Race: (What) Are They? (What) Do We Want Them to Be?', *Noûs*, 34/1, 31–55

Heywood, A. (2004) *Political Theory: An Introduction* (Basingstoke: Palgrave)

Hill Collins, P., and S. Bilge (2016) *Intersectionality* (Cambridge: Polity)

Hohfeld, W. (1919) *Fundamental Legal Conceptions as Applied in Judicial Reasoning and Other Legal Essays* (New Haven: Yale University Press)

Honneth, A. (1996) *The Struggle for Recognition* (Cambridge: Polity)

Honneth, A. (2007) *Disrespect: The Normative Foundations of Critical Theory* (Cambridge: Polity)

Horton, J. (2006) 'John Gray and the Political Theory of Modus Vivendi', *Critical Review of International Social and Political Philosophy*, 9, 155–69

Horton, J. (2010) 'Realism, Liberal Moralism and a Political Theory of Modus Vivendi', *European Journal of Political Theory*, 9, 431–48

Horton, J. (2011) 'Modus Vivendi and Religious Conflict' in M. Mookherjee (ed.) *Democracy, Religious Pluralism and the Liberal Dilemma of Accommodation* (Dordrecht: Springer)

Horwitz, P. (2009) 'Churches as First Amendment Institutions: Of Sovereignty and Spheres', *Harvard Civil Rights – Civil Liberties Law Review*, 44, 79–131

Ivison, D. (2020) *Can Liberal States Accommodate Indigenous Peoples?* (Cambridge: Polity)

Jaggar, A. (1999) 'Multicultural Democracy', *The Journal of Political Philosophy*, 7/3, 308–29

Jeffers, C. (2019) 'Cultural Constructionism' in J. Glasgow, S. Haslanger, C. Jeffers and Q. Spencer (eds.) *What is Race? Four Philosophical Views* (New York: Oxford University Press)

Jewkes, M., and J.-F. Grégoire (2016) 'Models of Citizenship,

Inclusion and Empowerment: National Minorities, Immigrants and Animals? An Interview with Will Kymlicka', *Political Theory*, 44/3, 394–409

Jones, P. (1994) 'Bearing the Consequences of Belief', *The Journal of Political Philosophy*, 2/1, 24–43

Jones, P. (2006) 'Toleration, Recognition and Identity', *The Journal of Political Philosophy*, 14/2, 123–43

Jones, P. (2015) 'Toleration, Religion, and Accommodation', *European Journal of Philosophy*, 23/3, 542–63

Joppke, C. (2004) 'The Retreat of Multiculturalism in the Liberal State: Theory and Policy', *British Journal of Sociology*, 55/2, 237–57

Joppke, C. (2013) 'Through the European Looking Glass: Citizenship Tests in the USA, Australia and Canada', *Citizenship Studies*, 17/1, 1–15

Joppke, C. (2015) *The Secular State Under Siege: Religion and Politics in Europe and America* (Cambridge: Polity)

Joppke, C. (2017) *Is Multiculturalism Dead? Crisis and Persistence in the Constitutional State* (Cambridge: Polity)

Joppke, C. (2018) 'War of Words: Interculturalism v. Multiculturalism', *Comparative Migration Studies*, 6/11, 1–10

Joppke, C., and S. Lukes (eds.) (1999) *Multicultural Questions* (Oxford University Press)

Kelly, P. (2005) *Liberalism* (Cambridge: Polity)

Kloss, H. (1977) *The American Bilingual Tradition* (Rowley, MA: Newbury House)

Koppelman, A. (2006) 'Is it Fair to Give Religion Special Treatment?' *University of Illinois Law Review*, 571–603

Koppelman, A. (2017) 'A Rawlsian Defence of Special Treatment for Religion' in C. Laborde and A. Bardon (eds.) *Religion in Liberal Political Philosophy* (Oxford University Press)

Kukathas, C. (1992) 'Are There Any Cultural Rights?' *Political Theory*, 20, 105–39

Kukathas, C. (1998) 'Liberalism and Multiculturalism: The Politics of Indifference', *Political Theory*, 26/5, 686–99

Kukathas, C. (2001) 'Is Feminism Bad for Multiculturalism?' *Public Affairs Quarterly*, 15/2, 83–98

Kukathas, C. (2003) *The Liberal Archipelago: A Theory of Diversity and Freedom* (Oxford University Press)

Kymlicka, W. (1989a) *Liberalism, Community and Culture* (Oxford University Press)

Kymlicka, W. (1989b) 'Liberal Individualism and Liberal Neutrality', *Ethics*, 99, 883–905

Kymlicka, W. (1992) 'Two Models of Pluralism and Tolerance', *Analyse & Kritik*, 14/1, 33–56

Kymlicka, W. (1995) *Multicultural Citizenship: A Liberal Theory of Minority Rights* (Oxford University Press)

Kymlicka, W. (1998) 'Introduction: An Emerging Consensus?' *Ethical Theory and Moral Practice*, 1, 143–57

Kymlicka, W. (1999) 'Liberal Complacencies' in S. Okin, M. Nussbaum, J. Cohen and M. Howard (eds.) (1999) *Is Multiculturalism Bad for Women?* (Princeton University Press)

Kymlicka, W. (2001a) *Politics in the Vernacular: Nationalism, Multiculturalism and Citizenship* (Oxford University Press)

Kymlicka, W. (2001b) 'Territorial Boundaries: A Liberal Egalitarian Perspective' in D. Miller and S. Hashmi (eds.) *Boundaries and Justice: Diverse Ethical Perspectives* (Princeton University Press)

Kymlicka, W. (2001c) *Contemporary Political Philosophy*, second edition (Oxford University Press)

Kymlicka, W. (2009) 'The Governance of Religious Diversity: The Old and the New' in P. Bramadat and M. Koenig (eds.) *International Migration and the Governance of Religious Diversity* (Montreal: McGill-Queen's University Press)

Kymlicka, W. (2015a) 'The Essentialist Critique of Multiculturalism: Theories, Policies, Ethos' in V. Uberoi and T. Modood (eds.) *Multiculturalism Rethought: Interpretations, Dilemmas and New Directions* (Edinburgh University Press)

Kymlicka, W. (2015b) 'Solidarity in Diverse Societies: Beyond Neoliberal Multiculturalism and Welfare Chauvinism', *Comparative Migration Studies*, 3/17, 1–19

Kymlicka, W. (2016) 'Defending Diversity in an Era of Populism: Multiculturalism and Interculturalism Compared' in N. Meer, T. Modood and R. Zapata-Barrero (eds.) *Multiculturalism and Interculturalism: Debating the Dividing Lines* (Edinburgh University Press)

Laborde, C. (2005) 'Secular Philosophy and Muslim Headscarves in Schools', *The Journal of Political Philosophy*, 13/3, 305–29

Laborde, C. (2008) *Critical Republicanism: The Hijab Controversy and Political Philosophy* (Oxford University Press)

Laborde, C. (2017) *Liberalism's Religion* (Cambridge, MA: Harvard University Press)

Lægaard, S. (2015) 'Disaggregating Corporate Freedom of Religion', *Netherlands Journal of Legal Philosophy*, 44, 221–30

Lægaard, S. (2017) 'What's the Problem with Symbolic Religious Establishment? The Alienation and Symbolic Equality Accounts' in C. Laborde and A. Bardon (eds.) *Religion in Liberal Political Philosophy* (Oxford University Press)

Laitin, D., and R. Reich (2003) 'A Liberal Democratic Approach to Language Justice' in W. Kymlicka and A. Patten (eds.) *Language Rights and Political Theory* (Oxford University Press)

Laycock, D. (1990) 'The Remnants of Free Exercise', *Supreme Court Review*, 1–68

Laycock, D. (2009) 'Church Autonomy Revisited', *Georgetown Journal of Law and Public Policy*, 7, 253–78

Lear, J. (2006) *Radical Hope: Ethics in the Face of Cultural Devastation* (Cambridge, MA: Harvard University Press)

Leiter, B. (2013) *Why Tolerate Religion?* (Princeton University Press)

Lenard, P., and D. Miller (2018) 'Trust and National Identity' in E. Uslaner (ed.) *The Oxford Handbook of Social and Political Trust* (Oxford University Press)

Lever, A. (2017) 'Equality and Conscience: Ethics and the Provision of Public Services' in C. Laborde and A. Bardon (eds.) *Religion in Liberal Political Philosophy* (Oxford University Press)

Levey, G. B. (2016) 'Diversity, Duality and Time' in N. Meer, T. Modood and R. Zapata-Barrero (eds.) *Multiculturalism and Interculturalism: Debating the Dividing Lines* (Edinburgh University Press)

Levrau, F., and P. Loobuyck (2018) 'Introduction: Mapping the Multiculturalism–Interculturalism Debate', *Contemporary Migration Studies*, 6, 13

Levy, J. (2000) *The Multiculturalism of Fear* (Oxford University Press)

Levy, J. (2007) 'Contextualism, Constitutionalism, and Modus Vivendi Approaches' in A. Laden and D. Owen (eds.) *Multiculturalism and Political Theory* (Cambridge University Press)

Levy, J. (2015) *Rationalism, Pluralism and Freedom* (Oxford University Press)

Lewis, H. (2017) 'Realising Linguistic Justice: Resources versus Capabilities', *Journal of Multicultural and Multilingual Development*, 38/7, 595–606

Locke, J. (2010) 'A Letter Concerning Toleration' in R. Vernon (ed.) *Locke on Toleration*, trans. Michael Silverthorne (Cambridge University Press)

McConnell, M. (1985) 'Accommodation of Religion', *Supreme Court Law Review*, 1–59

McConnell, M. (2000) 'Believers as Equal Citizens' in N. Rosenblum (ed.) *Obligations of Citizenship and Demands of Faith* (Princeton University Press)

Maclure, J., and C. Taylor (2011) *Secularism and Freedom of Conscience*, trans. J. M. Todd (Cambridge, MA: Harvard University Press)

McKinnon, C. (ed.) (2008) *Issues in Political Theory* (Oxford University Press)

McNay, L. (2008) *Against Recognition* (Cambridge: Polity)

Manent, P. (1996) *An Intellectual History of Liberalism* (Princeton University Press)

Margalit, A., and M. Halbertal (1994) 'Liberalism and the Right to Culture', *Social Research*, 61, 491–510

Margalit, A., and J. Raz (1990) 'National Self-Determination', *Journal of Philosophy*, 87, 439–61

Markell, P. (2003) *Bound by Recognition* (Princeton University Press)

Mason, A. (1990) 'Autonomy, Liberalism and State Neutrality', *The Philosophical Quarterly*, 40, 433–52

Mason, A. (1999) 'Political Community, Liberal Nationalism, and the Ethics of Assimilation', *Ethics*, 109/2, 261–86

Mason, A. (2000) *Community, Solidarity and Belonging* (Cambridge University Press)

May, S. (2012) *Language and Minority Rights: Ethnicity, Nationalism and the Politics of Language* (Abingdon: Routledge)

May, S. C. (2017) 'Exemptions for Conscience' in C. Laborde and A. Bardon (eds.) *Religion in Liberal Political Philosophy* (Oxford University Press)

Meer, N., and T. Modood (2012) 'How Does Interculturalism Contrast with Multiculturalism?' *Journal of Intercultural Studies*, 33/2, 175–96

Meer, N., and T. Modood (2015) 'Religious Pluralism in the United States and Britain: Its Implications for Muslims and Nationhood', *Social Compass*, 62/4, 526–40

Merry, M. (2013) *Equality, Citizenship, and Segregation: A Defense of Separation* (Basingstoke: Palgrave Macmillan)

Miller, D. (1995) *On Nationality* (Oxford University Press)

Miller, D. (2000) *Citizenship and National Identity* (Cambridge: Polity)

Miller, D. (2002) 'Liberalism, Equal Opportunities and Cultural Commitments' in P. Kelly (ed.) *Multiculturalism Reconsidered* (Cambridge: Polity)

Miller, D. (2016) 'Majorities and Minarets: Religious Freedom and Public Space', *British Journal of Political Science*, 46/2, 437–56

Miller, D. (2018) 'The Life and Death of Multiculturalism' in E. Goodyear-Grant, R. Johnston, W. Kymlicka and J. Myles (eds.) *Federalism and the Welfare State in a Multicultural World* (Montreal: McGill-Queen's University Press)

Miller, D. (2021) 'What's Wrong with Religious Establishment?' *Criminal Law and Philosophy*, 15/1, 75–89

Mills, C. (1997) *The Racial Contract* (London: Cornell University Press)

Modood, T. (2007) *Multiculturalism: A Civic Idea* (Cambridge: Polity)

Modood, T. (2009) 'Muslims, Religious Equality and Secularism' in G. B. Levey and T. Modood (eds.) *Secularism, Religion and Multicultural Citizenship* (Cambridge University Press)

Modood, T. (2013) *Multiculturalism: A Civic Idea*, second edition (Cambridge: Polity)

Modood, T. (2016) 'State–Religion Connections and Multicultural Citizenship' in J. Cohen and C. Laborde (eds.) *Religion, Secularism and Constitutional Democracy* (New York: Columbia University Press)

Modood, T. (2017a) 'Must Interculturalists Misrepresent Multi-culturalism?', *Comparative Migration Studies*, 5/15, 1–17

Modood, T. (2017b) 'Multiculturalism and Moderate Secularism', in J. Shook and P. Zuckerman (eds) *Oxford Handbook on Secularism* (Oxford University Press)

Modood, T. (2018) 'Interculturalism: Not a New Public Policy Paradigm', *Comparative Migration Studies*, 6/22, 1–8

Modood, T. (2019a) *Essays on Secularism and Multiculturalism* (London: ECPR / Rowman & Littlefield)

Modood, T. (2019b) 'A Multicultural Nationalism?' *Brown Journal of World Affairs*, 25/2, 233–46

Modood, T., and R. Kastoryano (2006) 'Secularism and the Accommodation of Muslims in Europe' in T. Modood, A. Triandafyllidou and R. Zapata-Barrero (eds.) *Multiculturalism, Muslims and Citizenship* (Abingdon: Routledge)

Mulhall, S., and A. Swift (1996) *Liberals and Communitarians* (Oxford: Blackwell Publishing)

Muñiz-Fraticelli, V. (2014) *The Structure of Pluralism* (Oxford University Press)

Murphy, M. (2012) *Multiculturalism: A Critical Introduction* (Abingdon: Routledge)

Norman, W. (1994) 'Towards a Philosophy of Federalism' in J. Baker (ed.) *Group Rights* (University of Toronto Press)

Norman, W. (2006) *Negotiating Nationalism: Nation-Building, Federalism, and Secession in the Multinational State* (Oxford University Press)

Nussbaum, M. (2008) *Liberty of Conscience* (New York: Basic Books)

Okin, S. (1998) 'Feminism and Multiculturalism: Some Tensions', *Ethics*, 108, 661–84

Okin, S. (1999) 'Is Multiculturalism Bad for Women?' in J. Cohen, M. Howard and M. Nussbaum (eds.) *Is Multiculturalism Bad for Women?* (Princeton University Press)

Okin, S. (2002) '"Mistresses of Their Own Destiny": Group Rights, Gender, and Realistic Rights of Exit', *Ethics*, 112/2, 205–30

Okin, S. (2005) 'Multiculturalism and Feminism: No Simple Question, No Simple Answers' in A. Eisenberg and J. Spinner-Halev (eds.) *Minorities Within Minorities: Equality, Rights and Diversity* (Cambridge University Press)

Ong, A. (1999) *Flexible Citizenship: The Cultural Logics of Transnationality* (London: Duke University Press)

Orgad, L. (2015) *The Cultural Defense of Nations: A Liberal Theory of Majority Rights* (Oxford University Press)

Pagden, A. (2000) 'Stoicism, Cosmopolitanism and the Legacy of European Imperialism', *Constellations*, 7, 3–22

Parekh, B. (1994) 'Superior People: The Narrowness of Liberalism from Mill to Rawls', *Times Literary Supplement*, February 25, 11–13

Parekh, B. (1999) 'The Incoherence of Nationalism' in R. Beiner (ed.) *Theorizing Nationalism* (State University of New York Press)

Parekh, B. (2000) *Rethinking Multiculturalism: Cultural Diversity and Political Theory* (Basingstoke: Palgrave Macmillan)

Parekh, B. (2005) *Unity and Diversity in Multicultural Societies* (Geneva: International Institute for Labour Studies)

Parekh, B. (2008) *A New Politics of Identity: Political Principles for an Interdependent World* (Basingstoke: Palgrave Macmillan)

Parekh, B. (with R. Jahanbegloo) (2011) *Talking Politics* (New Delhi: Oxford University Press)

Parekh, B. (2016) 'Afterword: Multiculturalism and Interculturalism – A Critical Dialogue' in N. Meer, T. Modood and R. Zapata-Barrero (eds.) *Multiculturalism and Interculturalism: Debating the Dividing Lines* (Edinburgh University Press)

Parekh, B. (2019) *Ethnocentric Political Theory: The Pursuit of Flawed Universals* (Cham, Switzerland: Palgrave Macmillan)

Patten, A. (2014) *Equal Recognition: The Moral Foundations of Minority Rights* (Princeton University Press)

Patten, A. (2016) 'The Normative Logic of Religious Liberty', *The Journal of Political Philosophy*, 25/2, 129–54

Patten, A. (2017) 'Religious Exemptions and Fairness' in C. Laborde and A. Bardon (eds.) *Religion in Liberal Political Philosophy* (Oxford University Press)

Patten, A. (2020) 'Populist Multiculturalism: Are There Majority Cultural Rights?' *Philosophy & Social Criticism*, 46, 539–52.

Phillips, A. (2007) *Multiculturalism Without Culture* (Princeton University Press)

Pinsky, R. (2002) 'Eros against Esperanto' in J. Cohen (ed.) *For Love of Country: Debating the Limits of Patriotism* (Boston: Beacon Press)

Pogge, T. (2003) 'Accommodation Rights for Hispanics in the US' in W. Kymlicka and A. Patten (eds.) *Language Rights and Political Theory* (Oxford University Press)

Pokorn, N., and J. Čibej (2018) 'Interpreting and Linguistic Inclusion – Friends or Foes? Results from a Field Study', *The Translator*, 24/2, 111–27

Pool, J. (1991) 'The Official Language Problem', *American Political Science Review*, 85, 495–514

Poulter, S. (1998) *Ethnicity, Law, and Human Rights: The English Experience* (Oxford University Press)

Quong, J. (2006) 'Cultural Exemptions, Expensive Tastes and Equal Opportunities', *Journal of Applied Philosophy*, 23/1, 53–71

Quong, J. (2011) *Liberalism Without Perfection* (Oxford University Press)

Rawls, J. (1996) *Political Liberalism* (New York: Columbia University Press)

Rawls, J. (1999) *A Theory of Justice: Revised Edition* (Cambridge, MA: Harvard University Press)

Raz, J. (1986) *The Morality of Freedom* (Oxford: Clarendon Press)

Raz, J. (1994) *Ethics in the Public Domain: Essays in the Morality of Law and Politics* (Oxford University Press)

Rubio-Marín, R. (2003) 'Language Rights: Exploring the Competing Rationales' in W. Kymlicka and A. Patten (eds.) *Language Rights and Political Theory* (Oxford University Press)

Rudas, S. (2019) 'The Paradox of Political Secularism' in J. Seglow and A. Shorten (eds.) *Religion and Political Theory* (London: ECPR / Rowman & Littlefield)

Ryan, A. (2012) *The Making of Modern Liberalism* (Princeton University Press)

Sager, L. (2016) 'Why Churches (and, Possibly, the Tarpon Bay Women's Blue Water Fishing Club) Can Discriminate' in M. Schwartzman, C. Flanders and Z. Robinson (eds.) *The Rise of Corporate Religious Liberty* (Oxford University Press)

Sargent, L. T. (ed.) (1997) *Political Thought in the United States: A Documentary History* (New York University Press)

Schaeffer, M. (2014) *Ethnic Diversity and Social Cohesion: Immigration, Ethnic Fractionalization and Potentials for Civic Action* (Farnham: Ashgate)

Schäffner, C. (2009) 'Does Translation Hinder Integration?' *Forum*, 7, 99–122

Scheffler, S. (2001) *Boundaries and Allegiances: Problems of Justice and Responsibility in Liberal Thought* (Oxford University Press)

Schragger, R., and M. Schwartzman (2013) 'Against Religious Institutionalism', *Virginia Law Review*, 99/5, 917–85

Schuck, P. H. (2009) 'Immigrants' Incorporation in the United States after 9/11: Two Steps Forward, One Step Back' in J. L. Hochschild and J. H. Mollenkopf (eds.) *Bringing Outsiders In: Transatlantic Perspectives on Immigrant Political Incorporation* (London: Cornell University Press)

Scruton, R. (1982) *A Dictionary of Political Thought* (London: Macmillan)

Seglow, J. (2017) 'Religious Accommodation: Responsibility, Integrity and Self-Respect' in C. Laborde and A. Bardon (eds.) *Religion in Liberal Political Philosophy* (Oxford University Press)

Shachar, A. (2001) *Multicultural Jurisdictions: Cultural Differences and Women's Rights* (Cambridge University Press)

Shorten, A. (2010a) 'Cultural Diversity and Civic Education: Two Versions of the Fragmentation Objection', *Educational Philosophy and Theory*, 42/1, 57–72

Shorten, A. (2010b) 'Cultural Exemptions, Equality and Basic Interests', *Ethnicities*, 10/1, 100–26

Shorten, A. (2014) 'Liberalism' in V. Geoghegan and R. Wilford (eds.) *Political Ideologies* (Abingdon: Routledge)

Shorten, A. (2015a) 'Federalism, Contractualism and Equality' in J. F. Grégoire and M. Jewkes (eds.) *Recognition and Redistribution in Multinational Federations* (KU Leuven Press)

Shorten, A. (2015b) 'Are There Rights to Institutional Exemptions?' *Journal of Social Philosophy*, 46/2, 242–63

Shorten, A. (2016) *Contemporary Political Theory* (London: Palgrave)

Shorten, A. (2017) 'Accommodating Religious Institutions: Freedom vs. Domination?' *Ethnicities*, 17/2, 242–58

Shorten, A. (2018) 'Justice in the Linguistic Environment' in M. Gazzola, T. Templin and B.-A. Wickström (eds.) *Language Policy and Linguistic Justice* (Cham, Switzerland: Springer)

Shorten, A. (2019) 'May Churches Discriminate?' *Journal of Applied Philosophy*, 36/5, 709–17

Shorten, A. (2021) 'Toleration and Religious Discrimination' in M. Sardoc (ed.) *The Palgrave Handbook of Toleration* (Cham, Switzerland: Palgrave Macmillan)

Shorten, A. (forthcoming) 'Immigration, Language and Disadvantage', *Nations and Nationalism*

Simpson, A. (2014) *Mohawk Interruptus: Political Life across the Borders of Settler States* (London: Duke University Press)

Skutnabb-Kangus, T., and R. Phillipson (eds.) (1994) *Linguistic Human Rights: Overcoming Linguistic Discrimination* (New York: de Gruter)

Smith, S. D. (2016) 'The Jurisdictional Conception of Church Autonomy' in M. Schwartzman, C. Flanders and Z. Robinson (eds.) *The Rise of Corporate Religious Liberty* (Oxford University Press)

Stichnoth, H., and K. Van der Straeten (2013) 'Ethnic Diversity, Public Spending, and Individual Support for the Welfare State: A Review of the Empirical Literature', *Journal of Economic Surveys*, 27/2: 364–89

Tamir, Y. (1993) *Liberal Nationalism* (Princeton University Press)

Taylor, C. (1979) *Hegel* (Cambridge University Press)

Taylor, C. (1985) *Philosophy and the Human Sciences: Philosophical Papers 2* (Cambridge University Press)

Taylor, C. (1989) *Sources of the Self: The Making of the Modern Identity* (Cambridge University Press)

Taylor, C. (1992) *The Ethics of Authenticity* (Cambridge, MA: Harvard University Press)

Taylor, C. (1993) *Reconciling the Solitudes: Essays on Canadian Federalism and Nationalism* (Montreal: McGill-Queen's University Press)

Taylor, C. (1994) 'The Politics of Recognition' in A. Gutmann (ed.) *Multiculturalism and the Politics of Recognition* (Princeton University Press)

Tebbe, N. (2017) *Religious Freedom in an Egalitarian Age* (Cambridge, MA: Harvard University Press)

Tomasi, J. (1995) 'Kymlicka, Liberalism and Respect for Cultural Minorities', *Ethics*, 105, 580–603

Tomasi, J. (2004) 'Should Political Liberals be Compassionate Conservatives? Philosophical Foundations of the Faith-based Initiative', *Social Philosophy and Policy*, 21/1, 322–45

Tremblay, A. (2019) *Diversity in Decline? The Rise of the Political Right and the Fate of Multiculturalism* (Cham, Switzerland: Palgrave Macmillan)

Triandafyllidou, A., T. Modood and N. Meer (2012) *European*

Multiculturalisms: Cultural, Religious and Ethnic Challenges (Edinburgh University Press)

Tully, J. (1995) *Strange Multiplicity: Constitutionalism in an Age of Diversity* (Cambridge University Press)

Tully, J. (2008) *Public Philosophy in a New Key*, Volume I: *Democracy and Civic Freedom* (Cambridge University Press)

Turner, D. (2006) *This Is Not a Peace Pipe: Towards a Critical Indigenous Philosophy* (University of Toronto Press)

Turner, T. (1993) 'Anthropology and Multiculturalism: What Is Anthropology That Multiculturalists Should Be Mindful of It?' *Cultural Anthropology*, 8/4, 411–29

Uberoi, V. (2018) 'National Identity – A Multiculturalist's Approach', *Critical Review of International Social and Political Philosophy*, 21/1, 46–64

Uberoi, V., and T. Modood (2013) 'Inclusive Britishness: A Multiculturalist Advance', *Political Studies*, 61/1, 23–41

US Census Bureau (2019) American Community Survey 1-Year Estimates, Table S1601 (https://data.census.gov/cedsci/table?hideP review=true&tid=ACSST1Y2019.S1601)

Van Dyke, V. (1977) 'The Individual, the State, and Ethnic Communities in Political Theory', *World Politics*, 29/3, 343–69

Van Dyke, V. (1982) 'Collective Entities and Moral Rights: Problems in Liberal Democratic Thought', *Journal of Politics*, 44, 21–40

Van Parijs, P. (ed.) (2004) *Cultural Diversity versus Economic Solidarity* (Brussels: De Boeck)

Van Parijs, P. (2011) *Linguistic Justice for Europe and for the World* (Oxford University Press)

Vertovec, S., and S. Wessendorf (eds.) (2010) *The Multiculturalism Backlash: European Discourses, Policies and Practices* (Abingdon: Routledge)

Vincent, A. (2010) *Modern Political Ideologies*, third edition (Oxford: Blackwell)

Waldron, J. (1995) 'Minority Cultures and the Cosmopolitan Alternative' in W. Kymlicka (ed.) *The Rights of Minority Cultures* (Oxford University Press)

Waldron, J. (2000) 'What is Cosmopolitan?', *The Journal of Political Philosophy*, 8, 227–43

Walsham, A. (2006) *Charitable Hatred: Tolerance and Intolerance in England, 1500–1700* (Manchester University Press)

Watts, R. (1996) *Comparing Federal Systems* (Montreal: McGill-Queen's University Press)

White, S. (1997) 'Freedom of Association and the Right to Exclude', *The Journal of Political Philosophy*, 5/4, 373–91

Williams, B. (1972) *Morality: An Introduction to Ethics* (Cambridge University Press)

Williams, M. (1998) *Voice, Trust, and Memory: Marginalized Groups and the Failings of Liberal Representation* (Princeton University Press)

Williams, R. (2001) *The Bloudy Tenent of Persecution, for the Cause of Conscience, Discussed in a Conference Between Truth and Peace* (Georgia: Mercia University Press)

Wind-Cowie, M., and T. Gregory (2011) *A Place for Pride* (London: DEMOS)

Wolfe, P. (1999) *Settler Colonialism and the Transformation of Anthropology* (London: Cassell)

Young, I. M. (1989) 'Polity and Group Difference: A Critique of the Ideal of Universal Citizenship', *Ethics*, 99, 250–74

Young, I. M. (1990) *Justice and the Politics of Difference* (Princeton University Press)

Young, I. M. (2000) *Inclusion and Democracy* (Oxford University Press)

Young, I. M. (2011) *Responsibility for Justice* (Oxford University Press)

Zapata-Barrero, R. (2016) 'Theorising Intercultural Citizenship' in N. Meer, T. Modood and R. Zapata-Barrero (eds.) *Multiculturalism and Interculturalism: Debating the Dividing Lines* (Edinburgh University Press)

Zapata-Barrero, R. (2017) 'Interculturalism in the Post-Multicultural Debate: A Defence', *Comparative Migration Studies*, 5/14, 1–23

Index

religious associations 16, 143, 152–3
  and collective integrity 159–61
  and discrimination 159–62
  locating jurisdictional authority
    156–62
  regulating 153–6
  and role of consent 161
  and self-governance 153–4
  and sovereignty 157–9
Rousseau, Jean-Jacques 56
Rushdie, Salman 100

Sarkozy, Nicolas 103
Scruton, Roger 98, 99
secularism 135–8
self-determination 16, 142
  national 144–8
self-government rights 7–8, 16, 41,
    141–3
  and minorities 16, 142–4, 146–8
  and national communities 144–8
  religious 153–62
  self-defence justification 148
  and territorial autonomy 148–52
separation principle 27–8
settler communities 2, 7, 114–15
Seventh-Day Adventists 32–3
Shachar, Ayelet 85, 162
Sherbert, Adell 32–3, 124
Sikhs 82, 83–4, 120, 121, 126
Skutnabb-Kangas, Tove 166
Slaughter of Animals Act (1933) 122
Slonimski, Antoni 177
social cohesion 2
  and shared values / political
    stability 115–18
  and solidarity 111–15
societal culture 35–6, 146–7
solidarity 111–15
  and belonging 113–14
  and common identity 111–13
  and Indigenous communities 114–15
Switzerland 165–6

Taylor, Charles 11, 13, 32, 49, 50–66,
    134, 136, 165
  and cosmopolitanism 98–9
  critique of 57–60
  and essentialism 91–2
  and recognition 50–7, 60–6, 173
  religious issues 126–9
  and solidarity 113
toleration 12, 16, 76, 146, 185
  as centre of liberal political
    morality 26
  concept/understanding of 23–4
  conscience argument 24–5
  as derivative not fundamental value
    25
  and dignity / moral dogmatism 65,
    67, 68
  and disputed practices 71, 73
  and ethical independence 25–6
  and gender 88, 101
  and group authority 45–6
  and language 166
  and minority/majority feelings 113
  peace and stability argument 24, 25
  as pure not derivative 43–4
  as radical/controversial 44–5
  and recognition 131–5, 139
  and religion/beliefs 24–5, 44, 45,
    116, 121, 130, 138
  and shared values 116, 118
  and stability of society 118
  state approach 46–7, 87–8
Tomasi, John 36, 159
Treaty of Westphalia (1648) 24
Tremblay, Arjun 105
Trilling, Lionel 55
Tully, James 61, 62, 95, 114
Turner, Dale 114–15
Turner, Terence 91

Uberoi, Varun 105
UK Equality Act (Sexual Orientation)
    Regulations (2007) 161